Indecision Points

The Belfer Center Studies in International Security book series is edited at the Belfer Center for Science and International Affairs at the Harvard Kennedy School and is published by The MIT Press. The series publishes books on contemporary issues in international security policy, as well as their conceptual and historical foundations. Topics of particular interest to the series include the spread of weapons of mass destruction, internal conflict, the international effects of democracy and democratization, and U.S. defense policy. A complete list of Belfer Center Studies appears at the back of this volume.

Indecision Points

George W. Bush and the Israeli-Palestinian Conflict

Daniel E. Zoughbie

BELFER CENTER STUDIES IN INTERNATIONAL SECURITY

The MIT Press
Cambridge, Massachusetts
London, England

Library of Congress Cataloging-in-Publication Data

Zoughbie, Daniel, 1984–
Indecision points : George W. Bush and the Israeli-Palestinian conflict / Daniel E. Zoughbie, Belfer Center Studies in International Security.
    pages   cm. — (Belfer Center studies in international security)
Includes bibliographical references and index.
ISBN 978-0-262-02733-5 (hardcover : alk. paper)
1. Arab–Israeli conflict—1993—Peace. 2. Arab–Israeli conflict—1993—Diplomatic history. 3. Bush, George W. (George Walker), 1946– 4. United States—Foreign relations—Middle East. 5. Middle East—Foreign relations—United States. 6. United States—Foreign relations—2001–2009. I. Title.
DS119.76.Z68   2014
956.05'4—dc23

                                                                                    2014012461

10 9 8 7 6 5 4 3 2 1

To my mother and father

...AND THE TRUTH SHALL MAKE US FREE.

CONTENTS

ACKNOWLEDGMENTS

✛

In a world that once again appears to be moving toward all sorts of terrible fanaticisms, with nuclear and chemical weapons programs in play, extremist militants flooding destabilized states, and chronic volatility threatening to disrupt regional and international economic stability, one cannot afford to ignore the relevance of the Israeli-Palestinian conflict for international affairs. The central aim of this book is to provide an explanation for changing U.S. policy toward the conflict during one of the most consequential periods in contemporary world history, and in doing so, to uncover the assumptions that shaped it. The book, and the thesis from which it eventuated, has evolved through many conversations with my doctoral supervisor at Oxford, Avi Shlaim, who, with tremendous knowledge, wisdom, and understanding, lighted my way. For his steadfast support and incisive criticism of my work, I must register my heartfelt gratitude; that it may still contain imperfections is something for which I am wholly responsible.

I'm grateful to Sean Lynn-Jones and Karen Motley, who provided excellent feedback on the entire book manuscript. I thank Graham Allison, Stephen Walt, Steven Miller, Susan Lynch, and the Belfer Center for Science and International Affairs at the Harvard Kennedy School. I am also indebted to Nezar AlSayyad and Emily Gottreich at the Center for Middle Eastern Studies and the Sultan Program at the University of California, Berkeley, and Larry Diamond and Lina Khatib at Stanford University's Center on Democracy, Development, and the Rule of Law for providing me with a community of support as I executed the many facets of this book project.

The faculty and staff of Exeter College, the Middle East Centre, and the Department of Politics and International Relations made Oxford a warm and stimulating intellectual home for me as I completed the doctoral research upon which this book is based. In particular, I wish to thank Yuen Foong Khong, Raffaella Del Sarto, and LSE's Fawaz Gerges for commenting on earlier versions of this research. On the administrative side, Amber Prime, Marga Lyall, Joan Himpson, Julia Cooke, and Daniel Meacoe helped me navigate through copious amounts of paperwork. At Oxford, I was made to feel welcome as part of a consortium of scholars and a community of friends. I owe special thanks to Seth Anziska, David Zarnett, Andrew Kerr, and Rajaie Batniji, who read through earlier chapters, and to Maher Bitar, who read through the entire manuscript. Andrew Elkhoury, an exceptionally gifted student of the law at the University of Chicago, scrupulously checked the manuscript for errors and read through it multiple times.

Outside of Oxford, I am also indebted to a large number of individuals. Mary Denyer and Elizabeth Martin helped me navigate my way around the United Kingdom while a graduate student. Nick Rengger of St. Andrew's University read and provided valuable feedback on some philosophical and theological concepts underlying U.S. foreign policy. In Washington, D.C., Thomas Banchoff and Thomas Farr graciously hosted me as a visiting researcher at Georgetown University's Berkley Center for Religion, Peace, and World Affairs, and the Reverend Earl Palmer enriched my understanding of complex theological concepts. I am thankful to the numerous interviewees from the United States, the Middle East, and Europe who, with great kindness and hospitality, made time to present their views. Though they will not necessarily agree with my conclusions, several provided extremely important information that shaped both the content and structure of this research. Here, I wish to acknowledge Archbishop of Canterbury Rowan Williams, Prime Minister Salam Fayyad of Palestine, Elliott Abrams, Sir Mark Allen, Sir Christopher Meyer, Tom DeLay, Chuck Hagel, Stephen Hadley, Marwan Muasher, David Welch, Colin Powell, William Burns, Lord Christopher Patten, William Inboden, David Wurmser, Kofi Annan, Condoleezza Rice, and Richard Perle.

The Marshall Commission, Exeter College, and the Institute for Strategic Dialogue (ISD) generously funded my research and travels at Oxford. In particular, I wish to thank Lord George Weidenfeld and Sir Ronald Grierson for creating the Weidenfeld Scholarships, John Adamson for intellectually enriching seminars at the Hartwell House, Lady Elizabeth Roberts for her advice, and the many ISD staff and benefactors who made the program possible.

Over the years, the late A.W. Clausen has been a valued mentor, and, together with Helen Clausen, a steady source of "common sense" and warm friendship. Ananya Roy and Raymond Lifchez have remained cherished tutors and friends. Here I also wish to mention Christopher Omran and his family, whose generosity of heart is known far and wide. I am thankful for the many friends and colleagues who labored with me to provide under-resourced communities in the Middle East (and elsewhere) with increased access to health care. It is the beneficiaries of these humanitarian activities, not simply those who have occupied significant positions of power, who have educated me about Middle East politics.

From my family I learned that "knowledge puffeth up, but love edifieth." In addition to supporting my academic pursuits. I am extremely grateful to my grandfather for teaching me to see both the lights and shadows of history. My ultimate obligation belongs to my excellent parents, whose greatest gift to their son is the lesson inscribed on the dedication page. Without their unconditional love, this book would not have been possible.

CHAPTER 1

⊕

Introduction

One morning, as President George W. Bush awoke, he discovered that his signature foreign policy initiative had morphed into something horrible. The date was January 26, 2006, and it was a very bad morning indeed. As usual, Secretary of State Condoleezza Rice awoke before 5:00 a.m. and started her morning exercise routine as she watched the news. Suddenly, the following story flashed on the screen: Hamas had won the Palestinian elections in a landslide victory. Strange. Her embassy staff in Tel Aviv and Jerusalem had not notified her of any major new developments. Why was she learning about this from the morning news? She picked up the phone and called Jacob Walles, a career diplomat serving as consul general in Jerusalem, to confirm that this was not some sort of terrible mistake. In Washington, Assistant Secretary of State David Welch was getting ready for work when he too received a call from his boss. Clearly, the story was no mistake. The bad news would now need to be conveyed to the president—that is, if he had not already heard what everyone else but Secretary Rice seemed to know.[1]

But then again, why should regional embassy staff have disturbed the secretary of state during the night? What could she have done? With mayhem in Iraq and Afghanistan and a myriad of other problems around the world, peaceful Palestinian elections would seem relatively low on the list of emergencies. And besides, the Bush administration, having been warned of Hamas's growing popularity by the Palestinians, Jordanians, and Israelis, had insisted that the democratic process be respected. The election results imminently threatened neither U.S. forces nor treasure. But the stakes were high for another important reason: the Bush administration's democracy experiment in the Middle East, which already lacked the support of many U.S. and foreign diplomats, would be deemed an abysmal failure not only in Palestine, but also in Iraq and beyond.

This experimental plan to create a new Middle East, dubbed the "freedom agenda," was hatched four years earlier by the president and members of his administration. The second Palestinian *Intifada* was destabilizing the Middle East, and Bush's war cabinet was bitterly divided about how the United States should respond. One Sunday, as the president was deciding what to do, Rice and Karen Hughes, two of the president's closest advisors, exchanged handwritten notes on the plan as they listened to their pastor's sermon. In their written exchange, Rice and Hughes expressed mutual agreement that the president should deliver a game-changing presidential speech on Palestine. Astonishingly, Hughes compared the controversial nature of the proposed speech to Lincoln's Gettysburg Address.

Bush had stated that he wanted to "change the way people think" about the Israeli-Palestinian conflict. He confided to Rice and Hughes that he saw Palestine as a "nice little laboratory" to test his hypothesis that freedom was the solution to the broader problems in the Middle East: freedom and democracy would be introduced on the rocky hills of the West Bank and in the deserts of Iraq.[2] As Rice put it, democracy, Iraq, and Palestine formed a "package."[3] In the heavily pro-Israel speech given on June 24, 2002, Bush placed the onus for change on the Palestinians, calling for a sequence of steps to be taken, which included the removal of Yasser Arafat, the dismantling of all terrorist organizations, and the organization of democratic elections as a precondition for peace negotiations. Even the president's mother expressed shock and disapproval when she learned of it, describing her son as the "first Jewish president."[4] After all, only two months earlier Bush had stood in the same Rose Garden and delivered a very different speech, which outlined the need for a process of parallel concessions made by both sides. And in November 2001, he seemed to be vying for "first Palestinian president" when he mentioned that unmentionable word—Palestine—before the United Nations General Assembly.

Such erratic shifts in the president's decision-making process were not an isolated occurrence; unfortunately, they were the norm. And this problem—the president's inability to make decisions on Israeli-Palestinian affairs—is the subject of this book. It argues that the president was paralyzed by the battles within his own administration and chronically confused and conflicted by his beliefs about the democratic Middle East as it should be versus the harsh truth of Middle Eastern political life as it really was.

Background

The significance of George W. Bush's presidency should not be understated. For over half a century, U.S. foreign policy has been a predominant force in shaping the development, course, and resolution of international conflict, especially in the modern Middle East. Before the 2003 invasion of Iraq, Fareed Zakaria described a unipolar world that was "shaped and dominated by one country—the United States." It took only five years for Zakaria to declare that a "post-American world" was fast emerging.[5] In the wake of a global economic crisis, the Arab revolutions, and an ongoing regional nuclear arms race, the stakes could have hardly been higher for U.S. statecraft in the Middle East.

This book focuses on Bush's Middle East policy *vis-à-vis* the peace process for several reasons. First, as mentioned above, the Bush administration viewed the Israeli-Palestinian conflict as its experimental "laboratory" for the entire Middle East. The president and his senior advisors argued that his hallmark "freedom agenda" would be vindicated first in the occupied Palestinian territories, then in Iraq, and so on. Second, the Bush era opened a new chapter in U.S.-Israeli relations. Since the Kennedy administration, the United States and Israel shared a "special relationship" that was held together by shared interests, shared cultural-religious ideas, and political lobbying. For more than fifty years, the United States has been involved in the conflict between Israel and the Palestinians, with very few successes. Yet Bush's policies were unprecedented in that they permanently changed the face of the conflict for the worse during a critical period in Middle East history. Before, there were two main parties to the conflict—the Palestine Liberation Organization (PLO) and Israel; now there are three parties—Hamas, the Palestinian Authority, and Israel. All three find it difficult to sit down and negotiate, and sometimes even recognize each other. Obtaining a peace agreement that is respected by all parties and supported by the public will prove to be a daunting task indeed.

Third, many commentators partially attribute U.S. regional decline to its failed leadership of the peace process. Unpopular U.S. policies toward the Palestinians during the Bush administration incited tremendous anger throughout the Arab and Muslim worlds, serving to bolster Iran's proxy militias, undermine U.S. allies, and endanger U.S. blood and treasure in the Middle East and South Asia. Equally important, Israel's continued defiance on issues like settlements, often citing "understandings" reached with Bush administration officials as justification, made the United States look weak. As Vice President Joe Biden put it to the Israelis in 2010, "This is starting to get dangerous for us. What you're doing here undermines the security of our troops who are fighting in Iraq, Afghanistan and Pakistan. That endangers us and it endangers regional peace."[6]

Perhaps most significantly, the Bush era was immediately followed by the "Arab Spring" or, perhaps more accurately, the "Arab revolutions"—a major shift in international power that is compared in importance to the ends of the Cold War, decolonization, and the Ottoman Empire. Due to shared economic and security interests, the Middle East is one of the most physically, politically, and economically penetrated areas of the world by the United States; therefore, presidential decision-making after 9/11 had a considerable impact on the decisions undertaken by both regional leaders and, perhaps more important, civilians.

Advocates of the Bush administration's policies have claimed that the president's freedom agenda, including the removal of Yasser Arafat and Saddam Hussein, catalyzed the Arab Spring. As Kanan Makiya claimed in the *New York Times*, "The removal of Saddam Hussein and the toppling of a whole succession of other Arab dictators in 2011 were closely connected—a fact that has been overlooked largely because of the hostility that the Iraq war engendered." Makiya argued that the Arab Spring started with the removal of Hussein, enabling the Arab communities to imagine a different world. Similarly, Vice President Dick Cheney stated, "I think that what happened in Iraq, the fact that we brought democracy, if you will, and freedom to Iraq, has had a ripple effect on some of those other countries." Rice also noted, "The change in the conversation about the Middle East, where people now routinely talk about democratization, is something that I'm very grateful for and I think we had a role in that."[7]

This view does not entirely square with reality. George W. Bush was possibly the most reviled U.S. president in the history of the modern Middle East; to say that his grand statements about freedom were causally linked to the Arab Spring is to commit the logical fallacy that what comes after the fact is because of the fact. Many careful observers of the region know that the people of the Middle East have been struggling for their rights for decades; the Bush administration did not open their eyes to the misery of their true condition. In fact, a quick Internet search will uncover vast numbers of Arab and Muslim commentators who readily point out what they describe as the hypocrisy of the Bush administration's freedom agenda: while praising democracy, the president supported autocratic regimes and cherry-picked election results, removing unfriendly yet democratically elected leaders from power.

Yet one cannot dismiss this linkage entirely. While it would be difficult to attribute the Egyptian people's revolution to a speech delivered by Condoleezza Rice in Cairo or to George W. Bush's second inaugural address, it is likely that Hosni Mubarak became less and less popular in Egypt precisely because of his cooperation with Bush on a range of regional issues, notably the war in Gaza and the fight against Hamas. It is also likely that some of the violence sweeping the region today is associated with the missteps of the Bush administration.[8] When a superpower conducts a regime-changing military operation against a major country like Iraq and attempts to remove two democratically elected leaders—Yasser Arafat and Ismael Haniyeh—in a situation as complex as the Israeli-Palestinian conflict, many things change—and the social, economic, and military changes that occurred destabilized the region. During the Bush years, Iran's influence grew, Iraq became a breeding ground for terrorism, Hamas and Hezbollah grew in stature, Jordan experienced significant financial and social challenges, autocratic U.S. allies became less popular as a result of their cooperation with the United States and Israel, and perhaps most important, the United States came to be seen as morally, militarily, and, especially, financially bankrupt.

Definitions

It would perhaps be instructive to offer a few notes on words and definitions used throughout this book. The term *neoconservative* identifies those who ostensibly believe that the United States has an international obligation to use its unipolar military preponderance to eliminate individuals who are regarded as tyrants and terrorists, and to replace them with democratic regimes, especially in the Middle East. *Nationalist conservative* identifies those who wish to use unipolar U.S. military power to remove tyrants and terrorists, but unlike the neoconservatives, use democracy promotion language more as a pretense in order to forward their goals. *Zionist conservative* identifies those who are not simply devoted to the idea of a Jewish state of Israel, but who also oppose a peace process and advocate for a more militaristic approach to Middle East affairs. *Theoconservative* identifies those who cite a Biblical justification for supporting Israel and rejecting a peace process, and who tend to advocate for the use of force in the Middle East conflict. The *conservative alliance* refers to the cooperation between all the aforementioned groups in opposing the peace process, advocating military attacks against Israel's enemies, and, at times, promoting democracy. *Moderate* and *realist* refer to those who are skeptical about imposing democracy in the Middle East, acknowledge the limits of U.S. military power, and tend to advocate for a diplomatic resolution to the peace process. Finally, the term *utopian* does not refer to individuals who aspire to high moral ideals; rather, it indicates people whose practical decision-making process is based on assumptions that do not measure up with the reality of political life. Of course, none of these broad categories captures all the nuances and debates that occur between like-minded individuals; however, they are nevertheless helpful analytical tools for understanding major debates and divisions during the Bush administration.

Overview

Following this introduction, the book is developed in seven additional chapters. Chapters 2 and 3 focus on the period from January 2001 to December 2002. During this time, the ABC ("anything but Clinton") approach of the new administration resulted in a hands-off Israeli-Palestinian policy, which divided conservatives and moderates. After 9/11, conservatives slowly gained more power as they presented the president with a black-and-white vision for a new Middle East. Driven by conservatives, the June 2002 Rose Garden speech introduced the *sequence* principle—the essence of Bush's freedom agenda for Palestine—which conditioned a political process upon the emergence of entirely new Palestinian leaders and institutions.

Chapter 4 covers the period from January 2003 to December 2004. During this time, the president more clearly developed his freedom agenda against the backdrop of his June 2002 Rose Garden speech and planning for war in Iraq. But with pressure from Europeans, Arabs, and administration moderates, Bush endorsed the Road Map and its principle of *parallelism*—the moderate view that reciprocal Israeli and Palestinian concessions must occur through a negotiated peace process—once major operations in Iraq were concluded. Without decisive leadership from the president, a series of unilateral Israeli actions, notably the construction of the separation wall and the Gaza withdrawal, marginalized the Road Map.

Chapter 5 discusses the period from January 2005 to December 2006. With conservative backing and the Gaza disengagement completed, Bush made freedom the centerpiece of his Middle East policy and returned to the sequence principle. With enormous losses in Iraq, however, conservatives started losing power to Condoleezza Rice, who gradually pushed for a return to the peace process. Conservatives urged strikes against Syria and Iran while Rice attempted to restart the diplomatic process. The election of Hamas, along with the U.S.-backed appointment of unelected Palestinian leaders and the war in Lebanon, marked the demise of Bush's freedom agenda.

Chapters 6 and 7 include the period from January 2007 to January 2009. After Hamas and Fatah acted as surrogates in a proxy war in Gaza, Rice eventually succeeded in restarting a political process between Palestinians and Israelis based on the principle of parallelism. Facing fierce conservative opposition, she returned to Bill Clinton's methodology of negotiations and made an eleventh-hour effort to forge peace between the two sides. Though the Israelis and the Palestinians once again came close, Israeli Prime Minister Ehud Olmert's corruption scandal was the major reason for the end of the negotiations. With a failed peace process, Israel returned to the sequence principle, and with Bush's backing, launched a devastating war in Gaza, the capstone for eight years of human tragedy. Chapter 8 provides some conclusions for the reader.

By way of concluding this introduction, it is worth stating the obvious: the Israeli-Palestinian conflict is a dispute many understandably view as ancient, intractable, and thoroughly hopeless. Some readers of this book may be tempted to embrace such a perspective and to see this study as further confirmation of the conclusion that the United States is incapable of playing a constructive role in the peace process. That would be a mistake. While this book identifies the many opportunities that were missed during the Bush administration, it also demonstrates that when the proper amount of political pressure was applied, peace—or at least the avoidance of human suffering—was well within reach. It has often been said that those who forget history are doomed to repeat it. But one must remember that those who cannot forget history are also doomed to repeat it. It is in this spirit that the reader might continue to engage the pages that follow; to learn from the mistakes of the past, but never to lose sight of that wonderful possibility when the children of the land that is called holy can live together in peace.

CHAPTER 2

⊕

A World Transformed

In the days leading up to Governor George W. Bush's formal announcement that he would run for president, British Ambassador to the United States Christopher Meyer and his wife Catherine made a visit to Texas. Their intention was to meet with Bush to scope out the changing U.S. political terrain for the UK government. The Meyers were having a jolly conversation when all of a sudden Bush pulled out a piece of paper from his jacket and asked Meyer, "What do you think of this?" It contained a short stump speech on the special role of the United States to spread democracy and freedom around the world.[1] Bush did not emphasize this theme during his campaign. Rather, he promised not to engage in nation-building and moved in the direction of a modest foreign policy and restrained use of U.S. power. He seemed to heed the advice of John Quincy Adams, who in 1821 famously warned against going abroad "in search of monsters to destroy."[2] In a major debate with Vice President Al Gore, he argued that "the United States must be humble, and must be proud and confident of our values, but humble in how we treat nations that are figuring out how to chart their own course."[3] Bush the candidate expressed his commitment to a more realistic foreign policy; after 9/11, however, Bush the president slowly rejected realism and exercised his belief in a much grander and more deeply held theology of the exceptional role of the United States in history. Though he indecisively vacillated back and forth between realist and utopian policies, his freedom agenda, heavily shaped by the conservative alliance, transformed the landscape of the Israeli-Palestinian conflict.

Clinton's Legacy

As the new administration moved out of transition mode, Bush was faced with his first major chance to act decisively. He had inherited an *Intifada*, a shattered peace process, and an explosive geopolitical situation in the Middle East, intensified by the death of Syrian President Hafez Al-Assad and the Israeli withdrawal from Leba-non.[4] Ariel Sharon, an Israeli general who regarded "Jordan as Palestine," was easily elected as prime minister in February 2001, despite the fact that his "provocative" visit with over one thousand Israeli police to the Temple Mount in September 2000 was strongly discouraged by U.S. and Israeli officials.[5] Sharon's controversial past was not limited to this one event. Known as the "Butcher of Beirut," he was held indirectly responsible by the Israeli Kahan Commission for failing to prevent the 1983 massacre of at least seven hundred Palestinian refugees in Lebanon and was subsequently forced to resign as defense minister.[6] Because Sharon fundamentally opposed a political process with the Palestinians based on reciprocal concessions, his Temple Mount visit was widely viewed as an effort to undermine then–Prime Minister Ehud Barak's negotiations, affirm Israel's sovereignty over the Temple Mount, and, ultimately, solidify his authority as the leader of the Likud Party.[7] According to former Jordanian Deputy Prime Minister Marwan Muasher, Sharon's actions were "deliberately provocative" in that he brought a "legion of snipers" and "made deliberations from the plaza about his birthright as a Jew."[8] Violent clashes ensued and Israeli Internal Security Minister Shlomo Ben-Ami was held responsible by the Or Commission—the group primarily charged with investigating clashes between state security forces and Palestinian citizens of Israel—for the conduct of his security forces as they confronted large numbers of unarmed demonstrators. According to the report, twelve Palestinian citizens of Israel, one Jewish citizen of Israel, and one resident of Gaza were killed; hundreds more were injured.[9]

The outbreak of the second Palestinian *Intifada* cannot be blamed on a single person—the Palestinian Authority President Yasser Arafat—or an isolated event—Sharon's visit—and must instead be viewed as a consequence of the Palestinian people's exasperation with the peace process. Ben-Ami, a political moderate trained as a historian, argues that the Palestinians as an "occupied people" believed they were entitled to fight for freedom and rights, and that with the ultimate failure of

Clinton's peace process to deliver any improvements for the Palestinians, the conditions were ripe for an outbreak of violence. Sharon's visit was widely seen as the "ignition" for the popular uprising.[10]

These broader conditions were not well understood by the Bush administration. Though the Israeli Or Commission did not focus on Arafat's role, senior U.S. officials such as National Security Advisor Condoleezza Rice held the Palestinian president responsible for the outbreak of violence within Israel and throughout the occupied Palestinian territories.[11] By contrast, the Or Commission held that Sheikh Ra'ed Salah, an Islamic leader in Israel, and other senior political figures contributed to the incitement of violence on the Palestinian side and that on the Israeli side, "neglectful and discriminatory" policies against Palestinian citizens of Israel constituted a "fundamental contribution to the outbreak of the events."[12] Similarly, the Mitchell Report, which was produced by a committee led by former U.S. Senator George Mitchell, investigated the reasons for the outbreak of the second *Intifada*. The report concluded that "we have no basis on which to conclude that there was a deliberate plan by the PA [Palestinian Authority] to initiate a campaign of violence at the first opportunity."[13]

Though Yasser Arafat certainly was not working to prevent the violence, and may have considered it beneficial to his bargaining position, he was not directing the masses of angry demonstrators within Israel and the occupied Palestinian territories whose passions could neither be ignited nor extinguished by the aging leader.[14] In the past, Palestinians had failed to heed Arafat's calls for demonstrations in occupied East Jerusalem; this time, with his visit to the Temple Mount, Sharon triggered what Arafat could not and Palestinian demonstrators converged to defend the area, which is also regarded as one of Islam's holiest sites, Al Aqsa. The second *Intifada* was born.[15]

Without taking the time to explore the full range of complex factors that led to the *Intifada*, Bush effectively ignored the Mitchell Report, adopted the ABC ("anything but Clinton") approach to the conflict, and subsequently showed little interest in remaining engaged in the peace process. Ironically, though, he did so in response to the historical narrative propagated by Bill Clinton. The political significance of Clinton's account was that it identified Arafat's rejectionism as the reason, and the fundamental reason, for the collapse of negotiations. Although the outgoing president had made a very clear promise to Arafat—who was reluctant to participate in the Camp David talks—that he would not fault anybody for failed negotiations, Clinton did just that.[16] As a former president, he used his political capital to place blame squarely on Arafat, characterizing the Palestinian leader as untrustworthy, aged, and "confused."[17] Prior to taking the oath of office, Bush was told by Clinton, "you can't trust Arafat."[18] Though it is commonly believed that Clinton's antipathy toward Arafat was simply a public relations stunt to help Ehud Barak get re-elected, it was actually something of a much more personal nature. When Clinton called Colin Powell to privately congratulate him on his appointment as secretary of state, he took the time to express his strong dislike for Arafat and conveyed his belief that the Palestinian leader could neither be trusted nor relied upon to conclude a peace agreement.[19]

The resounding mantra, as devised by Prime Minister Barak, was that Israel had no "partner for peace." Making this case in policy circles, Dennis Ross, Clinton's former negotiator and fellow at the pro-Israel Washington Institute for Near East Policy, argued that though the Palestinians were never shown a map, Yasser Arafat had turned down a generous offer consisting of 97 percent of the West Bank.[20]

But the portrayal of Arafat as a rejectionist was skewed. As Clinton's former special assistant Robert Malley and Yasser Arafat's advisor Hussein Agha warned, this distorted orthodoxy would constrain the Bush administration's policy options because it produced a convenient culprit rather than a realistic evaluation of complex dynamics between the United States, Israel, and the Palestinians. Agha and Malley concluded that the Arafat orthodoxy failed "to capture why what so many viewed as a generous Israeli offer, the Palestinians viewed as neither generous, nor Israeli, nor, indeed, as an offer."[21] As Ben-Ami later admitted, "If I were a Palestinian, I would have rejected Camp David as well."[22] Adding important historical perspective, Aaron David Miller, a senior State Department official who served in the George W. Bush, Clinton, George H.W. Bush, and Reagan administrations, candidly summed up the one-sided nature of Clinton's involvement in the peace process, saying that the administration worked as Israel's lawyer "before, during, and after the summit."[23]

In reality, negotiations did not end at Camp David with Arafat's rejectionism, and the Palestinian leader sent a team to Taba, Egypt, where intense talks with the

Israelis continued. But the Israeli and Palestinian negotiators were unable to conclude a deal on behalf of their leaders, partly because there was a fundamental disconnect between the Palestinians and Israelis and partly because Barak was leading a transitional government that was, in the words of Ben-Ami, "committing suicide."[24] Though blame for the failure of peace negotiations should be shared, it must be emphasized in light of the dominant narrative that it was ultimately Barak, not Arafat, who called off the Taba talks. As Ben-Ami explained, "the pressure of Israeli public opinion against the talks could not be resisted."[25]

Despite all the problems that beset Taba, the belief remained, as expressed in the summary of negotiations, that "solutions are possible" and that a political process should continue.[26] As the Israelis and Palestinians expressed in their Joint Statement concluding the negotiations, "The sides declare that they have never been closer to reaching an agreement and it is thus our shared belief that the remaining gaps could be bridged with the resumption of negotiations following the Israeli elections."[27] Because the Palestinians and Israelis had already traveled a considerable distance together, and because the alternative was more bloodshed and regional instability, sustained diplomatic pressure would be needed more than ever before.

Given Bush's uncritical acceptance of the "no peace partner" orthodoxy, he did not feel compelled to pursue solutions.[28] Although U.S. Ambassador to Israel Daniel Kurtzer understood that there was plenty of blame to go around for the failure of the Clinton peace talks, the narrative that Arafat was the main "obstacle to peace" received uncritical acceptance among both conservative and moderate principals in the new administration. No significant attention was paid to the Palestinian narrative of Camp David, and in a powerful symbolic statement of ambivalence, Bush eliminated the position of Middle East envoy, which was previously held by Dennis Ross during the Clinton administration.[29] As State Department Director of Policy Planning Richard Haass put it, Arafat came to be seen as "damaged goods."[30] Although the second *Intifada* was well under way, Bush started his presidency by ignoring his commitment to serve as an "honest broker" in the region, and instead embraced a hands-off approach coupled with symbolic—though not unqualified— support for Israel.

A "Hands-Off" Approach

As the *Intifada* intensified, a major fissure between moderate and conservative worldviews—and the president's perennial tendency to vacillate indecisively between the two—became clear. Because they had utopian visions of forcibly transforming the Middle East, conservative members of the Bush administration, led by Vice President Dick Cheney and his mentor, Secretary of Defense Donald Rumsfeld, strongly urged Bush not to restart a political process with Arafat, whom they regarded as illegitimate and part of a broader infrastructure of evil.[31] Rumsfeld was widely regarded as a "ruthless" but effective Cold War politician who, with the assistance of Cheney and the neoconservatives, had waged bureaucratic warfare for years against prominent realists from Henry Kissinger right up to Colin Powell.[32] Though Rumsfeld and Cheney were a bit more cynical about the idea of promoting democracy, when it came to the use of U.S. military preeminence, their views were virtually indistinguishable from the neoconservatives—and diametrically opposed to the realists.[33] As former UK Prime Minister Tony Blair lucidly encapsulated, the vice president believed that "the U.S. was genuinely at war; that the war was one with terrorists and rogue states that supported them; that it stemmed from a guiding ideology that was a direct threat to America; and that therefore the only way of defeating it was head-on, with maximum American strength, with the object of destroying the ideology and allowing democracy to flourish in its stead." Blair speculated, "He would have worked through the whole lot, Iraq, Syria, Iran, dealing with all their surrogates in the course of it—Hezbollah, Hamas, etc. In other words, he thought the *world had to be made anew*, and that after 11 September, it had to be done by force and with urgency."[34]

In previous administrations, the vice president and the secretary of defense had very limited involvement in the Israeli-Palestinian conflict and left things to be decided by the president, the national security advisor, and the secretary of state. In the Bush administration, neoconservatives such as Deputy Secretary of Defense Paul Wolfowitz, formerly dean of the School of Advanced International Studies at Johns Hopkins University, and nationalist conservatives such as Rumsfeld and Cheney diluted Powell's voice of moderation.[35] Neoconservatives dominated U.S. policy and the policy process. The Vice President's Office, the Pentagon, some parts of the National Security Council, and the U.S. Congress were stacked with optimists of all shapes and sizes who supported a revolutionary approach to foreign policy that sought to democratize the Middle East and free it from corrupt tyrants. Interagency coordination between them was deftly facilitated by neoconservative bureaucrats: Paul Wolfowitz, who was number two at the Pentagon; the Vice President's National Security Advisor and former Wolfowitz mentee I. Lewis "Scooter" Libby; and the National Security Council's Elliott Abrams.[36] These three individuals, who shared an emotional commitment to Israel, believed that the United States and Israel were projecting weakness in a dangerous world, that their moral stature was diminished by dealings with corrupt Arab and Muslim regimes, and that the U.S.-led peace process was symptomatic of these two shortcomings.[37]

This neoconservative worldview was circulated in conservative pro-Israel circles for many years and outlined in a 1996 study group paper to which Defense Policy Board Chairman Richard Perle, Undersecretary of Defense for Policy Douglas Feith, and Cheney's Principal Deputy National Security Advisor David Wurmser added their names. In establishing "a new intellectual foundation" for peace, they encouraged Israeli Prime Minister Benjamin Netanyahu to make "a clean break" with the stated policy of the U.S. government. Without addressing the negative ramifications of socially engineering a "realm" populated by over two hundred million people, the document optimistically conjectured that the royal Hashemite tribe, as descendents of the Prophet Mohammad, could simply usurp authority in Iraq and thereby diminish Iranian and Syrian influence.[38] In pursuit of a new beginning, the document advised Israel to prepare for an end to the Oslo political process, strike Syrian interests in Lebanon, find alternatives to Arafat who would remain accountable to the Palestinian people, engage in "hot pursuit" in Palestinian areas to prevent terrorist attacks, and work on removing Saddam Hussein. The strategy paper explicitly sought to kill the reciprocal "land for peace" strategy, and replace it with a sequential one that pursued "peace through strength" and "peace for peace."[39]

Moderates at the State Department tended to deride grand neoconservative strategies as dreams that were both deluded and dangerous for U.S. interests.[40] During his first National Security Council meeting, Powell was shocked by Bush's suggestion that the United States could reverse a thirty-year diplomatic effort and pull out of the Arab-Israeli conflict because the president did not "see much we can do over there at this point."[41] Powell did not like Arafat and was not eager to mediate an intensive peace process; however, as a decorated four-star general with an intimate knowledge of the Middle East, he knew that the president and secretary of state of the United States could not simply walk away and politically disengage from the Palestinian leader.[42] During a visit to the Middle East in February 2001, Powell gained first-hand exposure to the havoc being wreaked in the absence of serious diplomacy. Equally important, as the *Intifada* intensified, he realized that the president of the Palestinian Authority was losing "control of events."[43]

Despite the chaos, on Sharon's first visit to Washington as prime minister, he was warmly welcomed by Bush.[44] An Israeli general with a reputation for being a "bulldozer," Sharon and his conservative nationalist government shared some similarities with the conservative alliance in the United States. Like U.S. conservatives, Sharon's expansionism was in part powered by theoconservative U.S. Christians who viewed "Judea and Samaria"—the West Bank—as being their divine birthright. Like U.S. conservatives, Sharon had his own utopian visions of "Jordan as Palestine."[45] And like U.S. conservatives, Sharon had a strong aversion to a parallel process of negotiations and concessions.

If politics is the continuation of warfare by other means, in Washington, D.C., Sharon applied this principle time and again.[46] During his meeting with Bush, he issued a scathing critique of his archenemy Yasser Arafat and defined rogue states with missiles, not the Israeli-Palestinian conflict, as the region's gravest geopolitical threat. The Bush administration subsequently shocked the Palestinians by indicating that Arafat would not be invited to Washington. Instead, Powell stated the administration's policy was to "assist, not insist" in the peace process.[47]

Sharon interpreted Bush's warm welcome and hands-off approach as a green light for aggressive preemption—"hot pursuit"—into the occupied Palestinian territories, but he could not entirely evade the State Department's influence. Following Israel's April 2001 incursion into Gaza, Powell issued harsh criticism of Israel's "excessive and disproportionate" use of force, and the Israeli Defense Forces (IDF) quickly withdrew its soldiers within twenty-four hours. While Powell indicated that the attacks were provoked by Palestinian mortars, his criticism of Israel was also harsh. Yet in keeping with Bush's wishes, he rearticulated the administration's commitment to remain distant from the peace process, and to "facilitate" rather than "force" talks.[48]

Powell was not interested in forcing peace negotiations; as the violence in the Middle East escalated, however, he successfully moderated Bush's position and convinced him to address the chaotic security situation.[49] Against conservative wishes, Bush dispatched CIA Director George Tenet and the State Department's William J. Burns to negotiate a shaky ceasefire, known as the Tenet Plan, to which both sides reluctantly agreed.[50] As David Wurmser recounts, administration conservatives opposed the CIA's involvement in Middle East policy because it compromised the intelligence community's ability to provide accurate intelligence.[51] More than anything, however, conservatives opposed the Tenet mission because involving a Clinton appointee in Israeli-Palestinian affairs, along with a career diplomat from the State Department, meant that a political process based on the principle of parallelism was brewing. The Tenet Plan, which emphasized the revitalization of security cooperation and intelligence-sharing between the Israeli government and the Palestinian Authority, was an attempt to get the situation back to where it was prior to the outbreak of the second *Intifada*, and ultimately to get back to Mitchell's vision of a process with parallel negotiations and concessions.[52] According to George Tenet, his efforts ultimately failed because "there was no corollary political or incentive process."[53]

Despite Tenet's best efforts, violence continued to escalate toward the end of June 2001, and Sharon refused to accept anything less than "100 percent results" in preventing attacks against Israelis. But then his crusade went a step too far in describing Arafat as "our Bin Laden."[54] Although Sharon's argument would be the death knell for the Palestinians' public image following 9/11, in June 2001 Sharon's comments were unacceptable to Bush. The president stood with the moderates, rejected Sharon's incendiary remarks, and praised the CIA-brokered ceasefire and the progress being made on the ground, much to the disappointment of U.S. and Israeli conservatives.

In publicly opposing Sharon, Bush issued a "humiliating public blow" to the Israeli premier that compromised the latter's public standing in Israel.[55] On his way to the European Union summit, Bush "expressed himself in a pretty disparaging way about Sharon" because, as Christopher Meyer observed, "this was not some-body he enjoyed dealing with."[56] As violence continued to escalate amid continuing disregard for the Tenet Plan, Sharon ordered the permanent takeover of Orient House, the Palestinian Authority's presence in Jerusalem. The State Department described Israel's move as "a serious political escalation" and urged both sides to resist "incitement and provocations."[57]

International pressure mounted on Bush to do something about the vio-lence. UN Secretary General Kofi Annan dispatched his special envoy, Catherine Bertini, to the region; she subsequently produced a published report that stated, "there is a serious humanitarian crisis in the West Bank," one that is "inextrica-bly linked to the ongoing conflict and particularly to the measures imposed by Israel in response to suicide and other attacks against Israeli military and civilian targets."[58] In the Middle East, Crown Prince Abdullah of Saudi Arabia expressed his great disapproval "of the 'hands off'" approach by sending "one of the toughest messages in the history of the American-Saudi relationship." Alluding to petro-politics, he threatened not to take U.S. interests into account unless Bush dealt with the Palestinian problem. In response to mounting pressure from friends and allies, Assistant Secretary of State William Burns asked his senior Middle East advisor, Aaron David Miller, to start drafting a major speech for Powell on the Arab-Israeli conflict. To placate Saudi anger, moderate National Security Council Senior Director Bruce Riedel drafted the president's response to the crown prince, committing the United States to a "viable independent Palestinian state." Signifi-cantly, the response incorporated the language of Palestinian self-determination.[59]

Before 9/11, therefore, Bush's support for Israel was strong but not unquali-fied, and his commitment to the hands-off approach was sometimes set aside when broader U.S. interests throughout the Middle East were at stake. Though he vacil-lated between conservative and moderate worldviews, when push came to shove, he leaned more in the direction of moderation. Like many U.S. presidential can-didates, he did not follow through on his campaign promises to move the U.S. embassy from Tel Aviv to Jerusalem and did not always abstain from scolding Israel.[60] For example, Bush privately rebuked Sharon's continuing characterization of Arafat as Osama bin Laden.[61] While Cheney justified Israel's preemptive strategy of assassinations and Powell described them as "highly provocative," Bush took a middle ground, urging both Israelis and Palestinians to refrain from using violence.[62] Prior to 9/11, Bush was even planning on announcing a possible United Nations–based meeting with Arafat to shore up deteriorating relations with the Arab world.[63]

The Impact of 9/11

If the competition between a utopian vision for regional transformation and a more realistic vision of Middle East stability was beginning to grow apparent, the newly declared "War on Terror" cast these divisions into sharp relief. Most important, the utter devastation wreaked on the United States on September 11, 2001, had a profound psychological impact on Bush and his view of the Middle East. As Meyer recalls, Bush was an "emotional man," not a "cold calculating machine." The terrorist attack shocked the new president and suddenly presented him with the daunting responsibility of protecting three hundred million people from grave and imminent danger. He consequently came to see himself not simply as another world leader but in messianic terms, as "God's chosen instrument to spread freedom and democracy and to smite the terrorists."[64] Calling his War on Terror a "crusade," Bush stated that his purpose was nothing short of ridding "the world of evil-doers."[65] Though he would lead a "monumental struggle of good versus evil," Bush affirmed that "good will prevail."[66]

Outwardly the nation and the administration appeared united, but inwardly the administration's chasm between moderates and conservatives widened, with the president stuck in the middle, greatly bothered and at times bewildered by it all. According to Wurmser, the intellectual "fissure" between the two sides was primarily about how two fundamental questions were answered. First, what was the source of the terrorists' rage? Second, should the United States regard counterterrorism efforts as requiring more limited "police action" or all-out war against state sponsors of terrorism?[67] Interestingly, these are the same questions raised by Bernard Lewis, a recipient of the National Humanities medal from George W. Bush in 2006. Though not an entirely new argument, Lewis concluded that "Muslim rage" is rooted not in grievances against imperialism or Zionism, but in a fundamental rejection of secular modernity and individual liberty. For Lewis, only liberal democracy could save the suicide bomber from becoming a "metaphor for the whole region."[68]

Revered as the dean of Middle East studies, Lewis had a powerful impact on conservative members of the Bush administration.[69] Significantly, Lewis's commentary led to a single utopian policy conclusion: because the rage was rooted in the undemocratic nature of Muslim society, the only way the United States could prevent another 9/11 was to democratize the Middle East forcibly. Senior conservative officials and advisors like Rumsfeld, Cheney, Wurmser, Feith, Abrams, Wolfowitz, Perle, and Libby embraced Lewis's worldview. They argued that "deep bitterness exploded into rage" on 9/11, and that "disdain" for shared U.S. and Israeli values was at the very heart of the problem. Endemic rage was being channelled by corrupt Saudi, Egyptian, Syrian, Palestinian, and Iranian leaders to sustain their regimes. It followed from this conceptual framework that the United States should not simply engage in "police action," but should regard the problem of terrorism as a massive problem of "statecraft" that required, in the words of Cheney, the use of "overwhelming power in defense of freedom."[70] So-called "friendly" regimes like Egypt needed to be reformed and democratized, while dictators like Saddam Hussein and Yasser Arafat needed to be replaced with transparent, democratic institutions built from the "bottom-up."[71] Conservatives were fundamentally opposed to a parallel political process because they regarded the Israeli-Palestinian conflict as the symptom, not the cause, of the rage. Instead, they argued for a sequential approach: democratically elected leaders would be needed to remove terrorism from the Middle East. Then, and only then, could peace negotiations commence.

By contrast, administration moderates such as Powell, Burns, and Deputy Secretary of State Richard Armitage saw the roots of rage as "humiliation and grievances," with the continued suffering of Palestinians, a consequence of continued Israeli occupation, being first and foremost. For them, the conservative view of Palestinians confused freedom with democracy, and pursued the latter at the expense of the former. Powell was a distinguished general and an influential former chairman of the Joint Chiefs of Staff who fully understood the horrors of war, the limitations of force, and the necessity of diplomacy to secure stability.[72] Like Powell, Armitage was a military man who had seen combat during the Vietnam War, and over the years had gained first-hand field experience in the Middle East.[73] While Powell and Armitage did not diminish the virtues of individual liberty, they rejected utopian plans to impose Jeffersonian democracy on a region of the world that had developed its own political cultures and institutions over the centuries. More important, they understood that Arab societies value honor just as much as people in the United States value individual liberty, and that countries could not simply be ideologically transformed by "shock and awe." After 9/11, it followed from the moderate worldview that it was in the national interest of the United States to focus on resolving the Israeli-Palestinian conflict in order to maintain crucial alliances with friendly Arab states, explore strategic relationships with potential allies like Iran, and secure vital interests in the region and around the world.[74] The United States, it was argued, should pursue police action against terrorism, and engage imperfect Arab leaders, including Arafat, in the fight.[75] Because a political process based on reciprocal concessions was seen as a necessary precondition to regional progress, a parallel political process was preferred to a sequential process that required concessions first of the Palestinians. As Wurmser puts it, conservative and moderate worldviews were incompatible with one another, like two completely different languages.[76]

Caught in the middle of this bureaucratic battle, Bush wavered indecisively. Because of his pro-Israel inclinations and devoutly held belief in the God-given power of individual liberty, the president was predisposed to the conservative agenda.[77] But he also empathized with moderate arguments that highlighted the need for political progress. In matters of policy he relied heavily on the advice of his trusted National Security Advisor, Condoleezza Rice, an accomplished Stanford political science professor who unsuccessfully tried to referee the war within the administration. Rice was trained as a realist, but like Bush, had a strong tendency to support the conservative focus on individual freedom.[78] As the president's closest advisor, she was harshly criticized by both sides for not mediating disputes between conservatives and moderates, and for mixing and matching incommensurable worldviews.[79] She valued receiving diverse opinions, but, as Wurmser argued, mixing policies only works if starting assumptions are the same. Wurmser and Armitage, a conservative and a moderate, both concluded that in the absence of an effective arbiter, feelings of deep bitterness developed between the two administration camps and a "schizophrenic" Middle East policy emerged that confused Israelis and Palestinians alike.[80]

In this tense intellectual climate, the terrorist attacks of 9/11 not only polarized members of the administration; they also intensified Sharon's resolve to rid himself of Arafat. Rightly anticipating that moderates would deem Israeli-Palestinian negotiations to be a vital national security interest, Sharon continued to lobby for a green light to "go after Arafat" just as Bush was chasing down Bin Laden.[81] He argued that moderate plans to formally support a Palestinian state would reward Arafat and encourage terrorism.

Despite heavy conservative pressure, Bush rejected Sharon's on-going requests to chase down Arafat.[82] Incensed by moderate plans to give Arafat a Palestinian state, Sharon responded by accusing the president of capitulating to evil. The prime minister warned, "Do not repeat the dreadful mistake of 1938, when the enlightened democracies of Europe decided to sacrifice Czechoslovakia for the sake of a temporary, convenient solution. Don't try to appease the Arabs at our expense. We will not accept this.... Israel will fight terror."[83]

After receiving Sharon's threatening message, the White House replied to Sharon with harsh words, criticizing the prime minister's "unacceptable" comments and citing the president's eight-month record of support for Israel.[84] Sharon ultimately expressed regret for his comments but maintained his abiding concern that the United States would reverse its policy to "assist, not insist" and force a resolution to the conflict.[85] He was also upset that the United States was distinguishing between Al Qaeda on the one hand, and Hamas and Hezbollah on the other; the latter two organizations were not added to a list of terrorist groups whose financial assets would be seized.[86]

In a major blow to Sharon and conservatives, Bush listened to the counsel of moderates and took an unprecedented step in declaring his recognition of the Palestinian right to self-determination from the pulpit of the United Nations in November 2001. Despite Sharon's protests, and despite the Popular Front for the Liberation of Palestine's assassination of an Israeli minister following the assassination of one of their own leaders, Bush shocked the world by announcing his support for statehood. Based on the logic of parallelism, he declared his vision for a "just peace" based on previous UN Security Council resolutions and a two-state formula, and intentionally used the word "Palestine."[87]

The significance of this speech should not be underestimated. Rice recalls that the use of "Palestine" prompted a "really big fight" with conservative members of the administration and with the Israelis. The first draft of the UN speech used the "weasel language" that U.S. presidents had always used. Bush disliked this and asked his foreign policy team if there would be a Palestinian state if peace negotiations were successfully concluded. They said "yes," and then he asked what the state would be called. He was told "Palestine." Then the president firmly indicated that he would call for a State of Israel and a State of Palestine living side-by-side, but Rice knew that this was going to be a "huge problem" with the Israelis. She called Sharon's foreign policy advisor, Daniel Ayalon, who wanted Bush to use the words "new Palestine," not "Palestine." Despite pressure from the American Israel Public Affairs Committee (AIPAC), ultimately the president declared to the world, "we are working toward the day when two states—Israel and Palestine—live peacefully together within secure and recognized borders as called for by the Security Council resolutions."[88]

Bolstered by the president's move toward moderation, Powell declared that the Middle East peace process would be revived. His words were well received by Arab leaders, especially after a suicide bombing killed a British citizen in Saudi Arabia.[89] Meanwhile, Blair, King Abdullah II of Jordan, and other Arab leaders continued to place increasing pressure on the Bush administration to restart the peace process, especially since Arafat had made a more concerted effort to rein in violence.[90]

In an effort to halt Powell's momentum, conservatives intensified their efforts to link the Palestinian leadership and Al Qaeda; the fear generated by the 9/11 terrorist attacks presented the conservative alliance with just the fuel they needed. Following Sharon's lead, they argued that Arafat's terror and Bin Laden's terror were part of the same evil.[91] Despite Arafat's strong condemnation of 9/11, images of isolated Palestinian celebrations were broadcast on major U.S. news networks, reinforcing negative public perceptions of Palestinians in the United States.[92] And Pat Robertson's Christian Broadcasting Network never stopped reminding theoconservative audiences that Palestinians passed out candy in celebration while Israelis mourned the terrorist attacks.[93]

The work of the conservative alliance was paying off in the U.S. Congress, where the president needed support for his domestic and international agendas.

Eighty-nine senators, led by theoconservative Republican Senator Christopher S. Bond and Charles Schumer, a Democratic senator with conservative views on the Middle East conflict, sent a letter to Bush on November 17, 2001, urging him not to meet with Arafat and not to restrain Israel in retaliating against Palestinian terrorism. Indirectly referring to Powell, the letter stated, "The American people would never excuse us for not going after the terrorists with all our strength and might.... Yet that is what some have demanded of the Israeli government after every terrorist incident they suffer. No matter what the provocation, they urge restraint."[94]

But a moderate minority in Congress understood the dangers of isolating Arafat. Senator Chuck Hagel, a senior Republican member of the Foreign Relations Committee, did not sign the letter because he felt that it would be a mistake to "pick and choose who we deal with." Whatever one thought of Arafat as a person was "frankly irrelevant" because he was the "designated leader of a group of people that had to be dealt with in order to make any progress...[on] an Israeli-Palestinian problem that had vexed president after president in [a] world which was becoming more and more dangerous."[95]

Brushing conservative pressure aside, Powell followed up on his commitment to reignite the peace process in a major foreign policy address at the University of Louisville. Outside of the State Department, no top members of the administration, including Bush and Rice, wanted him to deliver the speech. But Powell fought for it and won, though he had to dilute some of his language.[96] His even-handed speech endorsed the principle of parallelism and, as such, made several points that infuriated the conservative alliance. First, he sought to disassociate Arafat from 9/11, noting that the terrorists do not "speak for the Palestinians, whose leaders have rejected Bin Laden's attempt to hijack their cause for his murderous ends." Second, he endorsed a return to a negotiated political process with the Palestinians and indicated that it was time for the United States to "recapture the spirit" of the Madrid talks that led to the negotiated Oslo accords.[97] Third, Powell emphasized that progress toward peace could not come from "violence and war," and condemned both Palestinian terrorism and Israeli violence against innocent civilians. Fourth, he indicated that the United States would return to its tradition of "serious diplomacy," and would provide "active American engagement" as it had done for half a century. Fifth, in an unprecedented statement, he declared that the "occupation must end," adding that settlement expansion must cease. Finally, he announced that he was dispatching General Anthony Zinni to the region as his special advisor.[98]

Conservative members of the administration were opposed to Powell's speech and the Zinni mission, precisely because these were viewed as a return to the loathed Madrid and Oslo methodology, which they believed appeased terrorism and made Israel and the United States appear weak. For them, it was based on the flawed logic that discrete final-status issues could be resolved by working with a "terrorist" and a "dictator" unrestrained by human rights organizations, a free media, and a supreme court.[99] Norway had given Arafat a Nobel Prize, Clinton had honored Arafat by making him one of the most frequent foreign visitors at the White House, and now Powell was going to hand him a state.

Arafat and the Axis of Evil

Bush's UN speech marked the height of Powell's influence, but the latter's political capital was rapidly diminishing. As Zinni noted, Bush displayed a good deal of intellectual capability, but lacked curiosity and avoided Powell's complexity when discussing Middle East politics. Because the president wanted things reduced to relatively "simple, linear" terms, and saw things in a "bifurcated" way, the conservative worldview, with its sharp good and evil categories, was far more appealing. Cheney and Rumsfeld tended to provide simplicity, and therefore, their views on Arafat gained more and more influence.[100] Most conservative members of the administration simply assumed that Arafat was an "authoritarian and a terrorist," not a legitimate representative of his people. They argued that one could not possibly embrace Arafat while condemning Al Qaeda.[101]

The conservatives seemed to have won for the moment. By December 2001, the president changed his mind and gravitated away from the moderates. Bush, Treasury Secretary Paul O'Neill, and theoconservative Attorney General John Ashcroft finally ordered the freezing of assets of three organizations linked to Hamas.[102] With a conservative victory in place, the Israeli cabinet decided to cut off relations with Arafat and brand him as "irrelevant." In a meeting with Jewish leaders in New York following the Israeli government's decision to marginalize Arafat, Bush placed the blame for continued violence squarely on the Palestinian leader.[103]

With U.S. pressure mounting, and after receiving repeated warnings from Powell, Arafat called on the Palestinians to cease suicide bombings against Israelis, although he emphasized that the rival Hamas party was not under his control.[104] In January 2002, his position hit a new low when the *Karine A*, a Gaza-bound ship carrying fifty tons of anti-tank missiles and other heavy explosives from Iran, was seized by Israel. Senior Palestinian security advisor Mohammad Dahlan contends that the *Karine A* incident was a "personal endeavour" because neither he nor Arafat knew about the shipment. When Arafat found out about the incident from Zinni in his Ramallah headquarters, he was reportedly "shocked" and agreed to punish those from within the Palestinian Authority who were involved.[105]

It is possible, but unlikely, that Arafat was unaware of the weapons shipment. Although "there wasn't evidence" linking the shipment directly to Arafat, it was widely believed, as Rice recalls, that Arafat had to know about "something of this magnitude."[106] Powell took a more cautious tone: "I cannot tie [the *Karine A* affair] directly to Chairman Arafat on the basis of the information that is available to me, but it is certainly a case where he should have known and may well have known. I just can't prove that he did know or had direct control over the operation."[107] Even if Arafat was personally innocent, as Powell noted, he still bore ultimate responsibility for actions undertaken by the Palestinian Authority and its leaders. Yet upon further reflection, as Powell's Chief of Staff Lawrence Wilkerson later disclosed, "we have all pondered on whether it was a hoax or not." The incident happened at exactly the moment when President Mohammed Khatami of Iran was seeking detente with the United States and Arafat was on the ropes. As Trita Parsi has suggested, it is possible that Israelis staged the shipment, or that rogue elements of the Iranian government initiated it in order to prevent a thawing of U.S.-Iranian diplomatic relations.[108]

If Bush perceived Camp David as Arafat's strike one and the launching of the second *Intifada* as his strike two, then the *Karine A* incident was his strike three.[109] Like Bush, Rice concluded that Arafat was the main problem in the Israeli-Palestinian arena and echoed the conservative view that he was the main obstacle to peace. When diplomats such as European Commissioner Christopher Patten discussed the matter with her, they conceded that Arafat was a problem, but emphasized that he was not the only problem. However, she responded forcefully by saying that he was "*the* problem."[110] Though the Bush administration, following Clinton's lead, had identified Arafat as the sole problem, in reality he was only a part of it. As Powell seemed to understand, the problem was far bigger and far more complex—a state without borders occupied by a people without rights in a territory without land through the patronage of an authority without power. Furthermore, as former U.S. President Jimmy Carter wrote in the *New York Times*, Arafat was democratically elected in 1996 in a competition that was "well-organized, open, and fair."[111]

Though Arafat should not be absolved from guilt, Carter argued that Sharon continued to disregard international law and the president of the United States in pursuit of dual aims: "to establish Israeli settlements as widely as possible throughout occupied territories and to deny Palestinians a cohesive political existence."[112] Regardless of what any Western leader thought of Arafat's antics, the majority of Palestinians, as former PLO representative Karma Nabulsi eulogized, hailed him as their democratically elected president and a symbol of their aspirations to be free from Israeli occupation.[113]

Despite resistance from moderates, complexity was reduced to simplicity. In black-and-white terms, conservatives characterized Arafat as nothing more than an unscrupulous dictator, "a terrorist," and the obstacle to peace.[114] By this time Arafat, who had been under siege from the Israelis in Ramallah since December 3, 2001, had lost control over the security situation and dissipated whatever international political capital he had left.[115] Seeking to restore legitimacy with the Bush administration, Arafat sent a letter to Powell accepting responsibility for the *Karine A* incident as head of the Palestinian Authority, but denied that he had prior knowledge of the shipment. The letter was received in a favorable light, but the damage was already done.[116] While Blair continued to see Arafat as "a necessary evil," Bush increasingly viewed Arafat "as just evil."[117]

As Bush's 2002 State of the Union address was prepared, the president was becoming more and more convinced that freedom was the antidote to evil in the Middle East and in Palestine specifically. The *Karine A* incident helped to frame Bush's controversial speech, which focused on state sponsors of terrorism such as Iran, Iraq, and North Korea. In lumping together bitter enemies within an "Axis of Evil," Bush sent a warning that he viewed the Middle East, including Palestine, in black-and-white terms.[118] Referring to the *Karine A* incident, Bush noted that Iran "exports terror," though he stayed away from mentioning Arafat or the Palestinians by name. Terrorism, Bush argued, would never stop the "momentum of liberty."[119] Though not stated, Bush came to believe that Arafat was blocking the progress of history; after Arafat was first associated with Bin Laden by Sharon, he was then linked to the "Axis of Evil" by Bush.

Arafat responded to the speech in a *New York Times* op-ed, stating his continued desire to pursue a viable two-state solution. He revisited the widely known fact that since the 1993 Oslo Accords, Israeli settlers in the occupied Palestinian territories had doubled.[120] Arafat asked, "How do I convince my people that Israel is serious about peace while over the past decade Israel intensified the colonization of Palestinian land from which it was ostensibly negotiating a withdrawal?" Furthermore, he argued that Sharon's "no peace partner" mantra should be turned on its head because it was Sharon who did not accept the Oslo Accords. For Arafat, the Palestinian people were "ready to end the conflict." Sharon was not.[121]

Bush's State of the Union speech was a portent of things to come. In February 2002, Jordanian Foreign Minister Marwan Muasher visited Arafat in Ramallah and warned him that Bush, unlike Clinton, saw things in black and white, and because he understood the magnitude of the damage done by the *Karine A* incident, Muasher urged immediate diplomatic action.[122] While Arafat was dealing with domestic and international political fallout, Sharon visited Bush in Washington, D.C., ostensibly to discuss Israeli-Palestinian relations. Publicly, the Israeli leader focused on Arafat as the major obstacle to the peace process. Because moderates had warned of serious damage to U.S. interests if Israel harmed Arafat, Bush decided to reject Sharon's request to replace the Palestinian leader, while reaffirming a "mutual desire to rid the world of terror."[123] The unofficial purpose of Sharon's visit, however, was to obtain assurances that Israel would be forewarned prior to a U.S. invasion of Iraq. He got what he wanted, and Bush promised to remove Scud missiles in western Iraq that could be used against Israel prior to an invasion.[124]

If Bush sought to accommodate Israel's concerns *vis-à-vis* Iraq, Sharon did not repay the courtesy. Amid pressure from Arab moderates, Bush asked Sharon to allow Arafat to attend the March 2002 Arab League Summit in Beirut, but Sharon refused.[125] Even as U.S. policy continued to lean significantly in the conservative direction in early 2002, Powell continued with a forceful message of moderation, demanding that Sharon withdraw from West Bank cities in advance of Zinni's arrival in the region. The administration was concerned that Sharon would launch a full-scale war, and that this would be counterproductive to Cheney's trip to the neighboring Arab states as he sought to build support for toppling Saddam Hussein.[126]

As a favor to the Saudi royal family, Cheney made an unusual concession and told Zinni that he would be willing to meet with Arafat, despite his utter disdain for the Palestinian leader.[127] But he did so with an Iraqi invasion on his mind. During the vice president's Middle East tour, he had heard a clear message that was consistent with the opinions expressed by Powell and General Tommy Franks, Commander in Chief of U.S. Central Command: the U.S. president must intervene in the Israeli-Palestinian conflict if any progress was to be made with Saddam Hussein. Saudi Crown Prince Abdullah and Kuwaiti Foreign Minister Sheikh Sabah al-Ahmad al-Jaber al-Sabah had asked Cheney to rescue Arafat from the Israelis so that he could attend the Arab League Summit.

In the end, Zinni recommended against the Cheney-Arafat meeting because he had met with the Palestinian leader on several occasions and felt that the Palestinian leader had a "sense of his own mortality." Arafat, who was prone to dramatic public displays, had described himself as the "last undefeated Arab general," a true revolutionary who was not going to leave a legacy of defeat.[128] More important, he was not allowing his senior aides to cooperate fully with the United States in the security arena, and this upset Zinni. But in passing up the Cheney-Arafat meeting, Zinni greatly undermined Powell's ability to challenge conservative orthodoxy. If nothing else, the meeting would have secured a diplomatic victory for his boss, Colin Powell.

Arafat's being forced to remain in his compound by Sharon was regarded as a powerful image of Arab humiliation that incited great hatred against the United States across the region. Arafat's situation was so miserable that Muasher had to bring him clean clothes on a diplomatic visit. While Arafat remained under siege, the rival Hamas organization, looking to subvert his power, carried out the tragic "Passover Bombings" in Netanya, Israel, killing 30 people and injuring 140. The international community strongly condemned the "morally repugnant" attacks; the Arab League endorsed the Saudi Peace Initiative the next day; and the following day Sharon launched Operation Defensive Shield, the largest offensive against the Palestinians since 1967.[129] To protest the unstable situation, on April 3, 2002, King Abdullah II of Jordan sent Bush a letter stating, "We have been instrumental in building consensus for the Saudi initiative, which has been translated into a collective Arab commitment to end the conflict with Israel, guarantee its security, and establish normal relations between all Arab states and Israel. Yet the actions of the Israeli government pose a serious threat to all the achievements we have jointly worked towards during the last ten years."[130]

In a momentary move back in the moderate direction, Bush softened his stance and delivered his first, soon-forgotten Rose Garden speech on April 4, 2002, to appease Arab anger. In it, he justified Israel's right to defend itself against terrorists, but also empathized with the humiliation that the Palestinians endured. The president endorsed the principle of parallelism, called for Israel to "withdraw" in accordance with UN resolutions, and announced that he would be sending Powell to the region.[131] Describing Sharon's actions as "unhelpful," Bush continued to criticize Israel's refusal to withdraw from the West Bank. Additionally, Zinni endorsed the Saudi peace plan, which was an unprecedented offer from Arab states, including Iraq and Libya, to normalize ties with Israel.[132]

Israel, however, continued its heavy-handed operations throughout West Bank cities. Burns called the aftermath of the fighting in Jenin, a refugee camp battleground, a "terrible human tragedy," and reported back to Powell that there was an unbelievable scene of "brick on brick rubble" in the West Bank. Burns's description "incensed [Powell and Armitage] quite a bit," but conservatives in the administration did not appear overly concerned.[133] In reports, the international community later determined that Israel violated international law. As a July 30, 2002, report stated, "the Israeli occupying forces have, without a doubt, committed serious violations of international humanitarian law. Also, without a doubt, war crimes, including grave breaches of the Fourth Geneva Convention, have been committed by Israel, the occupying Power, in several Palestinian cities, including in the Jenin refugee camp."[134]

At the urging of moderates and Christopher Meyer, Bush ordered Israel to "withdraw without delay."[135] For the time being, the U.S. and UK positions were briefly aligned, and Bush invited Blair out to his ranch in Crawford, Texas, where they conducted meetings on Iraq and held a joint press conference.[136] Blair's foreign policy advisor, David Manning, wanted the prime minister to use the Crawford meeting to push Bush on the Middle East peace process.[137] According to Meyer, the "immediate urgent issue" was the "out of control" situation in the West Bank, where bloodshed was inflicted on both sides. He remained very concerned that there would be a "train wreck" if the U.S. and UK leaders were not saying the same thing to Israel about withdrawal. For one thing, the president's conservative advisors were not happy at all about the "without delay" statement.[138]

Since their first meeting at Camp David, Bush and Blair developed a very close friendship, and the latter was sometimes able to influence the former to act on Israeli-Palestinian issues. Thus, with Blair's encouragement, Bush gave Powell marching orders to travel to the region and spend some "political capital."[139] Powell certainly did not volunteer for the trip, but the president said he needed Powell to show the world that the administration was doing something. Bush indicated that because Powell held an esteemed position in the United States, he could afford to lose a bit of political capital. But from the moment Powell left, administrative conservatives were "determined that [he] would not have much to work with."[140] In Meyer's words, he was "screwed right, left, and center by Wolfowitz's and Cheney's people."[141] Once Armitage got wind of their strategy, he called Powell and warned him, "they're eating cheese on you!"[142] Rumors were circulating that the Department of Defense and the Office of the Vice President were trying to "do him in."[143] Though Bush directed Powell to make the trip, even his White House staff did not forcefully back Powell's efforts because fundamentally Bush considered the visit a show.[144]

Though Powell's mission was compromised by conservatives, it was not a complete diplomatic failure. By making his presence known, he restrained Sharon and effectively saved Arafat's life, thereby preventing a regional crisis. Given the mood in Washington, however, he warned the Palestinian leader that this meeting could be their last.[145] During one of his lunches with Arafat, Powell asked for something tangible to work with—for Arafat to shut down the violent rhetoric, and to get the "terrorist forces under control." Arafat jumped up in a "light hearted manner" and said, "You are a general, I am a general, and I will obey!" But Arafat was "incapable of doing what [Powell] asked of him." For Powell, Arafat was the leader of a movement, not someone who could create a state or run a government.[146]

Powell personally disliked Arafat's lack of statesmanship and inability to deliver, but he also recognized that Arafat could never be sure if "Sharon was really serious about creating a [Palestinian] state." Powell recalls that when "you look at where the settlement blocks have gone in, when you look at how the West Bank has been sliced and diced with roads and tunnels and other things, you have to wonder whether anybody really intended for this to be a cohesive state." The Israelis were planning to "build more tunnels to sort of bisect the land that was supposed to be a contiguous state."[147] After all, Sharon had conveyed to both Zinni and Hagel on separate occasions that it would take twenty, thirty, fifty, even a hundred years before peace was possible.[148] It was Zinni's opinion that Sharon never lost sight of a non-contiguous Palestinian entity consisting of "Judea, Samaria, Gaza—three enclaves living in a Greater Israel with self-autonomy and the ability to move back and forth—some Indian reservations."[149]

Powell spent over a week in the region, and was able to reduce the tension, but did not succeed in getting a peace process started. First, the conditions were not right, and second, he did not have the support he needed from the president.[150] Clearly, Powell's State Department was becoming an increasingly marginalized voice as the conservatives once again gained ascendancy. But their rise was not without regional repercussions.[151]

CHAPTER 3

The Rose Garden and the Road Map

In mid-2002, the Bush administration's inability to act decisively in the Israeli-Palestinian arena was damaging U.S. relationships with Arab allies. Saudi Arabia's Crown Prince Abdullah declined an invitation to the White House because the kingdom was experiencing an internal political crisis due to popular outrage over the deteriorating situation in the West Bank. Subsequently, Saudi Prince Bandar, a close friend of the Bush family, briefed the president at the White House for five hours. He told Bush that the continuing violence in the West Bank and perceptions of U.S. support for Israeli actions against civilians would fuel greater extremism, adding that the United States and its moderate Arab allies "will pay a very high price." Prince Bandar warned, "The region is boiling and it's building and it's building."[1] Simultaneously, competing and much more forceful domestic pressure was being placed on the administration to give Israel a free hand to use force against the Palestinians. While Bush's "withdraw without delay" orders may have been directed at improving U.S. standing abroad, his words unleashed a firestorm among his conservative political base back at home. A backlash of this magnitude could not be ignored.[2]

Because of conservative support within the administration, Congress, and Bush's re-election base, Israeli Prime Minister Ariel Sharon brushed off the president's "withdraw without delay" orders as a strategy to obtain Arab support for the Iraq War. He wagered correctly that the conservative alliance in the United States, exceptionally motivated by a string of suicide bombings in Israel, would dwarf any European or Arab pressure being exerted on the president. As expected, conservative anger exploded into fury, and the president reversed course.

With considerable pressure from the conservative alliance, Bush's June 2002 Rose Garden speech established the sequence principle and effectively called for regime change in Palestine as a precondition of reestablishing the peace process. Though sequence came to be seen as a central pillar of Bush's freedom agenda for the Palestinians, the president continued to vacillate back and forth between the Rose Garden vision of sequence and the Road Map's vision of parallelism.[3]

Bush's Firestorm

Bush moved away from the moderate view on the Israeli-Palestinian conflict for several reasons. First, administration officials—mostly neoconservatives and nationalist conservatives—joined forces with conservative allies in Israel to make the case for regime change in Iraq and Palestine. Because a political process would involve relinquishing, in the words of Secretary of Defense Donald Rumsfeld, a "so-called occupied area…which [Israel] won," conservatives saw no need for Israel to deal with Yasser Arafat.[4] Instead, they argued that the tragedy of 9/11 sharpened the categories of good and evil, presenting the United States with the opportunity to remove Arafat from power, dismantle terrorist institutions, and nurture new Palestinian leadership. According to this sequence principle, no political process would commence until an entirely new, democratically elected Palestinian leadership was in place.[5] Until this happened, it was argued, the United States should focus on regime change in Iraq and Iran. The result would be a democratic domino effect that would transform the region into a "new Middle East."

Neoconservatives tended to view the Middle East as a *tabula rasa* upon which they would construct a new social order. In practical terms, they argued that regimes in Iraq and Palestine could be replaced with Hashemite solutions.[6] In October 2003, Bernard Lewis and former CIA Director James Woolsey suggested that because Hashemites were agnates of the Prophet, a monarch could simply be brought in to lead Iraq to democracy, just as King Juan Carlos had done for Spain.[7]

Though Hashemite monarchs were at one point seen by neoconservatives as the silver-bullet solution for both Iraq and the Palestinians, it became clear that installing a Hashemite king in Iraq was not being taken seriously by anyone else. Additionally, for fear of losing his dynasty, King Abdullah II categorically rejected the so-called "Jordanian option" for Palestine.[8] Neoconservatives searched elsewhere for alternatives to Saddam Hussein and Arafat. They found two exiles who spoke their language of democracy and freedom. For Iraq, they bet on Ahmad Chalabi, the infamous leader of the Iraqi National Congress, who promised that U.S. forces would be "greeted as liberators."[9] For the Palestinians they found Omar Karsou, an exiled Palestinian banker living in New York, who founded an obscure movement known as "Democracy in Palestine." Karsou was a harsh critic of Arafat's corruption, the Palestinian Authority, and the Oslo Accords. He was touted by Richard Perle and Bernard Lewis at the influential Hudson Institute, hailed in the *Wall Street Journal* as a "Palestinian Mandela," and designated by Israeli Deputy Prime Minister Natan Sharansky as an authentic representative "of the Palestinian middle class." After making his rounds with senior officials in Washington, Karsou was invited to a dinner with Vice President Dick Cheney and Deputy Secretary of Defense Paul Wolfowitz in Colorado.[10] The only problem with the neoconservatives' plan to liberate the Palestinians was that the latter had democratically elected Yasser Arafat as their leader, and unlike the real Mandela, very few people in the world knew of Karsou's existence.

The second reason Bush moved away from moderates was because Congress pressured him to.[11] Because there is little political risk associated with an aggressive pro-Israel policy, conservatives were able to play an influential role in shifting the congressional consensus to the right. This influence is clearly evident in the fact that by 2004, half of the U.S. Senate had received an 80 percent or higher approval rating from the Eagle Forum, a leading theoconservative organization.[12] During the Bush years, several powerful members of Congress aggressively promoted theoconservative views: Senate Republican Conference Chair Rick Santorum, Senate Majority Leader Bill Frist, Senate Republican Policy Chair Jon Kyl, House Majority Whip Roy Blunt, House Majority Leader Dick Armey, Senator Jesse Helms, and Senator Trent Lott.[13] Significantly, House Majority Whip Tom DeLay delivered a case for preemptive war in Iraq and Palestine, citing the "special destiny" of the United States to defend freedom and the centrality of Israel in God's plan to end the world. Lining up behind his friend Cheney, DeLay pledged that he would "lead the effort to provide President Bush the unified support of the House of Representatives" for the Iraq War. He also pledged to stand by Israel until the very end.[14]

In addition to theoconservatives, many influential Republican and Democratic members of Congress held views of the Middle East that were aligned with Zionist conservatives and neoconservatives.[15] As Chairman of the Defense Policy Board Richard Perle noted, while "the influence on the president of the Jewish community is greatly overstated…there's real influence in Congress."[16] European Commissioner Christopher Patten experienced this influence firsthand when he visited a group of U.S. senators in 2002. He was told "what you've got to understand, Commissioner, is that we're all members of the Likud Party here."[17]

In May 2002, both houses of Congress overwhelmingly passed resolutions expressing support for Israeli incursions into the occupied Palestinian territories, despite requests from the Bush administration to soften the language. With these sentiments, the congressional campaign to eliminate Arafat only intensified. Armey took to the airwaves and indicated that Israel should "grab the entire West Bank" and that the Palestinians should move to neighboring Arab countries.[18] Armey was the former leader of the Texas Republican Party, whose 2008 platform stated that Middle East policy should be "based on God's biblical promise to bless those who bless Israel and curse those who curse Israel." He once stated that his "No. 1 priority in foreign policy is to protect Israel."[19] Theoconservative Tom DeLay, who succeeded Armey as House Majority Leader, similarly opposed Israeli concessions and noted, "I've toured Judea and Samaria…and stood on the Golan Heights. I didn't see occupied territory. I saw Israel."[20] The policy objective of DeLay, Armey, and the theoconservatives was to change regimes throughout the region so that pro-Western democratic leaders would emerge, leaving Israel to rebuild the temple in Jerusalem. As DeLay argued, "Christ cannot return until the temple in Jerusalem is rebuilt. And then the temple in Jerusalem is not going to be rebuilt unless it's a Jewish state. So, I don't know. I mean, I'm not a biblical scholar, but it is quite obvious to me that, over time, and who knows what that time is, you have a Jewish state…and the prophecies can come true, because they have come true. And ultimately, Christ will return...there's one thing for certain, that the prophecies will be fulfilled." For Tom DeLay, that preordained moment would be the end (termination) of history.[21]

Members of Congress often disregard their own denominations' views in upholding theoconservative attitudes toward Israel because they or, at the very least, their constituencies hold to the Christian Zionist belief that God gave the Holy Land to the Jewish people.[22] For example, Senator James M. Inhofe, who is a member of the Presbyterian Church USA denomination that voted to divest from companies profiting from the Israeli occupation, expressed his opposition to Bush's more moderate policies, saying, "I believe very strongly that we ought to support Israel.... Because God said so."[23] Similarly, Senator Sam Brownback, a Roman Catholic who supported Israeli Minister of Tourism Binyamin Elon's plan for transferring Palestinians out of the West Bank, remarked in a speech before the Israeli Knesset: "I looked out the window of my hotel and saw the flag of Israel with the Star of David and the thought entered my mind, 'God does keep His promises!' That flag which had been absent in this land for nearly 2,000 years was now flying again."[24]

Congressional support for Israel's actions in the West Bank reflected the power of pro-Israel Jewish groups, working in tandem with theoconservatives, to shape foreign policy.[25] But the third reason Bush moved away from moderates was because conservative commentators placed enormous pressure on him.[26] Writers such as Charles Krauthammer, Norman Podhoretz, William Safire, Natan Sharansky (who was also an Israeli politician), and William Kristol enjoyed considerable influence within the administration.[27] In recognition of their influence, Bush awarded the coveted Presidential Medal of Freedom to Irving Kristol (William Kristol's father and the "godfather" of neo-conservatism) in 2002, Norman Podhoretz in 2004, and Natan Sharansky and William Safire in 2006.

In an effort to shift the public discourse to the right, commentators directed their harshest criticisms against the administration's lack of decisiveness in dealing with the Palestinian leadership's inability to stop terrorist attacks. Neoconservative *New York Times* columnist William Kristol criticized the administration for "turning a blind eye to Arafat's behavior."[28] Robert Kagan even slammed Cheney for appeasing the Saudis with his offer to meet Arafat.[29] *Washington Post* columnist Charles Krauthammer compared Arafat to the Nazis.[30] A *Wall Street Journal* lead editorial remarked that Sharon's aggressive strategy could only be faulted for not going far enough.[31] At the *New York Times*, William Safire criticized National Security Advisor Condoleezza Rice for "mollifying the press, dovish partisans and Gaza terrorists."[32] Fouad Ajami, in the *Wall Street Journal*, accused Arafat of feeding a "cult of terror."[33] In the *National Review*, John Derbyshire suggested that expulsion "might be the best option" for the Palestinians.[34] Meanwhile, numerous other talk show hosts, newspapers, and online media outlets intensified their campaign against Bush's moderate line.

The fourth reason Bush moved away from moderates was because conservative pro-Israel lobby groups organized public displays of political power. On April 15, 2002, the Israel Solidarity Rally, co-sponsored by the United Jewish Federation, attracted over 100,000 conservative activists from college campuses, synagogues, and churches to Washington, D.C. A long list of prominent speakers, including theoconservatives William Bennett, Janet Parshall, and Armey, reinforced a central point: Arafat was a terrorist and a dictator. Sharansky, the deputy prime minister of Israel, expounded on this theme, noting that Arafat was part of an evil "axis of terror." Former Israeli Prime Minister Benjamin Netanyahu followed Sharansky in describing Arafat as "Osama bin Laden with good PR."[35] Days before the demonstration, Netanyahu stood before the U.S. Senate and criticized Bush, demanding that "Yasser Arafat's terrorist regime…be toppled, not courted."[36]

In an effort to calm the popular outrage, Bush and his Deputy Chief of Staff Karl Rove decided to send Wolfowitz, a well-known pro-Israel conservative, to speak before the crowd of activists. The speech was intended to distance the White House from Secretary of State Colin Powell and to signal that the president had heard the voice of his political base. Wolfowitz reluctantly agreed to speak.[37] In his preapproved remarks, he linked Palestinian terrorism to 9/11 terrorism. He angered the crowd, however, by suggesting that innocents on both sides were suffering.[38] The furious crowd booed him amidst chants of "no more Arafat."[39] Such public displays of anger sent a powerful message to Bush that moderation would not be tolerated.

The fifth reason Bush moved away from the moderates was because his election base demanded it. He was looking to "quell a growing furor" from activists who were outraged with the administration's criticism of Israel and the apparent loss of "moral clarity" in Bush's handling of the "War on Terror."[40] Theoconservative support for Israel had always been strong, but it "took on a sense of urgency and an intensity that [had not] been seen before."[41] As Rove later disclosed to Jordanian Foreign Minister Marwan Muasher, such domestic pressure significantly constrained the ability of the United States to advance the peace process.[42] UK Prime Minister Tony Blair's chief of staff, Jonathan Powell, recalls that Rove was closely watching the views of theo-conservative activists, not only because they would help drive support for Republicans in the 2002 elections, but also because they were the ones who could turn out other voters who were ultimately "crucial in winning the 2004 election." Powell remarked that Bush would have been a "rather odd politician if he didn't respond to calls from his base to take a different line."[43]

The final and most significant reason why Bush moved away from the moderates was because he was more attracted to a utopian theological worldview. After all, according to him, "there is nothing bigger than world peace."[44] The president believed in the universal power of individual freedom not because it was "America's gift to the world" but because it "is God's gift to humanity."[45] He saw the United States as God's instrument to facilitate the spread of freedom. Following conventional neoconservative wisdom, he came to believe that the Middle East terrorism problem was due to a "freedom deficit," which was driven by despair and a lack of hope. For Bush, "the antidote to terrorism and the basis for permanent peace in the Middle East was freedom and democracy." He concluded that if the Palestinians could develop a "free state" with accountable leaders, then freedom would sweep the Middle East—first upon the rocky hills of the West Bank and then in the deserts of Iraq.[46]

As Rice recalled, though it's impossible to run an experiment and see how a statesman would have acted as a nonbeliever, faith was clearly very important to Bush and informed his view of "God as an agent."[47] Similarly, former Deputy National Security Advisor Elliott Abrams noted that Bush's faith influenced this view of freedom for the Palestinians because he believed that "rights are God-given. Rights do not come from the state. Rights do not even come from the democratic collectivity.... Rights come from God. Rights inhere in the individual and inhere in his or her relationship with God." This conviction informed his conclusion that "democracy should be universal." He rejected the view that democracy was something for Westerners and understood that "bringing democracy to these regions was the work of generations."[48]

Former National Security Advisor Stephen Hadley went so far as to say that the freedom agenda is the essence of "who [Bush] is." As Hadley summed up, Bush believed that "people have a God-given right to be free. It's the same principle as the radical belief in the individual and the right of individuals to be free that is the essence of this man. And it's why he thought we had terrorism coming out of the Middle East, because of the freedom deficit in the Middle East.... And for him then, *the antidote to terrorism and the basis for permanent peace in the Middle East was freedom and democracy.*" [49] In addition, Bush shared many beliefs with mainstream evangelicals in the United States, including their admiration of Israel. Tim Goeglein, a special assistant to the president and liaison to theoconservatives, believed "very strongly that President Bush is in the camp that believes that Israel is a special, unique country…with providential overlays," and that the United States and Israel share a common destiny.[50]

The Rose Garden Sequence

By temperament, Bush was decisively indecisive and at critical junctures such as this one, he exhibited a tendency to waver to and fro between moderate and conservative policy recommendations. Contrary to the view of his loyal aides, the president appeared to be easily influenced and at times confused by the many forceful opinions being presented by some of the most adept politicians in Washington. Amid continuing pressure from Sharon, conservative activists, pundits, members of Congress, and members of his own administration, Bush capitulated and declared Sharon to be a "man of peace."[51] It is clear that the shock of the 9/11 attacks, combined with a confluence of forces, nudged Bush in the conservative direction. Additionally, interpersonal relations between Sharon and Bush were steadily improving, and as the White House's chief speechwriter Michael Gerson recalls, the president started to develop a "growing, grudging admiration" for the prime minister's efforts to combat terrorism. As the two men moved toward a solid working relationship, Bush started to trust the Israeli leader more.[52] He gave up his calls for Israeli withdrawal and instead focused on the question of what to do about Yasser Arafat.

Bush decided to address the question of Arafat directly and charged Rice with overseeing the preparation of a major foreign policy address on the Israeli-

Palestinian conflict. In what came to be known as the Rose Garden Speech of June 24, 2002, Bush laid the foundation for his new Middle East.[53] There were several motivations driving the speech. First, Bush needed to pacify conservatives who were wary that he might once again lapse back into moderation. Secondly, as a prerequisite to obtaining support for the Iraq War, he was being pressured by European and Arab allies to act decisively in the Israeli-Palestinian arena. Blair, a crucial ally, was especially insistent on this.[54] Third, and most important, Bush retained a firm belief, informed by deep religious convictions, that the people of Palestine deserved to be freed from Arafat's tyranny and corruption.[55]

While Bush was theologically predisposed to the neoconservative notion of "democracy for peace," this was an old argument circulated for many years among those opposed to Israeli Prime Minister Yitzhak Rabin and the Oslo peace process.[56] After the 9/11 attacks, the case for democracy obtained a skillful evangelist in neoconservative Israeli Deputy Prime Minister Natan Sharansky.[57] One could be forgiven for mistaking Sharansky's words for those of a Palestinian human rights activist. He sang the song of freedom with the conviction and authority of a liberated gulag prisoner of conscience. He had enjoyed the praise of individuals ranging from former U.S. President Jimmy Carter to the Archbishop of Canterbury, but his foray into extreme right-wing Israeli politics lost him many prominent admirers in the West.[58]

Beneath the surface, Sharansky's case for democracy was viewed as a nightmare among Palestinians, precisely because it located their liberty within the negative space defined by Israeli liberty. Sharansky fundamentally opposed any compromises that would erode Jewish identity by removing settlements, dividing Jerusalem, and acknowledging the rights of Palestinian refugees. He categorically dismissed Palestinian claims of injustice and defended his religious nationalism by arguing that Israel's democracy depended on the maintenance of exclusive Jewish cultural and geographical boundaries. He fundamentally rejected the notion that the Israeli occupation was the primary obstacle to Palestinian freedom. Instead, he adapted a powerful idea from Rousseau; the people must be "forced to be free."[59]

Sharansky's intellectual influence within the Bush administration was substantial, and in many ways outshined Sharon's.[60] He translated his democratic peace theory into a simple but influential plan published in the *Jerusalem Post* on May 3, 2002.[61] And eventually, Sharansky's words touched the heart of the president. Administration conservatives in the Pentagon and the Vice President's Office also played a large role in shaping the aggressive direction of Bush's speech. Though they initially viewed it as an unnecessary concession to those demanding U.S. intervention in the Middle East conflict, if there was to be a speech, they wanted it delivered on their terms.[62] Undersecretary of Defense for Policy Douglas Feith, who co-founded One Jerusalem with Sharansky to prevent the holy city from being divided during future negotiations, worked on several drafts with Donald Rumsfeld. Feith was a vehement opponent of the Oslo-style process of dealing with Arafat and advocated the sequence principle.[63]

Predictably, moderates like Colin Powell, CIA Director George Tenet, Deputy Secretary of State Richard Armitage and National Security Council (NSC) Senior Director Flynt Leverett rejected Sharansky's vision of sequence. They wanted the Bush administration to keep its options open and to do more to address Arab and Palestinian grievances.[64] Though the moderates did not like Arafat, they did not believe that the United States "should eliminate someone that the Palestinian people had chosen." For them, the essence of democracy required that the United States should not pick whom it wanted to deal with. As Armitage noted, "People pick who we should deal with."[65] Given that Powell had previously articulated his vision for a balanced Middle East policy, he was concerned that the language of the June 2002 Rose Garden speech would appear "too rejectionist."[66] Powell, who initially called for a major international conference, did not want a speech that simply "criticized the Palestinians and told them that they had to get a government that people could work with." He also wanted a speech that "told them what was waiting for them if they moved in this direction." Moderates partially achieved this objective by successfully inserting a "very controversial" statement that a peace agreement "could" be reached within three years.[67] This timetable was important in that it established a political horizon, albeit in a highly conditioned way.

As national security advisor, Rice and her deputy Stephen Hadley supported the speech.[68] But they sided with conservatives when it came to sequence. Rice was an early "convert" to Sharansky's vision, and solicited his advice. As a Soviet specialist, she was impressed with what the Cold War veteran had to say about democracy and human rights for Palestinians.[69] Like Abrams and Sharansky, she agreed that the United States would have to reject "some of the premises of past peacemaking," namely that it would be possible to "make a deal between the Palestinian leadership and the Israeli leadership, even if the Palestinian leadership was tainted with terror." Rice observed that while previous administrations had argued that the geography of a Palestinian state mattered most, the president decided that the "internal nature of the state" mattered most. Palestine needed to be a democracy, not "a sort of authoritarian holdover of cronies of Yasser Arafat."[70]

Like Rice, the president was highly invested in the speech, and devoted significant amounts of time working through approximately thirty drafts.[71] Bush had stated that he wanted to "change the way people think" about the Israeli-Palestinian conflict and had confided in Rice and favored advisor Karen Hughes that he saw Palestine as a "nice little laboratory" to test his hypothesis that freedom was the solution to the broader problems in the Middle East. As Rice put it, democracy, Iraq, and Palestine formed a "package."[72] The 9/11 attacks had shifted the way in which the president viewed terrorism, with nations being either "with us or against us."[73] As Bush declared at the National Cathedral on September 14, 2001, his historic task was to "rid the world of evil."[74] Prior to 9/11 no one in the administration would have considered justifying the killing of innocents, but after the attacks, Al Qaeda's suicide hijacking in the United States and Palestinian suicide bombings in Israel began to be viewed as being "part of the same problem." When Hamas undertook the April 2002 Passover bombings, it became clear to Rice that one could not "denounce Al Qaeda and hug Hamas."[75] The only problem with this black-and-white approach was that Arafat was Hamas's chief rival. As moderates clearly understood, removing him from power would only bolster extremism and violence, not eliminate it.

Days before Bush was due to deliver his speech on the Israeli-Palestinian conflict, Sharansky spoke at a highly influential neoconservative conference, where he met separately with Cheney and Wolfowitz.[76] After a ninety-minute conversation with Cheney, Sharansky told the vice president that Arafat must be removed from the equation once and for all. Cheney indicated that he would pass along Sharansky's recommendation to the president.[77] According to Perle, who organized the speech, "Sharansky provided an important bit of last-minute affirmation" to those who believed that Arafat had to be politically eliminated.[78] The infighting continued until the very end, with Powell resisting the ultimate decision to "write [Arafat] off." But as Abrams put it, "he lost" the argument.[79]

The president made the decision to side with conservatives, but in light of both his subsequent conversations with the Jordanians and his approval of the Quartet's Road Map, it was not clear that Bush, as a non-specialist, fully understood the dramatic implications of the sequence principle. As Perle recalls, Bush was often engaged in a "wrestling match with the State Department. At times he didn't know it." Though Bush may have been the ultimate "decider" on Middle East policy, "there are limits to what a president can comprehend" and execute. [80]

The Isolation of Arafat

Muasher had heard from Powell that Bush was going to be "very tough" on Arafat in his speech, so he headed to Ramallah to warn Arafat the day before it was to be delivered. In a last-minute attempt to get the United States to soften the language of the speech, Muasher told Arafat that if he did not act to disassociate himself with radical groups, there would be serious international repercussions. Arafat did not act, and Bush proceeded to deliver his speech.[81]

The Rose Garden speech's central message, like Sharansky's peace plan, was that there would be a sequential formula: no political process would move forward until entirely new, democratic Palestinian leadership untainted by terrorism emerged. A comparison between Sharansky's words and Bush's reveals striking similarities:

> *Sharansky*: "The time has come for a new leadership, which, unlike Arafat, is interested in improving the lives of the Palestinian people in ways that include building peaceful relations with Israel. The time has come for a leadership that is dependent on the will of its people."
>
> *Bush*: "Peace requires a new and different Palestinian leadership, so that a Palestinian state can be born. I call on the Palestinian people to elect new leaders, leaders not compromised by terror. I call upon them to build a practicing democracy, based on tolerance and liberty. *If the Palestinian people actively pursue these goals, America and the world will actively support their efforts*" (emphasis added).

Sharansky: "We are in the midst of the first world war of the twenty-first century, waged between the world of terror and the world of democracy...."

Bush: "I've said in the past that nations are either with us or against us in the war on terror."

Sharansky: "...only democracy and economic prosperity for the Palestinian people can bring security for Israel."

Bush: "Israel also has a large stake in the success of a democratic Palestine.... A stable, peaceful Palestinian state is necessary to achieve the security that Israel longs for."

Sharansky: "In order to ensure our own security, the Palestinians must be encouraged to form an open and free society that is not burdened by the fear, hatred, and terror that have been sown in recent years by Arafat and his leadership.... This cannot happen overnight; for this we need a Transition Period."

Bush: "And when the Palestinian people have new leaders, new institutions and new security arrangements with their neighbors, the United States of America will support the creation of a Palestinian state whose borders and certain aspects of its sovereignty will be provisional until resolved as part of a final settlement in the Middle East."

Sharansky: "...the transitional administration must address two primary goals: dismantling terror and building economic infrastructure. This will require a great deal of money.... During this period, the educational, economic, and political systems, as well as the media, must be revamped—and set free from the current propaganda, terror, and violence."

Bush: "A Palestinian state will never be created by terror—it will be built through reform. And reform must be more than cosmetic change, or veiled attempt to preserve the status quo. True reform will require entirely new political and economic institutions, based on democracy, market economics and action against terrorism."[82]

In a bold declaration, Bush announced that "If liberty can blossom in the rocky soil of the West Bank and Gaza, it will inspire millions of men and women around the globe who are equally weary of poverty and oppression, equally entitled to the benefits of democratic government." Interestingly, he concluded his speech with an Old Testament reference about the restoration of the Israelites to the Promised Land: "The Bible says, 'I have set before you life and death; therefore, choose life.' The time has arrived for everyone in this conflict to choose peace, and hope, and life."[83] While Bush considered Arafat to be a terrorist, many Palestinians hailed him as a Palestinian Moses, leading his people from captivity into the Promised Land. However, with strong pressure from his aides, from Congress, and from his political base to reject Arafat once and for all, Bush made his Old Testament theology perfectly clear: like Moses, Arafat would never enter the Promised Land.

After months of battling conservatives, the president finally succeeded in pleasing his base. While the June 2002 Rose Garden speech lent additional backing to the idea of a Palestinian state, in reality the conservative alliance got exactly what they wanted: eliminating Arafat politically, dismantling the terrorist infrastructure, and electing an "entirely new" Palestinian leadership were made preconditions to any political process that would result in a Palestinian state. This sequence, as Sharon and his successor later made clear, made Israeli obligations dependent upon the Palestinians first meeting their obligations.[84]

Bush's plan was widely supported by both houses of Congress and by theoconservative leaders.[85] Christian Broadcasting Network founder Pat Robertson, who would later attribute Sharon's stroke to God's judgment for giving up Gaza, called Bush's plan "brilliant."[86] Theoconservatives even started utilizing the language of the neoconservatives in their criticism of the Palestinians, calling for democratic reform.[87] Israeli National Security Advisor Efraim Halevy described it as a "spectacular achievement" because in a few words, Bush had reshaped the international discourse so that "world leaders around the globe had all adopted the concept of alternative leadership for the Palestinian Authority without requiring the prime minister to travel the globe to gain support for it." Significantly, as Halevy noted, the speech "conformed to the basic view" of Sharon in that it did not impose demands, obligations, and timetables on Israel to advance a political process.[88] But no one was more elated than Natan Sharansky, who said that he was "almost pinching [himself]" in disbelief that Bush's language so closely paralleled his own ideas.[89] In announcing his support for a Palestinian state, Bush may have been trying to offer a concession to the neighboring Arab states. But at its heart, Bush was not speaking about the geographical coordinates of Palestinian statehood. His stated aspirations were nothing less than democratic transformation "around the globe"—the fulfillment and end (goal) of history.[90]

This freedom agenda for Palestine, though seemingly well intentioned, was born with irreconcilable contradictions. The first contradiction was that Bush's concept of liberty sought to bring democracy without freedom to Palestine. While Bush diagnosed the Palestinian problem as no sitting president had before—terrorism was rooted in a freedom deficit—he failed to grasp who the Palestinians wanted to be free from.[91] Though Sharansky conceded that if elections were held in 2002 Arafat would still win, Bush believed that average Palestinians, did they but know it, wanted to be free from the tyranny and terror of Arafat, not from the Israeli occupation.[92]

The second contradiction was that Bush's concept of freedom was conditional on total reform. As Palestinian Prime Minister Salam Fayyad remarked, "freedom is not conditional."[93] While there was wide recognition of rampant corruption in the Palestinian Authority and an ongoing effort to reform corrupt institutions, the Palestinians regarded the Israeli occupation, which exercised overall authority and control in the territories, as being the greatest impediment to the formation of transparent and democratic Palestinian institutions.[94]

The third contradiction, as many conservative opponents readily point out, was that those in the United States and Israel who were most persistent in pushing Bush to renounce Arafat as a corrupt tyrant were themselves accused of eroding transparency and democracy in their home countries.[95] In the United States and abroad, many critics who detected a double standard cited a long list of U.S. and Israeli scandals: prior to joining the administration, Elliott Abrams, though later pardoned by President George H.W. Bush, pled guilty to withholding information from Congress in 1991.[96] Paul Wolfowitz was forced to resign as president of the World Bank due to a scandal involving a compensation package for his partner, Shaha Riza.[97] Dick Cheney's closest advisor, I. Lewis "Scooter" Libby, was convicted "of four counts of perjury, obstruction of justice and lying to the FBI" in connection with his role in leaking the identity of a CIA officer.[98] Last but not least, House Majority Leader Tom DeLay was forced to resign in disgrace before being tried for money-laundering.[99]

As in the United States, corrupt and criminal practices also overshadowed top Israeli leaders who campaigned against Arafat's Palestinian Authority. Though Ehud Olmert called for Palestinian reform and the elimination of Arafat, criminal corruption charges were later brought against him, causing serious damage to U.S. interests in Israel.[100] According to Rice, Olmert's misdeeds ruined the possibility of a successful outcome to the 2008 peace negotiations.[101] Moreover, Olmert and his predecessor Sharon headed a government in which the president was convicted of rape and a tenth of the Knesset faced police investigations.[102] In 2005, Sharon's son Omri was accused of concealing illegal contributions to his father's 1999 election campaign.[103] Sharon's scandals were probably one reason why he tried to redirect attention away from his legal problems by withdrawing from Gaza in 2005.[104] Like Sharon and Olmert, Sharansky's reputation was stained. Despite his anti-corruption crusades against Arafat, Sharansky admitted accepting $100,000 from Gregory Lerner, a convicted member of the Russian-Israeli mafia.[105] As Movement for Quality Governance in Israel's Daniel Kayros observed, "there is a sense in Israel that the whole political arena is rotten from its foundation."[106]

Ignoring their own shortcomings, conservatives like Sharansky set out to create a new Palestinian society that would be free from Arafat's corruption and criminal behavior; but the problem with the tendency to demonize Arafat was that it prevented self-examination. As another gulag alumnus came to understand, "the line separating good and evil passes not through states, nor between classes, nor between political parties but right through every human heart...even the very best of all hearts."[107]

The Road Map: Land for Peace

On July 31, 2002, Rice met with Muasher to discuss the peace process. As moderates had predicted, writing off Arafat did not solve the problem and the political deadlock persisted. During his meeting with Rice, Muasher argued that the administration was being overly harsh on Arafat and that progress in the security arena would only happen if there was a political process, a "road map" with a Palestinian state at the end. Citing the sequence principle, Rice dismissed the idea and called it a "nonstarter," noting that Bush had given his speech, and now it was up to the Palestinians to deliver on security so that progress could be made. The next day, King Abdullah II of Jordan and Muasher met with Rice and Bush. Speaking directly to Bush, Muasher once again laid out his case for a political process that simultaneously dealt with security, humanitarian, and institutional concerns. Bush responded, "What do the Palestinians want from me? I gave them a vision. What more do they want?" Muasher responded by saying that most Palestinians were skeptical that the president's vision could be achieved. Building on the three-year timetable that the moderates had inserted into the Rose Garden speech, Muasher cleverly asked the president to take his "exact vision and translate it into steps." Because Bush did not fully appreciate the irreconcilable differences between sequentialism and parallelism, he reversed course and agreed with the Jordanians. After the meeting, Rice did as well.[108]

As moderates within the administration started working on the Road Map version of parallelism, Sharon confidently brushed it off. Instead, he focused on eliminating Arafat's presence from the West Bank. Lapsing back into moderation, the Bush administration provided a September 2002 draft UN Security Council measure calling for Israel to withdraw its forces from the Arafat compound in Ramallah, noting that the Israeli Army's actions "do not contribute to progress on comprehensive Palestinian civil and security reforms." Equally important, however, the administration's draft specifically reaffirmed a post-9/11 anti-terrorism Security Council resolution and condemned Hamas's and Islamic Jihad's terrorist activities by name. This was the first time the administration sought to equate suicide bombings in Israel with the 9/11 attacks.[109] Fearing political repercussions among Europeans and Palestine's neighboring Arab states if Arafat were forcibly removed from Ramallah, moderates continued to remind Israel of its promise not to expel the Palestinian leader. Although Bush had expressed frustration with Sharon's continued siege of the Arafat compound because it was undermining his efforts to build support for the Iraq War, relations between Israel and the United States were declared never to have been better.[110]

In an address in Herzliya on December 4, 2002, Sharon responded to moderates in the United States by reminding Bush of his commitment to the sequence principle as articulated in the June 2002 Rose Garden speech. Sharon called the sequential plan "a reasonable, pragmatic and practicable" solution, and repeated the idea that the Palestinians would be required to undergo significant reforms before a peace process could begin. To do this, Sharon outlined the actionable outcomes of the Rose Garden speech as he saw them: the Palestinians would appoint a chief executive officer for reforms. In the security arena, cooperation between Israelis and Palestinians would be renewed. The Palestinians would dismantle and consolidate existing security organizations under a unified command. A new minister of interior would be appointed to collect illegal weapons and outlaw terrorist organizations. Furthermore, a minister of finance would reform the Palestinian Authority's financial affairs. Additional reforms would be carried out in the Palestinian education, media, and justice systems. After these radical reforms took place, the Palestinians would hold "free, liberated and democratic elections," and only then would Israel proceed with a political process that would involve the Palestinians establishing a provisional demilitarized state.[111]

Because Israel learned that the Road Map discussions were getting serious, and that a final version would likely contain language they found objectionable, Sharon's trusted advisor Dov Weisglass was dispatched to Washington to convince Rice that the plan should not be published until after the Israeli elections. Changes were also being made to the Road Map language.[112] Weisglass had a very close relationship with Rice, and his visits would often disturb Armitage and Powell because they felt that Rice was overly influenced by some of the things he told her.[113] Israel was working very hard to ensure that the sequence principle of the June 2002 speech was included in the language of the Road Map, not parallelism. NSC Senior Director Flynt Leverett made the case against sequence, arguing that the settlement freeze should not be contingent upon Palestinian achievements, just as Palestinian action against terror should not be contingent upon Israel's behavior. But with pressure from Sharon, Bush and his senior aides "retreated on this pivotal issue." Moreover, no explicit reference was made to widely known final-status parameters, despite the fact that Leverett argued vociferously to have them included.[114]

After Muasher heard that the work-in-progress Road Map's principle of parallelism was being jeopardized by conservative intervention, he called Leverett and threatened that the Arabs would reject it unless the Arab Initiative—the Arab-Israeli peace plan proposed by the League of Arab States in 2002—was kept among the terms of reference. Although the United States deferred to many Israeli demands, including their desire that the Road Map not be published for another six months, the Jordanians ultimately pushed through important language: "The settlement will resolve the Israeli-Palestinian conflict, and end the occupation that began in 1967, based on the Madrid Conference, the principle of land for peace, UNSCRs 242, 338 and 1397, agreements previously reached by the parties, and the initiative of the Saudi Crown Prince Abdullah—endorsed by the Beirut Arab League Summit—for acceptance of Israel as a neighbour living in peace and security."[115]

As Road Map plans were fought out with conservatives, the White House continued to make the case for regime change in Iraq. Even as Bush was being turned against the Road Map by administration conservatives, European Commissioner Christopher Patten visited Bush along with EU Foreign Policy Chief Javier Solana and UN Secretary General Kofi Annan. Bush, with Cheney sitting behind him, was asked whether he accepted the Road Map. Bush responded very intentionally, "I am in support of *a* Road Map." The commissioner later remarked to one of his colleagues, "There is quite a difference between the definite and the indefinite article!"[116] As Annan observed, time and again parallelism slipped into sequentialism in the sense that the Road Map was sequenced "to death" by the Bush administration's continued insistence that the Palestinians make concessions before the Israelis move.[117]

Cheney and Rumsfeld, along with their senior advisors, were fundamentally opposed to the Road Map, and felt the whole plan was an unnecessary distraction.[118] Because the Israeli government chose a military rather than a political solution to the conflict, ongoing "hot pursuit" was needed to prevent Palestinians from attacking Israelis. Thus, conservatives argued that though an ongoing low-intensity Israeli-Palestinian conflict would not constitute a serious threat to U.S. national security, it remained vital to Israel's ability to secure itself against the threat of terrorism.[119] Instead, the United States needed to devote its attention to state sponsors of terrorism such as Iraq. This was precisely the case Sharon had made to Bush during his first official visit with Bush in 2001.

Outside the administration, theoconservative support for the sequential agenda grew. Calls for aggressive action in Iraq and the occupied Palestinian territories increased amid calls for limited U.S. involvement in Israeli affairs. In an October 2002 "60 Minutes" interview with Bob Simon, theoconservative Jerry Falwell said, "It is my belief that the Bible Belt in America is Israel's only safety belt right now." Simon went on to suggest that Christian support for Israel is larger than Jewish support in the United States.[120] That month the Christian Coalition hosted a rally on the Washington Mall featuring Jerry Falwell, Pat Robertson, Oliver North, and Jesse Helms, the South Carolina senator who served as chairman of the Senate Foreign Relations Committee and deacon in his Southern Baptist church.[121]

In an effort to undermine theoconservatives, Christian leaders from liberal and moderate Protestant, Evangelical, and Catholic congregations voiced their opposition to the Iraq War, arguing that it did not meet St. Augustine's "just war" criteria—which deals with issues such as proportionality, intention, and the likelihood of success—and would only inflame tensions between Israelis and Palestinians. In response to the liberal Christians' anti-war activism, theoconservatives attempted to construct their own Augustinian justification for preemptive war and identified Israel's safety as a point of consideration. Southern Baptist policy chief Richard Land, Campus Crusade for Christ founder Bill Bright, ex-Nixon advisor Chuck Colson, televangelist Reverend D. James Kennedy, and American Association of Christian Schools President Carl D. Herbster wrote a letter to Bush arguing that the proposed Iraq War fit within the "just war" framework.[122]

By the end of December 2002, conservatives thought that they had all but won the battle for supremacy within the White House. Bush's alliance with Israel seemed like the "right thing to do" and could also benefit the Republicans politically in the next election. In what was viewed as a personal favor to President Bush, Ariel Sharon agreed to appear with his brother, Governor Jeb Bush of Florida. Sharon's planned visit was an effort to boost Jeb Bush's popularity among Jewish voters who were growing increasingly concerned about Israel, but he ultimately cancelled his trip amid vocal opposition from Florida Democrats.[123]

The administration continued to declare that it would pressure Israel to stop settlement-building and release funds to the Palestinian Authority in order to alleviate human suffering and facilitate the implementation of the Road Map. But these were empty words; Congress held the purse strings and Bush remained indecisive.[124] For example, he appointed Abrams, one of the Road Map's greatest opponents, to head the NSC's Middle East policymaking team. Though Rice would end up crossing swords with Abrams in the second term, she ultimately offered Abrams the post after considering splitting the position between a conservative and a moderate.[125]

Abrams, a theoconservative ally and vocal opponent of realism, had published several books on the role of religion in international affairs.[126] Like Sharansky, Abrams was admired for his principled views on freedom.[127] However, as many were suspicious of Sharansky's intentions, many were suspicious of Abrams's as well.[128] Deputy National Security Advisor Stephen Hadley saw Abrams as having a bit of "his own agenda" when it came to Middle East policy.[129] Other members of the administration described Abrams's close relations with the Israelis as having "pros" and "cons."[130] As Rice's deputy Philip Zelikow put it, "[Abrams had] a fantastic relationship with the Israeli government, that's the pro. The con is that [Abrams had] a fantastic relationship with the Israeli government."[131] Regardless of the controversy surrounding Abrams, his appointment guaranteed that conservatives would have a highly skilled bureaucrat making the case for sequentialism to the president.

CHAPTER 4

✚

Politicide as Sequence

With the Iraq War on the horizon, the unattended tempest in Palestine raged on. Unmoved by the chaos, Bush remained steadfast in the belief that "an angel still rides in the whirlwind and directs [the] storm."[1] In his January 2003 State of the Union Address, the president affirmed his grand vision to "defend the peace, and confound the designs of evil men."[2] Borrowing words from a redemption hymn, Bush affirmed that there is "wonder-working power" in U.S. values and ideals.[3] The United States is "called," he declared, "to defend the safety of our people and the hopes of all mankind" against "man-made evil"; people in the United States "sacrifice for the liberty of strangers" because liberty is "God's gift to humanity." The speech implied that U.S. faith in freedom could redeem humanity, especially the Arab world.[4] Believing that the providentially established "end" (goal) of history was individual liberty, Bush more clearly defined his freedom agenda as the antidote to the tyranny and terrorism wrought by Yasser Arafat and Saddam Hussein. As the Iraq War commenced, Bush continued to vacillate between the sequentialism of the Rose Garden speech and the parallelism of the Road Map. Under conservative pressure, however, he ultimately abandoned the Road Map and accepted "politicide," Sharon's version of the sequence principle, as advancing the cause of freedom.

Iraq and Palestine: A Democracy "Package"

As the president defined his freedom agenda against the backdrop of planning for war in Iraq, it was growing increasingly apparent that the Israeli-Palestinian conflict was inextricably linked to the other two pillars of Bush's Middle East policy: democracy and Iraq. There were two major reasons for linking Iraq and Palestine under the democracy umbrella. First, the president made a connection between the liberation of Iraq and the liberation of Palestine. In conversations with National Security Advisor Condoleezza Rice, Bush expressed his belief that democracy would be introduced to the Middle East. According to Rice, the three pillars of a "new Middle East" created a "package." Once everybody turned against terrorism, Iraq would emerge as an "integrated" and "responsible member of the Arab world"; the conflict in Palestine would be solved without the use of force, and the Arab world would engage in "reconciling with its own people through democratic reform… [and in] reconciling [with] Israel."[5]

A second reason for the Iraq-Palestine link, as Secretary of State Colin Powell recalled, was that the conservative architects of the war saw the entire project in "Israeli-Palestinian terms"; they argued that the road to Jerusalem ran through Baghdad.[6] More specifically, the Israeli-Palestinian arena was viewed as a microcosm for how terrorism should be dealt with throughout the entire Middle East. Therefore, conservatives regarded the June 2002 Rose Garden speech as the "foundation for the war in Iraq."[7] They built their case for war on the sequence principle: no political process should be renewed until Palestinian society was entirely reformed. Instead, they believed that the Oslo-style method of pursuing diplomacy and negotiations should be replaced with aggressive action against state sponsors of Palestinian terrorism, notably Saddam Hussein.[8]

For conservatives, war was a way of producing Jeffersonian-style democracies throughout the Middle East region. The result would be regime change in Palestine and Iraq, then in Syria, then in Iran, and ultimately, a "more stable Middle East for Israel" would emerge.[9] Conservatives optimistically touted Iraqi National Congress leader Ahmed Chalabi's predictions that Iraq would become a "beacon of democracy," one that would reconcile itself with Israel while allowing its bases to be used against Iran.[10] As a main architect of the war, Deputy Secretary of Defense Paul Wolfowitz vehemently opposed more delays and noted that progress in Iraq would yield better results in the Israeli-Palestinian arena. It would protect U.S. interests by sending a powerful message throughout the region that terrorism would not be tolerated.[11]

Deputy Secretary of State Richard Armitage argued "vociferously" with Wolfowitz about such optimistic claims. For one thing, as a military man with on-the-ground experience in the Middle East, he regarded the notion that a liberated Iraq would recognize Israel as a "pipe dream."[12] Instead, moderates built upon previous calls for a renewed political process with the Palestinians and argued that the road to Baghdad ran through Jerusalem.[13] Furthermore, Armitage warned that the United States might be accused of acting on Israel's behalf. He believed that the Middle East peace process was going nowhere and that the United States could make Saddam Hussein its top priority once things were quiet on the Palestinian issue.[14] He and Powell wanted to delay war or avoid it altogether by getting another UN resolution to place international pressure on Saddam Hussein's regime.[15] Similarly, crucial international allies supported the moderate agenda and argued that something must be done in Palestine before they would support a war in Iraq.[16] It was argued that ideological support for terrorism would be reduced with progress in the Israeli-Palestinian arena.[17]

Wolfowitz and former Undersecretary of Defense for Policy Douglas Feith flatly reject the notion that the Iraq War was seen in strictly Israeli-Palestinian terms.[18] Taking the case a step further, Feith noted in an interview that what "you heard from the Israelis was not any kind of advocacy of war with Iraq."[19] This view, however, does not correspond to the public record. Though the Israelis and administration conservatives clearly regarded Iran as a major regional threat, they came to understand that the choice was Iraq or nothing. As Senator Chuck Hagel, former senior member of the U.S. Senate Foreign Relations Committee, stated, "there's no question that much of the Israeli leadership was very supportive and strongly, strongly urged America's involvement" in sending troops to Iraq.[20] Additionally, Rice advisor and former executive director of the 9/11 Commission Philip Zelikow asserted that the U.S. invasion of Iraq was largely motivated by "the threat that dare not speak its name," namely the threat that Iraq posed to Israel's security.[21] Thus, while the conservative alliance in the United States was making the internal case against delaying the invasion of Iraq, the conservative leadership in Israel was passionately presenting the same argument to a Western audience.

Despite the centrality of Israeli security concerns in the lead-up to the war in Iraq, the United States understood the danger of presenting the operation as a

U.S.-Israeli initiative. For fear of igniting a disastrous Israeli-U.S. war against Iraq, the United States asked Israel not to respond in the event that Saddam Hussein attacked. In return, Sharon demanded that the United States preemptively remove Iraq's Scud missiles and any potential dirty warheads in the western Iraqi desert.[22] Because Iraq had attacked Israel in the first Gulf War, Sharon and his key advisors warned that delaying the invasion would provide time for Saddam Hussein to accelerate his weapons of mass destruction program.[23] Sharon's National Security Advisor and former head of the Israeli Mossad Efraim Halevy delivered a lecture in Munich that echoed the "Baghdad to Jerusalem" claim of administration conservatives. Halevy argued that a U.S. invasion could make a "major contribution to stability in the region" because "the shock waves emerging from post-Saddam Baghdad could have wide-ranging effects in Tehran, Damascus, and in Ramallah."[24] Similarly, Major Amos Gilad, the Israeli coordinator of government activities for the West Bank and Gaza, argued that the Iraq War would set a precedent for "the removal of other dictators closer to [Israel] who use violence and terror."[25] Sharon's foreign affairs advisor, Zalman Shoval, argued that Israel would "pay dearly" for a delay in the Iraq invasion, noting that Saddam Hussein would use a delay "to develop non-conventional weapons" while Arafat "[intensified] terrorist attacks."[26] Because Sharon realized that Iran would be strengthened by the removal of Saddam Hussein, he urged the United States to deal with Iran the day after the Iraq operation was finished.[27]

At the time, Israel's conservative leadership believed that invading Iraq would achieve four aims: destroying a major Arab power that presented a geostrategic threat to Israel; teaching the Palestinians and other hostile regimes a lesson; postponing a political process that would extract unnecessary Israeli concessions; and providing a launching pad for attacks against Iran and Syria. Because the Iraq War dramatically strengthened Iran's position, Israelis later complained that the United States had fought the wrong war. But as David Wurmser, Vice President Dick Cheney's Middle East advisor, retorted, the choice was either Iraq or inaction.[28]

In addition to receiving support from administration conservatives and from Israel, the Iraq War also received strong support from the U.S. Congress. Three months before Powell's speech at the United Nations in February 2003, Congress had been provided with a "botched" National Intelligence Estimate, which "was even more definitive about the existence of weapons of mass destruction" than the intelligence provided to the administration.[29] In a memo to UK Prime Minister Tony Blair, Private Secretary for Foreign Affairs to the Prime Minister Matthew Rycroft commented that it appeared as if "intelligence and facts were being fixed around the policy."[30] Based on flawed intelligence, Congress granted the president the authority to go to war, and theoconservative House Majority Leader Tom Delay enthusiastically promised that "whatever the president deems necessary to fight" would be granted.[31]

With public support from the conservative alliance, Bush delivered a speech at the neoconservative American Enterprise Institute, where he discussed the role of Palestine in his new Middle East.[32] Echoing the conservative belief that "the road to peace in the Middle East goes through Baghdad," Bush once again cited the sequence principle: "Success in Iraq could also begin a new stage for Middle Eastern peace, and set in motion progress towards a truly democratic Palestinian state." This grand vision for the Middle East, which Bush considered a "personal commitment," would bring about nothing less than "an age of progress and liberty."[33]

Against great objections voiced by Powell, Blair, and other European and Arab allies, and despite the appointment of Palestinian Prime Minister Mahmoud Abbas, Bush declared that he would not publish the Road Map until the Iraq crisis was resolved.[34] He indicated that he wanted to use the political capital gained from an Iraq victory to advance the peace process.[35] If conservatives convinced Bush that the road to Jerusalem passed through Baghdad, the Europeans believed that the Quartet's Road Map was dead.[36] Confirming their view, Sharon remarked, "Oh, the Quartet is nothing! Don't take it seriously!" He went on to suggest there was another plan "that will work."[37]

The Road Map

By May 1, 2003, the conservative agenda seemed to have been vindicated in Iraq. Bush delivered his famous victory speech below a "Mission Accomplished" banner, lauding the armed forces, Commander in Chief of U.S. Central Command General Tommy Franks, and Secretary of Defense Donald Rumsfeld for serving the country and advancing the cause of global peace and liberty. Before concluding his speech, the president quoted a millennial passage from Isaiah that speaks of bringing "salvation unto the end of the earth."[38] Bush stated, "To the captives, 'Come out!' and to those in darkness, 'Be free!'" A few weeks later, Bush affirmed his belief in the unique destiny of the United States to fulfill its "moral purpose." Borrowing from Woodrow Wilson's theological optimism, Bush declared, "'America has a spiritual energy in her which no other nation can contribute to the liberation of mankind.' In this new century, we must apply that energy to the good of people everywhere."[39]

With Saddam Hussein's regime toppled, neoconservatives ascendant in Washington, and U.S. forces stationed next door, Iran's clerics had much to fear. At the highest levels of the Iranian government, a secret proposal was drafted and ultimately delivered through Republican Congressman Bob Ney to Bush's Deputy Chief of Staff, Karl Rove. The purpose of the document was to set in motion a process whereby the Iranian regime would reach a comprehensive peace agreement with the United States. The proposal, which also pertained to the Israeli-Palestinian arena, offered the potential of a major breakthrough in U.S.-Iranian relations. Powell and Armitage favored a response, but the moderate view was soon marginalized by Cheney and Rumsfeld, who were reportedly unwilling to negotiate with "evil." At the time, the conservative write-off of Iran's diplomatic overtures seemed to have been the crowning achievement of the Iraq War. But in retrospect, it would seem that pride had clouded their judgment. As Iran's Deputy Oil Minister Hadi Nejad-Hosseinian later summarized, U.S. handling of the Iraq War transformed Iran into a regional power: "Iraq couldn't have turned out better for us."[40]

Just when conservatives thought that they had won the war inside and outside the administration, Bush once again reversed course on Israel and Palestine, and headed in the moderate direction. With a perceived victory in Iraq on the table, Bush refocused his attention on the Road Map, despite fierce conservative opposition. As opposed to the June 2002 Rose Garden Speech, the Road Map offered a "performance-based and goal-driven" process aimed at producing results through a series of "reciprocal steps" overseen by the Quartet. Among other things, the Road Map required that both sides end incitement from official institutions, Palestinians reform their political institutions in preparation for elections, Israel withdraw to pre–September 2000 lines, Israel freeze settlement activity, and Palestinians "undertake an unconditional cessation of violence" accompanied by security cooperation with Israel.[41]

With the Road Map on the table, Palestinians initiated a process of internal reform. Though they indicated that it was impossible to create a constitution under military occupation, the Palestinian Legislative Council started transferring authority from Arafat to newly appointed Prime Minister Mahmoud Abbas. This resulted in a public power struggle between Arafat and Abbas because the former was elected by the people and enjoyed their support, while the latter was unelected, weak, and viewed as the architect of the failed peace process.[42] Palestinians accused Abbas of undermining Arafat in order to please Bush.[43] More important, as Feith recalls, Abbas was the favored candidate of the Israeli leadership. When Arafat died, Bush asked the *Israelis* who they wanted, and they said Abbas.[44]

With Palestinian reform underway, European and Arab allies once again mounted pressure on the Bush administration to push forward with a political process jump-started by an international conference.[45] Within the administration, Powell pushed to transform the June 2002 speech into a Road Map–initiated political process that fit within the stated three-year timeline.[46] Conservatives in the administration resisted. A sure sign of their rising influence was the fact that an April 2003 meeting between Bush and Sharon was attended by not only Powell and Rice, but also Cheney, Feith, and the Vice President's Chief of Staff, Scooter Libby.[47]

Though their agenda momentarily prevailed in Iraq, the conservative alliance was still not ready to accept the possibility of a Palestinian state, however democratic or free it might be. The disputes between Rumsfeld at the Pentagon and Powell at the State Department continued to overflow into the public arena.[48] Attacks on Powell intensified, with theoconservative former Speaker of the House and American Enterprise Institute Senior Fellow Newt Gingrich leading the way. As a close ally of Rumsfeld, Gingrich complimented the secretary of defense while deriding Powell: "The last seven months have involved six months of diplomatic failure and one month of military success." He further suggested that the idea of pursuing diplomacy with terrorists in Syria, another area of concern for the United States, and that engaging the Quartet to solve the Israeli-Palestinian conflict would throw away the lessons learned from a "hard won victory" that Rumsfeld had delivered in

Iraq. For conservatives, the State Department was broken and needed "transform-ing."[49]

In the *Washington Post*, Charles Krauthammer accused Bush of taking "his friend Sharon to the cleaners" by readopting the failed Oslo methodology, which pursued diplomacy instead of military force.[50] Conservatives were worried that the president was losing his moral mettle. After all, he had declared, "I want to change the way people think about the Arab-Israeli conflict," and in this sense, his freedom agenda had been conceived as something entirely new, a rejection of the Oslo meth-odology.[51] For the conservatives, the Road Map was Oslo all over again.

Adding to the fury, theoconservatives once again mobilized against moderates. During a visit to the United States, Israeli Minister of Tourism Binyamin Elon forged ties with the Christian Coalition leadership and pushed for the voluntary "relocation" of Palestinians to Jordan. His words were well-received by the annual gathering of the Christian Coalition, where thousands of theoconservatives cheered him on. Despite being rebuked by Sharon for advancing his own agenda, Elon was later invited by Sharon to attend a meeting with Bush and Powell. During the meeting, Sharon made it clear to Powell that the Road Map should not be pursued unless changes were made.[52] In a further show of support for the conservative Israeli position, two dozen influential theoconservative leaders led by Gary Bauer, a for-mer U.S. presidential candidate, encouraged the administration to "go back to the drawing board." They indicated that the Road Map forced Israel to make too many concessions and "could lead to a disaster for Israel and the United States."[53]

Despite heavy conservative criticism, Bush published the Road Map in a "low-key" manner, in hopes that he would not upset his conservative base as he had done in 2002. To anger conservatives further, Bush charged the State Department's John Wolf, a seasoned diplomat, with advancing the peace process.[54] But while the Palestinians fully accepted the Road Map, Sharon responded to the president's call for renewing the peace process by submitting fourteen reservations, which included, among other things, a demand that the "right of return" be waived prior to negotia-tions. His reservations emphasized the centrality of the sequence principle as stated in Bush's June 2002 Rose Garden Speech, and indicated that this U.S. policy, not the Quartet's, should guide the process. In keeping with the sequence principle, Sharon's reservations required Palestinians to first dismantle "terrorist organizations

(Hamas, Islamic Jihad, the Popular Front, the Democratic Front, Al-Aqsa Brigades and other apparatuses)," not simply "terrorist capabilities and infrastructure," before a political process could ensue.[55] Israel had already dealt a serious blow to the Palestinian Authority's security infrastructure during the 2002 Operation Defensive Shield, making it difficult for the Palestinian Authority to crack down on, much less dismantle, radical movements, which were rapidly growing in popularity amid Arafat's physical and political decline.[56]

After submitting his reservations to the president, Sharon expressed his "acceptance" of the Road Map, despite fierce opposition from Deputy Prime Minister Natan Sharansky and other members of his cabinet.[57] However, because Sharon's crippling reservations accompanied his acceptance, it should be underscored that Israel never fully accepted the Quartet's Road Map.[58] As George Clemenceau might have said, Moses gave ten commandments; Sharon delivered fourteen.

Disregarding the significance of the Israeli reservations, Bush moved in the moderate direction. With encouragement from Blair, a strong advocate of renewed negotiations, Bush used political capital gained from early successes in Iraq to pledge his support for the Road Map in Sharm El-Sheikh, Egypt, on June 3, 2003. He declared his desire for "true peace; not just a pause between more wars and intifadas, but a permanent reconciliation among the peoples of the Middle East."[59] At the Aqaba summit the next day, he affirmed his belief in a "viable, democratic, peaceful Palestinian state" existing in peace with Israel "and with every nation of the Middle East." In his prepared remarks, Abbas indicated that there would be "no military solution for this conflict," and in a highly symbolic statement, told his audience that the Palestinians "do not ignore the suffering of the Jews throughout history." Though the Palestinians accepted the Road Map without reservations, Sharon did not agree to freeze settlements, and instead committed himself to removing what he called "unauthorized outposts."[60] To complicate matters further, Sharon's spokesman, Raanan Gissin, held an off-the-record briefing with the Israeli press. Gissin indicated that Sharon was not serious about implementing Phase III of the Roadmap, which was about the establishment of a permanent Palestinian state and an end to the occupation. According to Marwan Muasher, "This explicitly contradicted the provision of the Road Map" and cast serious doubt on Sharon's intentions.[61]

As the Road Map was being unveiled in the Middle East, Sharansky met with Cheney in Washington, D.C. The Israeli leader, who voted against the Road Map in Sharon's cabinet meeting, was suspicious that Bush did not really mean what he said in his June 2002 Rose Garden speech. Sharansky wanted to be sure that the sequence principle was still guiding U.S. policy: Israeli concessions would be contingent upon the complete dismantlement of terrorist institutions and democratic reforms by the Palestinian Authority. Cheney assured Sharansky that the president's speech still governed U.S. policy. A month before, Elliott Abrams had described the Quartet's plan as a "road map to implement the president's vision of June 24, 2002."[62]

In the absence of decisive leadership, questions remained about whether Bush wanted parallel concessions or radical sequential change, i.e., "entirely new" Palestinian leaders and institutions. Bush and Rice indicated that the "reform" agenda of the Road Map was aligned with the Rose Garden speech.[63] However, Cheney, Rumsfeld, Wurmser, Feith, Abrams, Libby, Chairman of the Defense Policy Board Richard Perle, and other conservatives could not have disagreed more.[64] Because they had played such a prominent role in shaping the June 2002 speech, conservatives were adamant that it was about first establishing "entirely new" Palestinian leadership and institutions "untainted by terror."

Preserving Sequence

In an effort to salvage the sequence principle, Sharon dismissed the Road Map agenda and boldly moved ahead with his own unilateral plan for a separation barrier to penetrate deep into the West Bank.[65] On July 16, 2003, Israel began constructing a separation wall (also called a "security fence" by the Israelis and an "apartheid wall" by the Palestinians). The projected 709-kilometer barrier consisted of barbed wire fences, towering concrete walls, patrol roads, and advanced security systems. Israel justified the existence of the "security fence" as a preventive measure against Palestinian suicide bombers attempting to enter Israel. Because the proposed path of the wall significantly cut into Palestinian territory, however, effectively annexing about 9.5 percent of the West Bank, Palestinians regarded it as a unilateral land grab. Additionally, its path separated Palestinians from land, livelihoods, health care, schools, water, and each other.[66]

Although Bush eventually capitulated and allowed Sharon to move forward with construction of the wall, it was not at all clear that the president personally supported it. His speechwriter, Michael Gerson, recalls coming back from a trip to Ramallah with Rice during the second term. Upon his return, he had lunch with Bush and "pretty vividly described to him the situation with the wall." Though Gerson considered the wall to be "understandable and successful," he noted that "it creates a completely unviable Palestinian community" which "involves...a disturbing [kind of] of segregation that disturbs Americans' sensibilities." He noted that "you have to have a certain license plate to drive on certain roads" and "described this to the president." Bush "was deeply sympathetic" and several months later told Gerson that he remembered that conversation.[67] Given Bush's need to secure the support of pro-Israel voters in advance of the upcoming U.S. election, however, time and again Sharon was able to bulldoze his own agenda through with little resistance from the president. Armitage recalls that Sharon's aggressive tactics intimidated Bush. Brent Scowcroft, former chairman of the president's Foreign Intelligence Advisory Board, described Sharon as having Bush "wrapped around his little finger."[68]

While Israel convinced Bush administration officials that the not-yet-completed wall explained the decline in suicide bombings, there were several other compelling explanations. First, as former Jordanian Prime Minister Fayez Tarawneh noted, the Arabs placed a tremendous amount of pressure on the Palestinians to cease bombings because they were damaging the Palestinian cause. Second, the Palestinian preventive security forces were slowly becoming more effective in targeting terrorist activity.[69] Arafat adviser Hussein Agha cites a third reason for the reduction in suicide bombings: Operation Defensive Shield dealt radical groups in the West Bank a devastating blow from which they never fully recovered. Interestingly, former Likud Israeli Defense Minister and former advocate of the wall Moshe Arens offers a similar view. After initially writing an article in *Ha'aretz* justifying plans for the massive project, Arens wrote another article in 2008 criticizing the continued construction of the multi-billion dollar "fence." He attributed the cessation in suicide bombings to the Israeli army's reoccupation of the West Bank. Arens noted, "The fence will not keep terror away. If not controlled on the ground, it will return to Israel's cities—it will come over and under the fence."[70]

Though the wall may have presented additional challenges for Palestinian infiltrators, Shin Bet and the Israeli Defense Forces (IDF) eventually stopped attributing reductions in suicide bombings to the success of the wall. Palestinians still found other ways to penetrate porous checkpoints or uncompleted sections of the wall, as they had done in the past. Thus, a fourth reason for the reduction in suicide bombings was that Hamas eventually abandoned them as a strategy and entered into a truce with Israel.[71]

While Sharon created new facts on the ground, the conservative alliance escalated attacks against the moderate Road Map. Theoconservatives publicly affirmed their theological conviction that Israel must become Greater Israel and that the territory relinquished would be nothing resembling a viable state for the Palestinians. Pat Robertson argued: "Judea and Samaria were given to the Jews by God, and I cannot see the United States of America taking this land and giving it to a known terrorist." Gary Bauer launched a Safe Israel campaign in support of a "one-state solution" that sponsored billboards and bumper stickers with the following reference from the book of Genesis: "And the Lord said to Jacob.... 'Unto thy offspring will I give this land.'"[72]

Like conservative voters, conservatives in Congress became a major stumbling block for the moderates. When the Bush administration attempted to provide financial aid to support Abbas in 2003, the U.S. Congress restricted direct aid to the Palestinians. Members of conservative Zionist and conservative Christian groups were concerned that the money would be funneled toward violence against Israelis. Citing national security concerns, Bush indicated that he would invoke a waiver and bypass the congressional ban. He unsuccessfully attempted to pacify Tom DeLay by giving the funds to the hand-selected Palestinian Finance Minister Salam Fayyad (who would later become prime minister).[73]

As conservative activists continued to exert pressure on the White House, theoconservatives in the U.S. Congress fired another warning shot. House Majority Leader Tom DeLay traveled to the Middle East to remind the president, once again, not to disregard his conservative base. DeLay declared, "In my faith, fighting for right and wrong, and understanding good and evil, is pretty apparent and pretty straightforward."[74] He went even further, calling himself "an Israeli at heart" and indicating that the blame for the Israeli-Palestinian conflict should be placed squarely upon the Palestinians. He flatly opposed the Road Map: "I can't imagine this president supporting a state of terrorists."[75] DeLay's visit was viewed as an overt attempt to undermine Bush's ever-changing vision for a Palestinian state.[76] And his words empowered Sharon, who continued to ignore pressure from Bush to halt construction of the wall.[77] As Israeli Ambassador to the United States Daniel Ayalon stated from John Hagee's megachurch pulpit in Texas, the Israeli government needed theoconservatives.[78] Time and again, Tom DeLay proved to be the most reliable among them.

DeLay's extreme stance not only forced the Bush administration to pay more attention to theoconservatives, but also forced Democrats in Congress to the right. Several Democrats had angered members of the Jewish community by voting "no" or "present" on a 2002 congressional resolution expressing solidarity with Israel. Following DeLay's increasingly vocal support of Israel, Democratic House Whip Steny Hoyer indicated that he could not "imagine in the near future that a Palestinian state could ever happen." He subsequently led a Democratic delegation to visit Israel during the summer recess, a move regarded as a "significant statement" by Howard Kohr, executive director of the American Israel Public Affairs Committee (AIPAC).[79]

Despite heavy support for Israel within the U.S. Congress and among theoconservatives, moderates continued to exert "guarded" pressure on Israel to cease construction of the separation wall. They even considered reducing billions of dollars in loan guarantees approved by Congress. Being careful not to further upset the theoconservatives, Powell followed up with light pressure in expressing that the United States is "concerned when the fence crosses over onto the land of others."[80] His words fell on deaf ears, as there was growing speculation that Powell was on his way out.[81]

Instead of using financial leverage to get Israel to cease construction of the wall as the State Department had previously suggested, Bush did the opposite. He employed financial leverage against the Palestinians. Bush ordered the U.S. Treasury to block and freeze assets associated with Hamas leaders and supporting charities.

This move was seen as a significant victory for Sharon, who had been trying to get the U.S. government to take stronger action against Hamas fundraising activities ever since he was elected.[82]

True to form, Bush had moved back in the conservative direction. He and Congress embraced the line that full responsibility for the continued violence rested on the Palestinians. Although Abbas enjoyed verbal support from the United States, he received little tangible support. Bush was growing impatient with Abbas's inability to deliver on security and suggested that he had "bet" on the wrong guy.[83] In September 2003, when the Israeli government decided in principle to "remove" Arafat, the Bush administration issued no overt criticism.[84] When Abbas resigned in September 2003, Bush placed the blame squarely on Arafat.[85] When Israel engaged in strikes against Syria in October 2003, Bush indicated that "Israel must not feel constrained in terms of defending the homeland."[86] The administration further aligned itself with conservatives in abandoning its long-standing opposition to an act of Congress that would impose economic and diplomatic sanctions on Syria.[87] These sanctions were supported by administration conservatives like Wolfowitz and Wurmser.[88] Despite the fact that Powell was still continuing "intensive diplomacy" with the Syrian government, the White House gave up its opposition to the sanctions bill following weeks of negotiations with DeLay.[89] With the State Department presenting itself as the last stumbling block to conservatives, it is no wonder that Pat Robertson suggested, "Maybe we need a very small nuke thrown off on Foggy Bottom to shake things up like Newt Gingrich wants to do."[90]

In November 2003, moderates threatened to deduct $289.5 million in loan guarantees to Israel. Deputy Assistant Secretary of State David Satterfield followed up the threat with harsh words: Israel had "done too little for far too long" to advance peace talks.[91] Sharon did not flinch. He responded by placing blame on the Palestinians and threatened that if they did not follow the Road Map, he would unveil his own.[92]

On December 18, 2003, Sharon delivered his second Herzliya speech. He noted that Israel was "willing to proceed toward the implementation of the Road Map: two states—Israel and a Palestinian State—living side by side in tranquility, security and peace." Sharon reemphasized, however, that his interpretation of the Road Map, along with his fourteen reservations, was premised upon the June 2002

Rose Garden speech's sequence principle. For Sharon, Oslo-style political processes and peace agreements would not produce security. He declared, "only security will lead to peace. And in that sequence. Without the achievement of full security within the framework of which terror organizations will be dismantled, it will not be possible to achieve genuine peace, a peace for generations."[93]

Sharon warned that if the Palestinians were incapable of delivering security, he would implement yet another unilateral security policy called the "Disengagement Plan" in full coordination with the United States. The Disengagement Plan would involve "the redeployment of IDF forces along new security lines and a change in the deployment of settlements, which will reduce as much as possible the number of Israelis located in the heart of the Palestinian population." Sharon indicated that Israel would continue with the hasty construction of the wall, and that if he decided to proceed with disengagement, the Palestinians would "receive much less than they would have received through direct negotiations as set out in the Road Map."[94]

In keeping with traditional U.S. policy, the administration initially opposed the unilateral nature of the plan.[95] By February 2004, however, Bush was willing to change his mind. Moderates continued to voice concerns that the United States would be seen as walking away from peace negotiations because serious diplomacy was never given a chance. But Bush came around and supported Sharon's plan. Henceforth, the only negotiations that moved forward were the "functional equivalent of negotiations" between Abrams, Deputy National Security Advisor Stephen Hadley, and seasoned State Department official William J. Burns on how Israel might proceed with a unilateral withdrawal.[96]

Members of the administration such as Rice and Abrams believed that the Herzliya speech represented an ideological shift in Sharon's thinking, and their evaluation clearly influenced the president's.[97] Bush declared that Sharon's plan was "a bold initiative that could advance the cause of peace," and in an address to AIPAC, the president reinforced his support for Sharon, reaffirmed the sequence principle, and emphasized a common U.S. and Israeli appreciation for freedom. He noted that "[Israel and the United States] must be strong in our firm belief that every human heart desires to be free."[98]

In the United States, Sharon was rebranded as a courageous moderate committed to freedom who would move against his radical political base in the interest of offering "a new way of looking at the situation."[99] Unlike Bush, conservatives and moderates—for different reasons—were convinced that Sharon held ulterior motives. Wurmser, who strongly opposed any Israeli concessions to the Palestinians, speculated that Sharon created the Disengagement Plan to distract from the corruption charges being brought against him.[100] Armitage believed that Sharon still viewed "Jordan as Palestine."[101] U.S. Special Envoy General Anthony Zinni and Senator Chuck Hagel remained doubtful that Sharon ever lost sight of a fragmented territory for the Palestinians.[102] Similarly, U.S. Ambassador to Israel Daniel Kurtzer, who had extensive personal exposure to Sharon, did not believe that the unilateral disengagement from Gaza was a genuine attempt to establish a Palestinian state based on the Road Map. Kurtzer speculated that it was a strategic move. Sharon's plan to use Gaza settlements as a "security buffer" was failing. The settlers were not an adjunct to the Israeli army; instead, the army was being drawn into protecting settlers. He realized that the security and demographic trends in Gaza were not on Israel's side, so he decided to leave it without "any larger purpose in mind." Sharon also pulled out of a few isolated settlements in the northern West Bank, largely because the Bush administration "demanded it" and because "it was a small price to pay."[103] According to Rice, the United States "forced" Israel to make the connection between Gaza and the West Bank "so it would be clear that it wasn't going to be Gaza only."[104]

Though military strategy and domestic concerns played a role in the disengagement, above all Sharon's withdrawal was, in the words of Israeli scholar Baruch Kimmerling, a policy of "politicide": the prime minister would not give politics a chance to work.[105] As Sharon saw it, the Palestinians failed to live up to the requirements of the June 2002 Rose Garden speech, which set "forth the correct sequence and principles for the attainment of peace." Until the Palestinians "institut[ed] true reform and real democracy and liberty, including new leaders not compromised by terror," there would be no partner for peace. Instead, Israel would bypass the Road Map and proceed with its Disengagement Plan.[106]

If there was any ambiguity about Sharon's dubious intentions, his closest advisor, Dov Weisglass, provided abundant clarification. In a lengthy interview with *Ha'aretz*, he explained that the prime minister's Disengagement Plan was in no way intended to advance the peace process. He wanted to kill it and the Road Map once and for all. Sharon's plan created a new political reality by reshaping the discourse and agenda of the president of the United States, the U.S. Congress, and the international community. Sharon did not believe that a piece of paper would end 104 years of conflict; rather, the Palestinians "had to undergo a deep and extended socio-political change." In a telling statement that referenced the June 2002 Rose Garden speech, Weisglass explained how the Gaza disengagement was intended to freeze Bush's political process: "The disengagement plan is the preservative of the sequence principle," which states that there will be no political process until the Palestinians reform. "[The disengagement] is the bottle of formaldehyde within which you place the president's formula so that it will be preserved for a very lengthy period. The disengagement is actually formaldehyde. It supplies the amount of formaldehyde that's necessary so that there will not be a political process with the Palestinians." Weisglass summarized the cynical purpose of the disengagement: "We received a no-one-to-talk-to certificate. That certificate says: (1) There is no one to talk to. (2) As long as there is no one to talk to, the geographic status quo remains intact. (3) The certificate will be revoked only when this-and-this happens—when Palestine becomes Finland. (4) See you then, and shalom."[107]

After reaffirming Sharon's version of the sequence principle, Bush mistakenly believed that the Gaza withdrawal would later be seen as a foreign policy victory, an easy way of breaking the Israeli-Palestinian impasse. In hindsight, the unilateral nature of the withdrawal contributed to the eventual fragmentation of the Palestinian Authority. Also, because Sharon was experiencing domestic political fallout over the withdrawal, the prime minister indicated that he needed something from the United States to give to his conservative political base. He requested a U.S.-Israeli understanding on several large West Bank settlements.[108] Hailing Sharon's plan for unilateral withdrawal as "historic" and "an opportunity" that would lead to a Palestinian state, Bush agreed to provide Sharon with a conditional commitment on some sensitive final-status issues.[109]

In what followed, top Cheney aide Scooter Libby and NSC Senior Director Elliott Abrams were intimately involved in shaping the deliberations that led to an exchange of letters between the United States and Israel.[110] According to Kurtzer, the United States did not have a coherent policy, yet for the first time in history it offered a "conditional commitment on a final status issue unilaterally" to Israel.

Moreover, "there was no effort…whatsoever to consider the Palestinian view on these issues."[111] As with the sequence principle embedded into the June 2002 Rose Garden speech, the highly nuanced language shaped by Abrams and Libby was subject to later reinterpretation by moderates. Consequently, two narratives emerged which expose the tension between what Bush, Rice, Kurtzer, and Hadley had intended to accomplish on the one hand, and what Libby and Abrams intended to accomplish on the other.

As represented by Kurtzer, moderates contend that there was "no such understanding" on settlements. First, the intention of meetings held in 2003 was to discuss an outer boundary on the perimeter of the settlements, within which Israel would be free to build. According to Kurtzer, "This draft was never codified, and no effort was made then to define the line around the built-up areas of settlements."[112] Sharon, however, interpreted these discussions as he saw fit and regarded U.S. silence on settlement activity as tacit consent.

Second, in a letter dated April 14, 2004, Bush "gave Sharon two highly-conditioned commitments." The first commitment conveyed U.S. support for an agreed outcome of negotiations in which Israel would retain "existing major Israeli population centers" in the West Bank "on the basis of mutually agreed changes." Kurtzer emphasizes that a "key provision of this letter was that U.S. support for Israel's retaining some settlements was predicated on there being an 'agreed outcome' of negotiations."[113] Thus, in the context of a negotiated agreement between Israelis and Palestinians, the United States would support an outcome that allowed Israel to retain heavily populated settlement areas. It did not give Israel permission to build. The second commitment stated in this letter was that when a Palestinian state would be established, such a state would be the place where Palestinians would exercise their "right of return."[114]

Third, Weisglass sent a letter to Rice a few days later. He addressed "the issue of the 'construction line,'" saying that "within the agreed principles of settlement activities, an effort will be made in the next few days to have a better definition of the construction line of settlements in Judea and Samaria." According to Kurtzer, no such "agreed principles of settlement activity" existed, and the "effort to define the 'construction line' was never consummated." Weisglass also promised that "unauthorized outposts" would be removed, but Israel removed "almost none of them."[115]

Unlike moderates, administration conservatives, as represented by Abrams, assert that the United States and Israel came to an agreement on settlements between 2003 and 2004. First, Abrams argues, Bush's letter did not refer to settlements beyond the "1967 borders" as being "illegal" as many past administrations had done. Instead of referring to borders, he referred to the armistice lines of 1949 where fighting had ceased. Bush stated, "In light of new realities on the ground, including already existing major Israeli population centers, it is unrealistic to expect that the outcome of final status negotiations will be a full and complete return to the armistice lines of 1949." Abrams maintains that the United States and Israel "agreed on principles that would permit some continuing growth."

In a follow-up letter dated April 18, 2004, Weisglass indicated that he wanted to "reconfirm" understandings between the United States and Israel: "Restrictions on settlement growth: within the agreed principles of settlement activities, an effort will be made in the next few days to have a better definition of the construction line of settlements in Judea and Samaria." Weisglass supported Abrams's claims, and indicated that he and Abrams came to a "verbal understanding" supported by Rice and Sharon. In addition to an agreement on settlements, Abrams also asserted that the president's letter indicated that there would be "no 'right of return' for Palestinian refugees."[116]

Because the nuanced language of the letters required interpretation, the moderate version ultimately prevailed late into Bush's second term. However, the primary drivers of the U.S. letter, Libby and Abrams, clearly differed from Rice, Hadley, and Kurtzer in their interpretation. At the time, administration conservatives believed that they had won a major victory by convincing the president to take settlements "off the table."[117] Regardless of the legal status of the letters, the peculiar fact of their very existence is evidence that the president had momentarily shelved the Road Map and felt moved to reward unilateralism as the fulfillment of his June 2002 Rose Garden speech.

The Gaza Withdrawal

With the Quartet's Road Map in "formaldehyde," Bush took Sharon's "road map" to the world, hailing it as the only way to peace.[118] In an effort to boost his domestic support, Sharon argued that the withdrawal would only require Israel to remove fewer than 8,000 settlers from the Gaza Strip while solidifying its hold over the West Bank, where over 230,000 settlers illegally live.[119] As Israel prepared for its withdrawal from Gaza, the government announced its intention to demolish hundreds of Palestinian homes along the Egyptian-Gazan border to allow for an expanded patrol road. These new demolition plans followed the destruction of 88 buildings, which left over 1,000 Palestinians without homes.[120]

Sharon looked to pacify the hardliners in his government further by issuing tenders for 1,001 new government-subsidized housing units in the West Bank.[121] After returning from a vacation in Israel where he met with Weisglass, Abrams convinced the U.S. administration to amend its policy for the last three years, which called for freezing "all settlement activity." In yet another unprecedented step driven by Abrams, the Bush administration was reported to have expressed its tacit acceptance of settlement expansion within already-built-up areas in the West Bank. Unnamed U.S. officials explained to the *New York Times* that the president needed the support of pro-Israel conservatives in the next election and was thus reluctant to criticize Sharon.[122] Abrams reported that the president trusted the Israeli government on settlement-related issues.[123] Bush's actions in support of Sharon may not have been contributing to an Israeli-Palestinian peace accord, but they were helping to attract pro-Israeli Jewish voters in Florida, where Cheney had campaigned earlier in the year.[124]

As the U.S. elections approached, Bush continued to side with the conservative alliance. He blamed the Palestinians and praised Sharon's efforts to fight terror "just like we will." Rearticulating the sequence principle, Bush argued that the solution for the Palestinians was not Israeli concessions but internal democratic reform.[125] Just as Sharon sought to pacify the hardliners in his party, so Bush looked to satisfy the demands of conservatives within his own party. Pat Robertson warned that if Bush did not support Jewish sovereignty over all Jerusalem, he would lose the support of his base in the 2004 election. Robertson argued that theoconservatives would consider forming a third party.[126] Having barely won the 2000 election, Bush was not willing to risk the possibility of upsetting a few thousand conservatives, much less his entire base, as he had done in 2002 by pushing for the Road Map.

As support for Israel shifted to the right among Republicans, so did support among the Democrats, who were becoming increasingly aware that they could lose Jewish voters to Bush. Thus, conservatives continued to push bipartisan support for Israel to the right in the lead-up to the elections.[127] With the announced departure of Powell following Bush's reelection victory, there could be little doubt that the conservative alliance had emerged victorious and would define the freedom agenda for Bush's second term.[128]

CHAPTER 5

⊕

The Lost Year

George W. Bush started off his second term much as he ended the first—by mixing and matching conservative utopian and moderate realist policies. Drawing from conservatives, Bush partially adhered to the sequence principle by focusing on democracy, but he did not demand the complete dismantling of militant organizations prior to elections. Drawing from moderates, he referred to the obligations of Israel under the Road Map, but did nothing to bring Sharon into compliance.

On November 11, 2004, following Bush's re-election victory, the ubiquitous Natan Sharansky was once again received at the White House by future Secretary of State Condoleezza Rice. She was holding a copy of his new book, *The Case for Democracy*, which she and others in the administration had been reading on the advice of the president. Bush's friend Tom Bernstein, a prominent New York real estate developer, had given the president a copy of the book, which was an impassioned defense of the sequence principle: no peace process until Palestinian terrorist institutions were entirely dismantled and Palestinian society was democratically transformed. After meeting with Rice for forty minutes, Sharansky was ushered into the Oval Office and received by the president. Referring to Bush as a "dissident among the leaders of the free world," Sharansky praised him for remaining steadfast in his belief that the power of freedom would overcome tyranny and terror. Impressed by Sharansky's personal story, Bush later disclosed to a reporter, "If you want a glimpse of how I think about foreign policy, read Natan Sharansky's book, *The Case for Democracy*."[1]

A Balance of Power that Favors Freedom

Bush began his second term by affirming his commitment to the conservative vision of sequence as the end (goal) and means of Middle East policy. In his triumphant 2005 Inaugural Address, Bush's political theology of natural right and history was unambiguously defined. Every "man and woman on this earth has rights, and dignity, and matchless value, because they bear the image of the Maker of Heaven and earth." The cause of freedom was thus seen as the purpose and "calling of our time." Bush argued:

> When our Founders declared a new order of the ages; when soldiers died in wave upon wave for a union based on liberty; when citizens marched in peaceful outrage under the banner 'Freedom Now'—they were acting on an ancient hope that is meant to be fulfilled. History has an ebb and flow of justice, but history also has a visible direction, set by liberty and the Author of Liberty."

Because democratic ideals and interests were indistinguishable to Bush, it followed from his worldview that U.S. service members were not simply defending the nation; they were also serving an "idealistic" purpose to "raise up free governments" in a "world moving toward liberty."[2]

Bush's political theology not only expressed his own religious convictions, but also the secularized theology of leading neoconservative intellectuals such as Charles Krauthammer, William Kristol, Irving Kristol, and especially Natan Sharansky.[3] As with the June 2002 Rose Garden speech, Bush's second Inaugural Address echoed Sharansky's utopianism in a striking way:

> *Sharansky*: "Promoting peace and security is fundamentally connected to promoting freedom and democracy."
>
> *Bush*: "The best hope for peace in our world is the expansion of freedom in all the world."

Sharansky: "Yet when it comes to promoting democracy and human rights around the globe, the values and interests of the free world are one and the same."

Bush: "America's vital interests and our deepest beliefs are now one."

Sharansky: "But I do believe that there can be an end to lasting tyranny—that we can live in a world where no regime that attempts to crush dissent will be tolerated."

Bush: "So it is the policy of the United States to seek and support the growth of democratic movements and institutions in every nation and culture, with the ultimate goal of ending tyranny in our world."

Sharansky: "Just as the institution of slavery has been all but wiped off the face of the earth, so too can government tyranny become a thing of the past."

Bush: "We do not accept the existence of permanent tyranny because we do not accept the possibility of permanent slavery."[4]

Early in his second term, Bush restated his commitment to the conservative vision of targeting state sponsors of terrorism. Because he saw Middle East politics in terms of freedom, and because freedom was conceived of as the antidote to terrorism, Bush saw the need to replace tyrants who sponsored terrorism in Iran and Syria with democratic regimes. Echoing his previous commitment to fight for those seeking liberation from "the rulers of outlaw regimes," Bush affirmed, "we must confront regimes that continue to harbor terrorists and pursue weapons of mass murder." After highlighting the role of sanctions against Syria in opening "the door to freedom," he went on to declare that "Iran remains the world's primary state sponsor of terror—pursuing nuclear weapons while depriving its people of the freedom they seek and deserve." In a warning to the ayatollahs, he promised the Iranian people, "As you stand for your own liberty, America stands with you."[5]

Like Bush, Rice seems to have been persuaded by Sharansky's worldview.[6] In remarks before the U.S. Senate Foreign Relations Committee, she explicitly referenced Sharansky's work and declared that her preeminent goal as chief diplomat would be to "spread democracy and freedom throughout the world." For Rice, Bush had made an admirable break with six decades of realism, in which the U.S. leadership had hoped to "purchase stability at the price of liberty." She argued that with the recent successes in the Palestinian and Afghan elections, there could be no doubt that "freedom is on the march" in the Middle East and that "the future of the region is to live in liberty." In particular, she believed that democracy would help end the conflict in Palestine. And as with the epic battle against communism, it was her "deepest conviction" that "tyranny and terror" would be overcome by "a similar triumph of the human spirit." This is what she described as a "really bold" new vision for U.S. foreign policy.[7]

In an administration lacking Colin Powell's sober realism, Rice and Stephen Hadley offered moderate resistance against the radical war plans coming from the Office of the Vice President and the Pentagon. But Powell's departure from the State Department left the administration wide open to the dominance of utopian conservatives. In Powell's absence, Rice gradually became the *de facto* leader of the moderates; unlike the decorated general, however, Rice's moderation was heavily tainted by the utopian worldview. While she distanced herself from some aspects of the sequence principle by pushing the president to restart peace negotiations, she was also a fervent proponent of the freedom agenda.[8] Like the president, she sought to bridge utopian and realist doctrines by building "a balance of power that favors freedom."[9] But as in Bush's first term, she unsuccessfully mixed and matched two theories which, at fundamental levels, offered two opposing views of the world.[10]

Rice's utopianism was tempered by career diplomats at the State Department, notably Assistant Secretary of State for Near Eastern Affairs David Welch, who suffered no delusions about democratizing the Middle East. A former U.S. Ambassador to Egypt who was often accused of cynicism, Welch acknowledged the existence of a "Palestinian cause," opposed "unrealistic" conservative plans to expand the U.S. War on Terror, and understood the value of diplomacy. While conservatives wanted an anemic Palestinian Authority, Welch wanted to properly train and equip Palestinian forces so that through force or the threat of force they might take out Hamas and other militant organizations, thereby diminishing Iran's sphere of influence.[11]

Because of Rice's close relationship with Bush, her move to replace Powell at the State Department only increased her influence, especially with the simultaneous promotion of her trusted deputy Stephen Hadley to the position of national security advisor. Hadley was discreet, deferential, and fiercely loyal to the president's freedom agenda.[12] Significantly, Elliott Abrams, who had initially maintained a good relationship with Rice and Hadley, was named the White House's deputy national security advisor for global democracy strategy—a telling job title—and in this capacity was charged with democracy promotion and human rights while simultaneously overseeing the National Security Council's Directorate of Near East and North African Affairs.[13] Unlike Welch, however, Abrams was known for his resolute support of Israel and used bureaucratic leverage to oppose attempts to restart a political process.[14] Citing the conservative sequence principle, he argued that there should be absolutely no peace process—no political process of any sort—until Palestinian society was democratically reformed and terrorist organizations were completely dismantled.[15] As the White House's point person for the Israeli-Palestinian conflict, Abrams worked with Welch, his State Department counterpart, and together they reported back to Rice and Hadley. Welch typically dealt with the Arabs and Abrams with the Israelis.[16]

Mildly restrained by Rice and Hadley, conservatives started off the second term by renewing their insistence on sequence. They wanted the Israeli-Palestinian conflict taken off the agenda and regime change in Iran placed front and center.[17] As Vice President Dick Cheney speculated in an inauguration day interview, Iran was "right at the top of the list" of high danger areas.[18] Though outwardly the conservative alliance seemed to be ascendant, some of its core members were suffering serious setbacks. It soon became public that the moderate intelligence community and the neoconservatives were at "war." The Federal Bureau of Investigation (FBI) was watching several prominent individuals, including former Chairman of the Defense Policy Board Richard Perle, who were suspected of giving classified information to the American Israel Public Affairs Committee (AIPAC), to Iraqi National Congress leader Ahmad Chalabi, and to the Israelis. In the end, Larry Franklin, who worked under Douglas Feith in the Office of Special Plans at the Pentagon, received a twelve-year prison sentence for passing classified intelligence concerning Iraq, Iran, and other sensitive issues to pro-Israel lobbyists and an Israeli official.[19]

In the midst of the espionage controversy, Feith, one of the greatest opponents of the peace process, announced that he would leave the administration later that year.[20] It was eventually determined by the Pentagon's inspector general that Feith's Office of Special Plans had acted inappropriately in developing, producing, and disseminating "alternative intelligence estimates on the supposed relationship between Iraq and al-Qaeda, which included some conclusions that were inconsistent with the consensus of the intelligence community."[21] Additionally, the Senate's Select Committee on Intelligence reprimanded Feith's office along with Hadley and Deputy Secretary of Defense Paul Wolfowitz for acting inappropriately in withholding information from the Central Intelligence Agency (CIA) and the State Department.[22] Last but not least, John Bolton, a conservative State Department official who was nominated to be UN ambassador, was accused by a former colleague of attempting to distort intelligence on Syria in 2003.[23]

As in his first term, Bush continued his practice of wavering back and forth between realist and utopian policy recommendations. While Bush embraced the conservative focus on liberty, he and Rice also realized that the conditions could not have been better for a political process, and they met privately to discuss what could be done to take advantage of the circumstances.[24] First, Palestinian Authority President Yasser Arafat was not only out of office; he was dead (and perhaps assassinated).[25] Second, the Iraq War was not going as planned and the administration needed a victory for the freedom agenda. Third, the Palestinians had responded to Bush's June 2002 Rose Garden speech and, in the words of Prime Minister Salam Fayyad, had "passed the test" by undertaking widespread institutional reform and developing new levels of accountability and transparency. Additionally, the Palestinian security forces were reorganized and praised by Giora Eiland, director of Israel's National Security Council, and by the U.S. State Department.[26] Fourth, a ceasefire was declared by Israeli Prime Minister Ariel Sharon and Palestinian Prime Minister Mahmoud Abbas in Egypt on February 8, 2005.[27] And finally, and perhaps most significantly, Abbas, the architect of the Oslo peace accords and an outspoken opponent of the *Intifada*, was elected president of the Palestinian Authority in free, democratic elections. As Assistant Secretary of State Welch and State Department Counselor Philip Zelikow observed, the administration could not have asked for a more perfect window of opportunity to push forward a political process.[28]

But the opportunity was not seized. Unable to act decisively and practically, Bush offered little more than rhetoric. Ignoring the significant number of Hamas officials who were democratically elected in municipal elections, Bush praised Abbas's election to the Palestinian presidency in his 2005 State of the Union Address as a landmark in the "history of liberty" and praised the "power of freedom to break old patterns of violence and failure." Much to the disappointment of conservatives, the president asked Congress for $350 million in aid to the Palestinian Authority and dispatched Rice to hold meetings with Abbas and Sharon.[29] This move dramatically enhanced the marginalized State Department's significance within the administration, and was a public indication that Rice had not completely signed on to the conservative agenda.[30]

In a further push toward moderation, State Department officials suggested that renewed calls would be made for an Israeli settlement freeze and an increase in aid to the Palestinians. In keeping with her vision to renew the peace process, Rice met with Sharon and subsequently called upon Israel to make "hard decisions" in order "to promote peace and to help the emergence of a democratic Palestinian state." She called upon Israel to withdraw its forces from the West Bank and not to take actions that would undermine the authority of the newly elected Abbas.[31]

Faced with fresh opposition from the State Department, the conservative alliance once again seized a crisis to undermine moderation. On February 14, 2005, former Lebanese Prime Minister Rafiq Hariri was killed in a sophisticated assassination carried out in Beirut. Immediately, Syria was blamed for the attack and a popular movement dubbed the "Cedar Revolution," which was backed by Western powers, pushed Syrian forces to withdraw from Lebanon. Because Bush was not interested in pursuing stability at the expense of freedom, he recalled the U.S. ambassador to Syria and cut off diplomatic lines of communication. Citing UN Resolution 1559, which called for the removal of all foreign troops from Lebanon, Bush urged Syria to extricate its political and military operations from Lebanon.[32] For Rice, the reaction from anti-Damascus Lebanese activists was evidence that freedom was on the move in the Middle East. For conservatives such as Elliott Abrams and Secretary of Defense Donald Rumsfeld, the Hariri assassination provided an opportunity to establish pro-Western governments in Lebanon and Syria. But as former NSC Senior Director Flynt Leverett warned, conservatives were unaware of the potential chaos that would ensue after Syrian President Bashar Al-Assad's departure.[33] As predicted, in the wake of Syria's withdrawal from Lebanon, Hezbollah emerged as a formidable political force and immediately pledged its allegiance to Syria.[34]

On February 21, 2005, Bush delivered a speech in which he once again spoke of the "movement of liberty" spreading throughout the Middle East. Without Syria's involvement, he predicted that the upcoming Lebanese elections could become another "milestone of liberty" in the Middle East's march toward freedom. Concerning Iran, Bush took a more conservative tone, arguing that though diplomacy was being pursued, "no option can be taken permanently off the table." He called for the Iranian leaders to reform and join in the move toward liberty, for only "the advance of freedom within nations will build a peace among nations." But concerning Palestine, Bush once again moderated his position. In keeping with the Road Map principles, he called for an Israeli settlement freeze and expressed his determination to see two democratic states living side by side, not "a state of scattered territories." He argued that "only a democracy can serve the hopes of Palestinians and make Israel secure and raise the flag of a free Palestine." If Arafat's Palestinian Authority was previously associated with the "Axis of Evil," the Palestinians were now part of Bush's "Arc of Reform," the poster child for the freedom agenda.[35]

Bush followed up by sending Rice to an international meeting convened in London by UK Prime Minister Tony Blair on February 28, 2005. But the meeting, initially conceived of as a major international "conference" to bolster peace talks, quickly devolved into a one-sided charade focused on Palestinian reform. Under pressure from Israel and administration conservatives, Blair realigned the agenda with the sequence principle and removed language in the final declaration that referred to the Road Map's principle of parallelism. A rare opportunity to address final-status negotiations was squandered.[36]

At the meeting, Rice spoke about a "new chapter" in the Palestinian national story, where "genuine peace will only blossom when rooted in genuine democracy." She concluded by citing her utopian belief in the inevitable power of freedom to drive social progress: "The course of human liberty is often uneven. But from the long perspective of history, the forward movement of freedom is clear."[37] Though the freedom agenda was essentially about democratic reform, Rice and Welch saw the need for a simultaneous process of security reform. Because Israel's 2002 Operation Defensive Shield essentially destroyed the Palestinian Authority's preventive security force infrastructure, its forces were severely demoralized and were not fully equipped or trained to take on Hamas and Islamic Jihad.[38] To address these concerns, Rice had already formally announced the appointment of Lt. General William Ward as security coordinator for Israel and the Palestinian Authority. In light of the U.S. focus on Palestinian reform, it is worth mentioning that Ward was later investigated by the Defense Department inspector general for lavish spending while in charge of U.S. operations in Africa.[39]

Coordinating the Withdrawal

Because the Bush administration was preoccupied with instability in Lebanon and Syria, Israel seized the opportunity to enhance its position *vis-à-vis* the Palestinians. In flagrant disregard of its obligations under the Road Map, Israeli Defense Minister Shaul Mofaz approved the construction of 3,500 new housing units in the West Bank's largest settlement, Maale Adumim, on March 21, 2005. Palestinian Authority negotiator Saeb Erekat called upon Bush to "intervene directly." Erekat remarked, "The land that is supposed to be for a future Palestinian state is being eaten up. With this settlement building, and the wall that is being built, the question for President Bush is: What is left to be negotiated?" Yariv Oppenheimer of Peace Now similarly stated, "This project may be one of the biggest obstacles to reaching a two-state solution."[40]

Adopting a moderate approach, Rice condemned the announcement as being "at odds with American policy" and noted that Israel had not provided a "satisfactory" explanation for its actions. Rice offered her own moderate interpretation of the 2004 Bush-Sharon letters which seemed less favorable to the conservative view: "The American view is that while we will not prejudice the outcome of final status negotiations, the changes on the ground, the existing major Israeli population centers, will have to be taken into account in any final status negotiations."[41] Meanwhile, U.S. Ambassador to Israel Daniel Kurtzer's statement that the United States supports "the retention by Israel of major Israeli population centers as an outcome of negotiations" raised fears in Israel that the conservative interpretation, which favored Israel's retention of major settlement blocks, of the Bush-Sharon letters was being challenged.[42]

Instead of heeding Bush's calls for Israel to adhere to its obligations under the Road Map and cease settlement expansion, Sharon cited the sequence principle, arguing that the Road Map would only take effect once the Palestinians had fulfilled their obligations. In another show of defiance to moderates, the Israel Lands Authority announced that it had approved the construction of fifty new homes in the West Bank settlement of Elkana prior to Sharon's trip to Bush's ranch in Crawford, Texas in April 2005.[43] At the ranch, Bush once again adopted a moderate position and opposed the settlement expansion: "I've been very clear [that] Israel has an obligation under the Road Map. That's no expansion of settlements. I look forward to continuing to work and dialogue with Israel on this subject." But as in the first term, he only offered words, not deeds: "There is a road map, there is a process, and *we've all agreed to it*. And part of that process is no expansion of settlements."[44]

Contrary to what Bush stated, Sharon had never agreed to the terms of the Road Map. He had agreed to them only in conjunction with his fourteen reservations, which clearly noted that the sequence principle and the June 2002 Rose Garden speech would be guiding Israel's actions. At Crawford, Sharon made the principle of sequence very clear: "Only after the Palestinians fulfill their obligations—primarily a real fight against terrorism and the dismantling of its infrastructure—can we proceed toward negotiations based on the Road Map." Faced with Sharon's stubbornness, Bush failed to assert once and for all which policy he was following: the conservative Rose Garden speech's sequence principle or the moderate Road Map's principle of parallelism.[45]

Instead, Bush glossed over the gaping philosophical differences between the two approaches and capitulated to Sharon. In a confirmation of sequentialism, the president ignored the Road Map and predicted that the Gaza withdrawal, once completed, would produce the beginnings of a nascent democratic and peaceful Palestinian state. He reasoned that once this happened, Sharon would gain the confidence to move the political process forward.[46] Because Israel demanded that Abbas disarm Hamas and Islamic Jihad, Bush charged Ward with an "expanded mandate" to negotiate security arrangements between the Israelis and Palestinians. Yet even with Ward overseeing the "train and equip" program, the Palestinians were not able to access funds and sufficient levels of equipment in a timely manner.[47]

In an effort to show support for the democratic government in Palestine, Bush received Abbas at the White House and pledged financial support to the Palestinian Authority. Congress had previously approved $50 million for Israel to build a Gaza border crossing and $150 million in aid to the Palestinians. But because House Majority Leader Tom DeLay and other conservatives in Congress were theologically opposed to Bush's plans for a Palestinian state, they stipulated that the aid be given to nongovernmental organizations and charities, not Abbas's Palestinian Authority. This significantly undermined Abbas's efforts to reform and rebuild the Palestinian Authority's security infrastructure, as his forces lacked training, supplies, and weapons needed to combat the growing influence of Hamas and Islamic Jihad.[48] In a foreshadowing of events to come, Palestinian Interior Minister Nasser Youssef warned that "only the Palestinian Authority should have weapons" and if Hamas rejects past understandings, the Palestinian Authority was "not going to allow anybody to meddle with peace and the agreements we have made."[49]

In a brief moment of moderation, Bush called upon Israel to withdraw its forces to their positions as of September 28, 2000, "remove unauthorized outposts, and stop settlement expansion." Additionally, he emphasized that the barrier "must be a security, rather than a political, barrier." Moving against conservative wishes, Bush pledged his support for the Quartet's special envoy, James Wolfensohn, who was charged with economic development in Gaza.[50] As former president of the World Bank, Wolfensohn enjoyed a high level of international credibility. But as a Quartet negotiator, the distinguished banker found himself in an adversarial position with administration conservatives, especially Abrams, who represented the "opposition to the Quartet's serious involvement in the peace process." Abrams was able to influence Rice on this issue, and Wolfensohn's mandate was consequently reduced from the economics of the peace process to a more limited economic agenda. As Wolfensohn recounts, the Quartet simply became a "veneer" that gave U.S. and Israeli unilateralism the appearance of multilateralism.[51] Or, as the Europeans were fond of saying, the group of four was really the "Quartet *sans trois*."[52]

With the peace process in limbo, Bush did not seem particularly interested in crossing swords with Sharon. More important, he did not seem to believe that sustained management of the situation was necessary. By the summer of 2005, the president's freedom agenda for the Middle East appeared to be vindicating itself. At the invitation of President Hosni Mubarak, thirteen Palestinian factions visited Egypt in March and agreed to extend a truce with Israel until the end of the year on the condition that Israel "stop all forms of aggression" against Palestinians and free their prisoners.[53] The Egyptians agreed to hold their first multi-candidate elections, the Syrian withdrawal from Lebanon was to be consummated with free and fair elections, and the Iraqis successfully conducted free and fair elections. These developments, combined with the upcoming Israeli withdrawal from Gaza and the Palestinian Legislative Council elections, all seemed to be a clear indication that tyranny and terrorism were on the decline; the progress of liberty could not be contained.[54]

Channelling Bush's optimism, Rice traveled to Cairo to deliver a highly anticipated and historic speech on freedom and democracy. On June 20, 2005, she spoke of a rapidly changing modern world in which "a growing number of men and women are securing their liberty." Because "the ideal of democracy is universal," she argued, people choose to "create democratic governments to protect their natural rights." Echoing the president's 2005 Inaugural Address, she once again noted that "for 60 years, the United States pursued stability at the expense of democracy in the Middle East—and [it] achieved neither." Under Bush's leadership, the United States was "taking a different course." She praised the Iraqi elections and called upon the Syrian and Iranian leadership to trust and respect the aspirations of their people. She recognized efforts to reform political systems in Kuwait, Saudi Arabia, and Jordan, and praised Mubarak for allowing multi-candidate elections in Egypt. Borrowing from Sharansky's *Case for Democracy*, Rice argued that undemocratic institutions, like the institutions of slavery and colonialism, would one day be abolished. With unfettered optimism she declared, "The day is coming when the promise of a fully free and democratic world, once thought impossible, *will also seem inevitable.*"[55]

While Bush and Rice rightly sensed that something dramatic was happening in the Middle East, it was not the "something" that conservatives had hoped for. Contrary to what they believed, the freedom agenda was not unleashing pro-U.S. democratic energies across the region. Rather, in Iraq, pro-Iranian politicians won the elections. In Lebanon, Hezbollah swept the south of Lebanon, claiming to speak in "one voice to protect the resistance and its weapons." In Egypt, the elections were fraudulently conducted.[56] And in Palestine, Islamic fundamentalism was becoming increasingly popular, as evident in the Hamas victory in the historically Christian city of Bethlehem.[57] Because of these startling trends, Abbas postponed the legislative elections to buy Fatah, the major political part of the Palestine Liberation Organization, more time to get organized. As former Jordanian Prime Minister Fayaz Tarawneh and former Palestinian National Security Advisor Mohammad Dahlan recall, Palestinian officials were well aware of Hamas's strength and warned Bush administration officials time and again.[58] But surprisingly, as Abrams noted, no one in the U.S. administration "thought Hamas was going to win."[59] Disregarding statistics and advice, Bush did not reflect on the consequences of forcing the Palestinian elections and instead expressed confidence that Hamas would not be voted into power.[60]

Because of the unilateral nature of Israel's disengagement plan, Sharon's move to delay the withdrawal made it very difficult for the Palestinian Authority to coordinate and plan the takeover of security services in the Gaza Strip.[61] Wolfensohn's involvement, however, helped to facilitate a smoother transition than would have otherwise transpired, and he helped resolve disagreements through skillful diplomacy. He also popularized the notion that Israeli restrictions on movement were responsible for economic decline in the Palestinian territories.[62]

Sharon used his domineering stature to remove settlers in an efficient manner. Despite the uncertainty surrounding the event, on September 12, 2005, Israel completed the removal of its troops and settlers from Gaza. It is important, though, to underscore that while Israel dismantled settlements and its military infrastructure, the Gaza disengagement plan, as adopted by the Israeli Knesset on June 4, 2004, provided Israel with continued control over Gaza.[63] As Yoram Dinstein noted, the proposition that Sharon's Disengagement Plan ended the Israeli occupation of Gaza is not valid. Although Israel withdrew its forces and settlers from Gaza, it still retained overall control over the territory's airspace, coastline, borders, telecommunication networks, sewage systems, and electrical grids.[64] Therefore, Israel did not shed its obligations under the Fourth Geneva Convention to facilitate the provision of food, medical supplies, and humanitarian assistance so as not to inflict collective punishment on the population.[65]

With the Gaza Strip emptied of Israeli soldiers and settlers, Abbas unsuccessfully attempted to counter Hamas's propaganda campaign by claiming the withdrawal as his victory.[66] The Israeli prime minister delivered his own victory speech at the United Nations. Implicitly referencing number eight on his list of fourteen Road Map reservations, Sharon once again committed Israel to "the *sequence* of the Road Map."[67] As far as Sharon was concerned, because the sequence principle required that the Palestinians first undertake a radical sociopolitical transformation, Israel had no further duties to fulfill until this was complete. The day after his speech, Sharon blatantly disregarded Israel's obligations under the Road Map and announced that there would be no settlement freeze in the immediate future.[68] The Israeli warrior had successfully put Israeli-Palestinian politics into a deep freeze.

Missed Opportunities

In the wake of the Gaza disengagement, Sharon continued his stubborn refusal to accept the Road Map, and Bush was unwilling to stand up to him. Instead, Bush focused on the two major doctrines of sequentialism: democratic elections and dismantling terrorist organizations and institutions. Meanwhile, in the absence of any political process, conservatives, led by Cheney, pushed for a more aggressive posture against Iran and its nuclear program.[69] They argued that if Iran were to get the bomb, President Mahmoud Ahmadinejad could fulfill his apocalyptic dreams of wiping "Israel off the map."[70] Led by the "bomber boys" Charles Krauthammer and William Kristol, a conservative chorus put forward ideas for a war against Iran. For David Wurmser, a trusted member of Cheney's inner circle, an imaginative "Shiite strategy" would pit Iraqi Shiites against Iran.[71] As Wurmser speculated, "the Iraqi Shiites, if liberated from [Saddam Hussein's] tyranny, can be expected to present a challenge to Iran's influence and revolution," and consequently, would end Iran's monopoly over the region's Shiite minority. It followed from this line of reasoning that resentful Lebanese Shiites would turn against both Iran and Syria.[72] Given the reality of Iran's rising influence among both Shiite and Sunni communities through-out the Middle East, it is hard to imagine a strategy that could have been more spectacularly mistaken.

Though conservatives hoped for an immediate military attack against Iran, domestic politics turned in a more moderate direction. First, the president's theoconservative base was weakened by the mainstream evangelical community's decision to take a moderate stance on Middle East politics. Following the Presbyterian Church USA's 2004 decision to take a formal stand against the Israeli occupation and an ecumenical statement sent in January 2005 from Christian, Jewish, and Muslim religious leaders in the United States to Bush endorsing a two-state solution, it became clear that pro-Israel theoconservatives were losing some political capital.[73] Second, by late September, the conservative alliance suffered another severe blow. Powerful theoconservative House Majority Leader Tom DeLay was indicted on a charge of conspiracy and stepped down from his position. As Chairman of the U.S. Holocaust Memorial Council Fred Zeidman observed, "No one has been a bigger supporter of Israel than Tom DeLay." Although theoconservatives and Zionist conservatives remained supportive of DeLay, he did not return to Congress.[74] Third, Feith's departure from the Pentagon in August 2005 left the conservative alliance susceptible to accusations that hawkish U.S. policy was severely dysfunctional at best.[75]

With the conservative alliance weakened, Rice worked to bolster Abbas's credibility. So as not to put on a "farcical election, where [one does] not allow [one's] opposition to run," Abbas invited Hamas and Islamic Jihad to participate.[76] Bush pushed Abbas to disarm Hamas prior to the legislative elections, but the latter pushed back, arguing that he wanted to integrate Hamas into the political process rather than starting a civil war.[77] With the very real possibility that Hamas could win up to 40 percent of the vote, Sharon threatened to undermine the elections. Delicately sidestepping the matter, Rice sided with Abbas, saying, "This is going to be a Palestinian process…and I think we have to give the Palestinians some room for the evolution of their political process."[78] Though elections would have been seen as illegitimate without the participation of Hamas, conservatives in the administration were upset that Bush allowed an armed militia to take part.[79]

Lost between incommensurable moderate and utopian policies, Bush was unable to provide a clear way forward. He continued to embrace the freedom and democracy requirement of the sequence principle, but did not demand the complete dissolution of terrorist institutions as a prerequisite for holding elections in Palestine. Simultaneously, he also advocated for a return to the peace process without taking the necessary steps to bring Israel in line with its obligations under the Road Map.

Without a firm sense of direction from the president, Rice continued to move Middle East policy toward moderation.[80] She offered public displays of support for Abbas and turned her attention to the deplorable economic situation in the Palestinian territories, especially Gaza. Knowing that the Israeli withdrawal could turn disastrous if Palestinians did not have the ability to move goods and services to and from the narrow strip of land, Wolfensohn had been diligently trying to secure an agreement between Israel and the Palestinian Authority on movement and access. But because the disengagement coupled with negotiations would have left Palestinians with control over an outlet to the outside world, any agreement on movement and access was highly contested. Israel was concerned that the open border would be used to smuggle weapons into Gaza and did not want to relinquish its control. Wolfensohn and his capable team traveled a great distance in putting together a difficult compromise, but as noted by UN Special Envoy to the Quartet Alvaro de Soto, Wolfensohn's mission was "intercepted" by Rice, who wanted more control over the process.[81]

Impatient with the slow-paced Gaza negotiations, Rice let Abrams and Welch know that she was displeased with the lack of progress on the agreement. After briefly shuttling to Jordan to pay her respects to the victims of suicide bombings that shook Amman in November 2005, she returned to Jerusalem and drafted an agreement, negotiating line by line of the proposed text with the respective parties. Wolfensohn was particularly unhappy with Rice's attempt to move into his already limited domain and confronted Abrams in the lobby of the hotel before publicly threatening to quit. Abrams and other administration conservatives did not like Wolfensohn and sought to undermine him whenever possible.[82]

In the end, Wolfensohn was "elbowed aside at the crowning moment."[83] After staying up most of the night, Rice announced on November 15, 2005, that Israel and the Palestinian Authority had concluded an unprecedented agreement on movement and access, which would improve humanitarian conditions in the Gaza Strip. The agreement accomplished several crucial aims: First, the Palestinians were to be given access to the outside world through the establishment of an international crossing at Rafah. Second, Israel and the Palestinians agreed to "upgrade and expand" other crossings such as Karni in order to facilitate the export of Gaza's agricultural products. Third, Israel agreed to let bus and truck convoys through to the West Bank. Fourth, both parties agreed to remove obstacles to movement in the West Bank. Fifth, both parties agreed to the construction of a Gaza seaport, and an airport was to be discussed in the near future.[84] This Agreement on Movement and Access (AMA) demonstrated not only Rice's tremendous diplomatic abilities but also her potential to make a significant contribution to Israeli-Palestinian peace—if and only if the United States was willing to commit itself to the task.

Unfortunately, in the end the AMA also demonstrated what happens without continued U.S. involvement. If executed successfully, the AMA would have delivered a significant victory to Abbas's Palestinian Authority prior to the legislative elections. But soon after securing the historic agreement, Rice moved on to other pressing international affairs; without sustained U.S. diplomatic pressure, the agreement fell apart. Millions of dollars in Gazan produce rotted at border crossings due to Israeli closures. Qassam rockets were fired into Israel. Bush's favored Palestinian security chief, Mohammad Dahlan, and his loyalists engaged in rampant corruption. And in the absence of a robust Palestinian Authority security force, Palestinian militants destroyed the greenhouses that Wolfensohn, Bill Gates, and other wealthy donors had purchased from departing settlers on behalf of the Palestinians.[85]

Though Wolfensohn warned that the Israelis were not allowing the free movement of goods and services in and out of Gaza, no one heeded his voice.[86] One year after the AMA was signed, movement in the Palestinian territories was more restricted than before, and the humanitarian situation went from bad to worse. Disregarding its commitments, Israel never opened the Rafah crossing for the export of goods, did not allow more than 4 percent of harvested goods to be exported through the Karni crossing, did not allow the passage of convoys from Gaza to the West Bank, increased obstacles to movement in the West Bank by 44 percent, imposed a permit system on Palestinians, did not allow construction to begin on the seaport in Gaza, and did not continue discussions on the construction of a Gazan airport. Due to the lack of movement and access between 2005 and 2006, unemployment in the Gaza Strip rose from 33.1 to 41.8 percent.[87]

If Hamas campaigned under the slogan, "Three years of *Intifada* beat ten years of negotiations," the failure of the AMA only seemed to confirm the futility of negotiations and the inability of Palestinian negotiator-in-chief Abbas to stand up to the Israelis.[88] Having refused to enforce the AMA, Bush sent Rice on her fourth visit to Israel in November 2005 to break the diplomatic deadlock.[89] But the differences, once again, fundamentally rested on which U.S. policy—sequentialism or parallelism—was governing Israeli-Palestinian affairs. Sharon believed he was obliged to act only in sequence once the Palestinians dismantled terrorist organizations, while Abbas believed that Israel and the Palestinians were expected to take reciprocal measures toward peace, including freezing Israeli settlements and facilitating Palestinian movement and access. Because Bush continued to confuse the two policies and failed to come down on one side or the other, the situation was left in utter disarray.[90] Due to disagreements between the two parties, Abbas's and Sharon's third summit meeting was cancelled and the Israeli government arrested five hundred militants, mostly from Hamas, over a period of ten days.[91]

Having successfully achieved what no other Israeli prime minister had done with the Gaza withdrawal, Sharon decided to free himself from the naysayers within his own party who wanted to rein him in. He founded the Kadima (Forward) Party on the unwritten platform that he, Sharon, would successfully lead Israel to unilaterally withdraw from other undesirable parts of the West Bank while retaining control over a united Jerusalem, major settlement blocs, and probably the Jordan Valley. In this effort, he was joined by senior and junior statespersons Shimon Peres, Haim Ramon, Ehud Olmert, and Tzipi Livni.[92]

As the year drew to an end, there was very little indication that Bush was going to take a stand and break free from the conservative mold. Though he continued to waver back and forth, mixing and matching realist and utopian policies, Bush leaned more toward sequentialism as 2005 came to a close. Although no strike was made against Iran (or its ally Syria), the conservative vision for democratic transformation was still a superior force; as Rice restated in the *Washington Post*, U.S. policy for a world transformed was a "balance of power that favors freedom." In this "new world," she argued, "the fundamental character of regimes matters more today than the international distribution of power." The goal of U.S. statecraft, therefore, was "to help create a world of democratic, well-governed states that can meet the needs of their citizens and conduct themselves responsibly in the international system."[93]

In such a world, Rice did not recognize the distinction between democratic ideals and national security interests. They were one and the same. Though the Middle East was suffering from a "freedom deficit," she once again expressed confidence that "democracy [would] succeed in [the] region not simply because we have faith in our principles but because the basic human longing for liberty and democratic rights has transformed our world." Were it not for this vision, Rice argued, the Lebanese would still be under Syrian occupation, Iraqis would still be suffering under the brutal dictatorship of Saddam Hussein, and the Palestinians would still be living under the rule of a corrupt Palestinian Authority. She concluded, "I have an abiding confidence that we ...have laid a firm foundation of principle—a foundation upon which future generations will realize our nation's vision of a fully free, democratic and peaceful world."[94] With faith in freedom, and a faith-based policy in hand, she and the president optimistically looked to 2006 as the year of liberty.

CHAPTER 6

✛

A New Middle East

Prior to the Palestinian elections in January 2006, U.S. Secretary of State Condoleezza Rice delivered a lecture on "transformational diplomacy," a process that "not only reports about the world as it is, but seeks to change the world itself." As democracy permeates a world in which "centuries of international precedent are being overturned," she argued, a new diplomacy is required to "build a true form of global stability"—the proverbial "balance of power that favors freedom." As Rice saw it, "security, development, and democracy were to be viewed as a single, immutable foreign policy package." The traditional aims of statecraft were reconceived by Rice as an international project "to build and sustain democratic, well-governed states that will respond to the needs of their people and conduct themselves responsibly in the international system."[1] The approaching Palestinian elections were to be a testing ground for this new diplomatic U.S. posture. Still trying to reconcile soft utopianism with a realist worldview, Rice's transformational diplomacy did not stray very far from the sequence principle, which stated that no political process would occur until entirely new democratic Palestinian leadership replaced and dismantled terrorist institutions. After the outcome of the Palestinian election, however, George W. Bush exchanged one half of the sequence principle for the other by abandoning democracy promotion and attempting to dismantle Hamas through force.

The World As It Is

The new year had commenced with two game-changing events in the Israeli-Palestinian conflict. After forming his new Kadima Party, Israeli Prime Minister Ariel Sharon suffered a massive stroke on January 4, 2006, leaving his followers under the leadership of his deputy, Ehud Olmert, who first became acting prime minister then prime minister.[2] As Israelis adjusted to the new leadership, Palestinians braced for their own political earthquake. Expecting Hamas to do well in the upcoming elections, Mohammad Dahlan had warned the U.S. State Department that Hamas was going to win. Additionally, Palestinian President Mahmoud Abbas had spoken with Bush over the phone and conveyed a similar message. Days before the election, Assistant Secretary of State for Near East Affairs David Welch met with Abbas in Ramallah, where the latter once again sought to postpone the elections for fear of losing. Abbas and Sharon had previously devised a plan whereby Israel would publicly ban East Jerusalemites from fully participating in the elections, thus providing Abbas with a pretext for calling them off. Because Bush believed that elected office would make Hamas more accountable to the people, however, he insisted via Welch that further delays from Abbas were unacceptable.[3]

Though Sharon had stated in unequivocal terms that Hamas was an organization whose status as a terrorist entity disqualified it from electoral participation, the Quartet, like Bush, supported including Hamas in the Palestinian elections. Additionally, UN Secretary General Kofi Annan had read out a statement of support for the elections the year before.[4] But according to the testimony of UN Special Envoy Alvaro de Soto, who assisted Kofi Annan with the peace process, the secretary general also read an important sentence on behalf of the Quartet "not included in the written statement that was issued—in which the view was expressed that the forthcoming Palestinian legislative elections should be seen as a stage in the evolution toward democracy, and that the question of participation should be left to the Palestinians themselves, notwithstanding the 'fundamental contradiction' between participation in elections and the possession of militias." This, according to De Soto, was an endorsement of Abbas's co-option strategy and "a pass on the requirement, spelled out in the first stage of the Road Map, to disarm militias."[5]

With strong pressure from the United States, the Palestinian Authority moved forward with the elections. But Bush's vision of the democratic world that should be was utterly shattered by the reality of the world as it was on January 25, 2006. Condoleezza Rice was up before 5 a.m., working out at her private gym at the Watergate, when all of a sudden a headline appeared on the television stating that Hamas had won. Certain that it must be in error, Rice called both the Department of State and Consul General Jacob Walles in Jerusalem only to find out that Abbas's and Sharon's predictions had been right on target. Indeed, in free and fair elections, Hamas had won a large majority of seats—76 out of 132—in the Palestinian parliament.[6]

Rice spoke with Bush, who characterized the victory as being part of "the democratic process." Taking an optimistic tone, Bush publicly indicated that the world was "watching liberty begin to spread across the Middle East." The Palestinian elections served as a reminder of "the power of democracy" and the democratic mechanism as a means by which the people expressed their opposition to the corruption of the "Old Guard" of the Palestinian Authority. He praised the "competition of ideas" and saw the elections as a wake-up call to the aspirations of the Palestinian people, stating, "The people are demanding honest government. The people want services. They want to be able to raise their children in an environment in which they can get a decent education and they can find health care." While praising the election, Bush also cautioned that a political party with an "armed wing" could not be a "partner in peace." When asked whether or not he would rule out working with Hamas, Bush declined to "speculate."[7]

Like Bush, Rice optimistically praised the election but reiterated that the United States would require Hamas to renounce violence and recognize Israel's right to exist. She remarked, "You cannot have one foot in politics and the other in terror. Our position on Hamas has therefore not changed."[8] Two days later she still seemed to leave the door open for change by Hamas, emphasizing, "this is a transitional period, but anyone who wants to govern the Palestinian people and do so with the support of the international community has got to be committed to a two-state solution, [and] must be committed to the right of Israel to exist."[9]

Within the administration there was a mixture of blame and confusion, and the conciliatory tone toward Hamas lasted for but a moment. Rice indicated that the administration had grossly underestimated the popularity of Hamas. She asked her staff why they did not see this coming and stated that she did not know of anyone who was not surprised by the results. But contrary to what Rice recalled, Deputy Assistant Secretary of State for Near Eastern Affairs J. Scott Carpenter had sent around a pre-election memo indicating that predictions were far from certain, especially since Fatah was planning on running more than one candidate per ticket.[10] This would dilute the Fatah vote and strengthen Hamas's position.

Carpenter described Rice as being absolutely "befuddled" by the results.[11] While the Bush administration deliberated about how it should respond, the Arabs, the Israelis, and the international community also seemed unsure about what direction to take. Arab moderates pressured Hamas to recognize previous agreements, including Israel's right to exist. Tzipi Livni, the new Israeli foreign minister, indicated that "the Israeli position is not to try to punish somebody, but to find a way for the future to work together"; however, the Israeli government immediately froze $50 million in tax and customs revenue that belonged to the Palestinian Authority.[12] As De Soto notes, this action not only violated the framework for interim economic relations—the Paris Protocol—signed between Israel and the Palestine Liberation Organization (PLO), but it also made it impossible for the Palestinian Authority to pay teachers, doctors, nurses, and security personnel, who were left without income indefinitely. De Soto's report to the United Nations stated, "economic activity in Gaza came to a standstill, moving it into survival mode."[13]

In a move that irritated Israel and the United States, Russian President Vladimir Putin indicated that Russia, a member of the Quartet, had "never regarded Hamas as a terrorist organization" and that his government was willing "to invite the authorities of Hamas to Moscow to carry out talks."[14] The European Union's High Representative for Common Foreign and Security Policy, Javier Solana, indicated that "the European Union will not abandon the Palestinian people." In an effort to build a unified coalition against Hamas, Rice traveled to the Gulf to convince the Arabs not to fund the Hamas-led Palestinian Authority, which employed approximately 140,000 people and 58,000 security personnel.[15] The Saudis and the Egyptians rejected Rice's calls to withhold aid from the Palestinians and instead urged her to move forward with the peace process. In response to the threat of U.S. sanctions against the Palestinians, Iran stepped into its newly upgraded role as U.S. nemesis and committed its support to the new Hamas-led government.[16]

In the midst of the uncertainty, De Soto left a January 13, 2006, meeting with the sense that the United States was not completely opposed to the idea of "drawing on the flexibility of Russia and the UN" to moderate Hamas. His boss, UN Secretary General Kofi Annan, similarly opposed plans to ignore Hamas, especially given the West's longstanding insistence on democratic reform. Ultimately, the moderate view was rejected, and on January 30, 2006, the Quartet issued a statement on the elections: "It is the view of the Quartet that all members of a future Palestinian government must be committed to nonviolence, recognition of Israel, and acceptance of previous agreements and obligations, including the Road Map." In the statement, which reveals the level of discord within the Quartet, Annan tried to distance the United Nations from the other members of the Quartet—to effectively say "we are not with them"—by making a subtle distinction between donor and non-donor members. Echoing Annan's frustrations, De Soto's leaked report laments the fact that the Quartet was transformed from a "foursome guided by a common document (the Road Map) into a body that was all-but-imposing sanctions on a freely elected government of a people under occupation as well as setting unattainable preconditions for dialogue."[17]

The State Department and the Europeans were caught off guard by the elections, but Middle East specialists were not surprised for six reasons. First, in the weeks and months leading up to the elections, Israelis, Palestinians, Jordanians, and other Arab leaders had consistently warned that Hamas could win. Fundamentally, this was the main reason why Abbas had postponed the elections from 2005 to 2006. All indicators pointed to Hamas's growing popularity; of special mention were the municipal and university election results, in which Hamas did extremely well.[18] Second, because the withdrawal from Gaza was not negotiated or coordinated with the Palestinian Authority, Hamas succeeded in attributing Israel's disengagement to the Islamic movement's strategy of violence.[19] Third, because Hamas operated a massive social service program, a significant proportion of the Palestinian population was dependent upon their schools, health care facilites, orphanages, food programs, and social clubs. As Shaul Mishal and Avraham Sela observed, while

Hamas is internationally infamous for its murderous suicide bombings, it is known among Palestinians primarily as a "social movement" that has "directed its energies toward providing services to the community, especially responding to its immediate hardships and concerns."[20] Most polls showed that the majority of people voted for Hamas because they were looking for better governance and security, not an Islamic state. Additionally, while Hamas was cutting ribbons and feeding people, U.S. aid was diverted away from Abbas's Palestinian Authority to the non-governmental sector or blocked altogether by conservatives in Congress.[21]

Fourth, and related to the previous point, many Palestinians regarded Abbas as politically weak, unable to deliver economically, deferential to Israel, and incapable of ensuring basic goods, services, and freedom of movement for the Palestinian people. Fifth, because the Palestinian Authority had not organized a proper election strategy, it split the vote by running more than one candidate on the same ticket. And finally, because the Palestinian Authority was known for its corruption, Hamas successfully convinced the electorate that it would bring genuine transparency and reform to politics.[22]

As members of the administration blamed each other for failing to predict the election outcomes, they also blamed Abbas for not disarming Hamas and other Islamic movements by force.[23] Despite strong Israeli and U.S. pressure, Abbas had previously refused to do so for several valid reasons. First, since heavily armed wings of the Islamic movements in the territories enjoyed support from a significant proportion of the population, Abbas believed that confronting them by force would inevitably spark civil war.[24] Second, as his former National Security Advisor Mohammad Dahlan recalls, approximately 70 percent of all official headquarters and command centers for the Palestinian Authority's security infrastructure were destroyed during Sharon's Operation Defensive Shield in 2002. The Palestinian Authority lacked the equipment, training, and confidence needed to defeat Hamas.[25] Third, a political solution was needed to deal with Hamas, not a military solution. One could try to disarm militant groups, but as Israel might have learned over half a century, if no political solution existed, there could be no lasting security.

Though political solutions did exist, faith in sequence and the sword prevailed. In a meeting convened to discuss the Hamas crisis, Welch, Carpenter, and Deputy National Security Advisor Elliot Abrams reviewed the range of possible responses for

U.S. policymakers. Carpenter suggested that the administration could "let [Hamas] fail" at governing. After all, as he reasoned, the "last unexploded myth in the Middle East" was that "Islam was the solution." As Carpenter recalls, Abrams and Welch looked at him like he was "the biggest moron on the face of the planet." Abrams and Welch disagreed "on everything except…putting…pressure on Hamas…. They agreed 100 percent on that." Together, they worked to get international support for a consensus that "these guys need to be squeezed."[26]

As De Soto recounted, the Bush administration completely reversed its support for Abbas's co-option strategy, and "the U.S. clearly pushed for a confrontation between Fatah and Hamas."[27] Welch wanted the new security coordinator, Lt. General Keith Dayton, to equip Abbas's hawkish security chief, Mohammad Dahlan, and to give him free reign over Hamas. As Carpenter recalls, Welch would say something to the effect that Dahlan is the "biggest bastard in the battle out there, but he's our bastard and he's gonna kick their ass now." To his colleagues, Welch seemed "pretty hardcore when it came to this kind of stuff" and wanted things to "come to blows" so that Hamas would "get its head cut off." Initially, Abrams, as democracy promotion chief, was more skeptical of Dahlan's abilities and the "military strategy." He distrusted the Palestinian strongman and was concerned about what an armed Palestinian security force would mean for Israeli security. In addition, he was utterly conflicted by his devotion to Israel and by the apparent need to prepare Abbas's security forces for a confrontation with the democratically elected Hamas government.[28] In the end, Abrams had no choice but to agree with Welch. For him, it was either arm Fatah or talk with Hamas.[29]

Surprisingly, the decision to pursue a military strategy created a major fissure within the hawkish conservative alliance. In the Office of the Vice President, national security aides John Hannah, David Wurmser, and other hard-liners were vehemently opposed to arming the Palestinians because they believed that weapons intended for use against Hamas could just as easily be turned against Israel. They were highly critical of Abrams for breaking ranks with the conservative alliance and going forward with Welch and the State Department.[30]

With a military strategy in hand, Welch and Abrams received approval from Rice, National Security Advisor Stephen Hadley, and ultimately the president to proceed with the revamped security program.[31] Humiliated by the election debacle,

Bush all but abandoned his democracy promotion strategy for Palestine and instead desperately looked to autocratic Arab allies, who were by then experiencing a fair bit of post-election *schadenfreude*. The United States, with the help of the Arab states, developed a plan to rehabilitate the Palestinian security forces through technical assistance and the provision of equipment. As Dahlan saw it, the Palestinian forces needed to be equipped "with all defensive means and tools that would allow them to protect the Palestinian national scheme of independence and freedom."[32]

From these discussions emerged a highly secretive and controversial mission that aimed to build upon the "train and equip" program for the Palestinians and to take it in an ambitious new direction. Officially, the plan was to coordinate funds from international donations, advise the Palestinian Authority on security matters, and help ensure Israel's safety. Unofficially, however, the program's ultimate mission was to dismantle Hamas's military capabilities and establish Fatah's monopoly over the use of Palestinian force.[33] Fighters loyal to Abbas were vetted and received special training and arms from Jordan and Egypt. Because conservatives in the U.S. Congress prohibited the Bush administration from arming the Palestinians, the State Department sought funding from other sources, namely Prince Bandar of Saudi Arabia, a close friend of the Bush family, and from the United Arab Emirates. They agreed to bankroll the arms sales if Jordan and Egypt would deliver the weapons to the Fatah forces.[34]

The Diet of Gaza

On January 31, 2006, Bush delivered his fifth State of the Union Address, stubbornly declaring freedom to be the means and ends of his Middle East policy, "the future of every nation in the Middle East," and "the right and hope of all humanity." Bush indicated that "the leaders of Hamas must recognize Israel, disarm, reject terrorism and work for lasting peace." He accused Iran of continuing to sponsor terrorism in Lebanon and in the Palestinian territories, and promised the Iranian people that "our nation hopes one day to be the closest of friends with a free and democratic Iran."[35] Whereas in previous speeches Bush had declared liberty to be the preordained destination of history, now he radically qualified his philosophy of history, declaring that "the destination of history is determined by human action, and every great movement of history comes to a point of choosing." Yet he remained confident that the United States would "lead freedom's advance" throughout the world.[36]

In the weeks and months following the elections, Israel, the United States, and the European Union squeezed the Hamas-led Palestinian Authority. The Quartet's Special Envoy, James Wolfensohn, warned, "Unless a solution is found, we may be facing the financial collapse of the PA within two weeks.... I know I do not need to tell each of you that the failure to pay salaries may have wide-ranging consequences—not only for the Palestinian economy but also for security and stability for both the Palestinians and the Israelis." He concluded, "If we don't get this right, I am afraid past investment in the Palestinian development will be lost, a Palestinian economy will not be sustainable, the Palestinian people will live off humanitarian hand-outs, and security for both Palestinians and Israelis will be in greater jeopardy than it has been for years."[37] In response to Wolfensohn's letter, the European Union released $144 million to the Palestinian Authority prior to Hamas's formal takeover of the government.[38]

Though administration moderates understood that democracy promotion efforts, contrary to conservative expectations, were not producing governments more favorably predisposed to U.S. interests, conservatives were too blinded by their ideological commitments to see the consequences of their actions.[39] On March 7, 2006, Vice President Dick Cheney addressed the American Israel Public Affairs Committee (AIPAC) and echoed the president's belief that "best hope for peace in the world is the expansion of freedom throughout the world." The goal of Middle East policy, therefore, was "to replace hatred and resentment with democracy and hope" across the Middle East. He remarked that Israel and the United States are "fellow democracies, both founded in struggle" that have shown "devotion to the ideals of liberty, equality, and the dignity of every person." In keeping with Bush's interpretation of history, Cheney argued that world "events are moving in the direction of human liberty."

While affirming the president's focus on liberty even after the Palestinian election debacle, the vice president's speech highlighted an ever-widening fissure between Cheney's national security team and the more moderate teams of Rice and Hadley, who were investigating ways to engage Iran and arm Fatah. In what was seen as a veiled threat to Iran, Cheney declared that the United States was keeping "all options on the table."

Concerning the Israeli-Palestinian conflict, Cheney dismissed the notion that democracy promotion was "destabilizing the region and undermining hopes for peace." He argued, in what perhaps was a reference to a neoconservative policy paper, that "a clean break" was needed in the Palestinian territories. The United States could no longer trust a "tiny elite" to advance peace, as was done in the previous decade. Once again echoing the sequence principle, Cheney stated, "There is simply no way to achieve that peace until all parties fight terror."[40]

In an act of defiance to the United States, Hamas formed its democratically elected government, but Rice warned that any government that emerged must declare its intention to cease violence, recognize previous agreements, and commit itself to the Road Map if it wanted international support. According to State Department Legal Advisor John Bellinger III, to an extent, the administration had its hands tied. Even if Rice wanted to continue to supply the Palestinian Authority with aid, there was a "criminal prohibition on providing material support to terrorism." Additionally, the International Economic Emergency Powers Act named Hamas as a terrorist organization, making it even more difficult for the U.S. government to support a Hamas-led Palestinian Authority.[41] Domestic restrictions aside, however, if Rice wanted to engage Hamas, she still had the option of working through the United Nations, Russia, and to a lesser extent the European Union.

In the United States, engagement was set aside for hardball politics. If war is the continuation of politics by other means, then so is inter-national development. As the Hamas-led government formally assumed power, Bush declared that U.S. aid would continue to flow to the Palestinian people but not to Hamas.[42] Recognizing that Hamas gained much of its popular appeal from its social service programs, the State Department announced that it would increase aid to the Palestinians by bypassing the government and delivering funds directly to nongovernmental organizations and international institutions like the United Nations Relief and Works Agency (UNRWA). As a further precaution, all U.S. Agency for International Development (USAID) recipients were required to sign an "anti-terrorism certificate."[43]

With an embargo in place, Bush turned his attention to defending the freedom agenda at the neoconservative Foundation for Defense of Democracies. In a reiteration of the conservative sequence principle, he argued that the "war on terror is a struggle between freedom and tyranny, and that the path to lasting security is to defeat the hateful vision the terrorists are spreading with the hope of freedom and democracy." Despite the instability in Iraq, Lebanon, and Palestine, Bush affirmed, "America is committed to an historic long-term goal: to secure the peace of the world, we seek the end of tyranny in our world. We're making progress in the march of freedom, and some of the most important progress is taking place in a region that has not known the blessings of liberty, the broader Middle East."[44]

But Bush's freedom agenda, as Philip Zelikow notes, was simply a "rhetorical policy," not a program, and at times was "negligent."[45] Zelikow, the former executive director of the 9/11 Commission, a former member of the president's Foreign Intelligence Advisory Board, a top advisor to Rice, and a University of Virginia historian, took a realist approach to international relations, and his willingness to challenge administration orthodoxy frequently put him at odds with members of the conservative alliance.

Despite the declining influence of conservatives within his administration, Bush continued to act indecisively. Faced with the task of reconciling lofty principles with reality, Bush condemned the democratically elected Palestinian government for wanting to "destroy its neighbor" right after he cited democratic peace theory: "I believe democracies don't war with each other, and I believe a Palestinian democracy is in the interests of the Palestinian people, the Israelis, and the rest of the world." The *non sequitur* was followed up with what seemed like a severe misremembering of the process that was undertaken in Palestine in January of 2006. Just a few months after the Palestinian people democratically elected Hamas, Bush explained, "And now is the time for strong leaders to stand up and say, we want the…people to decide." In what came across as a disingenuous attempt at empathy, Bush condemned the shortcomings of Palestinian leaders and stated, "I weep about the suffering of the Palestinians."[46]

Indeed, the Palestinians were suffering tremendous hardships due to Israeli restrictions on movement and access, coupled with devastating international sanctions. As Israeli Prime Minister Ehud Olmert's aide Dov Weisglass summarized,

"The idea is to put the Palestinians on a diet, but not to make them die of hunger."[47] The United Nations Office for the Coordination of Humanitarian Affairs projected that with over 152,000 unemployed Palestinians, the poverty rates could rise from 56 to 75 percent, primary health clinics and major hospitals would lack the ability to pay their workers, and thousands of unpaid security personnel could "lead to a highly volatile security situation."[48]

Faced with a looming disaster, the European Union expressed concern that the situation was leading to greater instability. Breaking with the United States, the French Foreign Minister stated, "Our position is to oppose punishing the Palestinian people just because they voted badly." In response to European pressure, Rice called for a temporary mechanism to alleviate the humanitarian needs of the population.[49] Concerning the release of $50 million in taxes which Israel had collected on behalf of the Palestinian Authority, Olmert refused to budge. Though he was later indicted on corruption charges (and convicted of one such charge), he would not release the Palestinian funds, saying, "This money would disappear into the private pockets of the corrupt administration of the Palestinian Authority." Instead, he cited the sequence principle and called upon Abbas to "dismantle Hamas as an armed terrorist group."[50]

Eventually, the European Union put together a proposal for a mechanism that the United States, Israel, and the Arab states could use to maintain support for "essential supplies" and vital social, educational, and health services for the Palestinians.[51] But the mechanism was initially received with skepticism from the United States, and newly appointed World Bank President Paul Wolfowitz expressed concern that it could inadvertently violate U.S. law. Because of the far-reaching implications of U.S. sanctions against Hamas, non-U.S. banks—especially Arab banks—did not want to be accused of, much less prosecuted for, funnelling money to terrorists.[52] Under pressure from the Europeans, however, the Bush administration compromised and agreed to a special mechanism to transfer funds to poor Palestinians.[53]

With the Palestinian economy headed toward total collapse, the proxy war for the new Middle East neared its climax. Iranian President Mahmoud Ahmadinejad sent a letter to Bush, reminding him that Iran was a force to be reckoned with. The freedom agenda had dramatically increased Iran's influence among Iraqi Shiites and strengthened strategic ties between Iran and Syria. Additionally, Iranian-backed opposition movements in Lebanon, Palestine, and to some extent, the Gulf states, undermined U.S. interests to an unprecedented degree. Ahmadinejad took the opportunity to eulogize the freedom agenda: "Many people from around the Middle East manage to contact me," he said. "They do not have faith in these dubious policies either." He declared, "Those with insight can already hear the sounds of the shattering and fall of the ideology and thoughts of the liberal demo-cratic systems." For him the Middle East was gravitating not toward liberty, but "towards faith in the Almighty."[54] If the generally imperceptive Ahmadinejad seemed unusually perceptive, it was only because he said what everyone else in the region already knew—and had been saying for quite some time. George W. Bush's concept of liberty was dead, and in its place rose a dangerous form of religious extremism.

Olmert's Unilateralism

The "New Middle East" was a perilous place for Israel, and Ehud Olmert knew it. Extremists of all varieties claimed God as the co-signer on their deeds to the land that is called holy. Hamas indicated that they could not give away God's land, while U.S. and Israeli theoconservatives said the same thing.[55] But as the pragmatic Olmert would later reveal, he was concerned not about God's real estate but with Israel's very existence: "If the day comes when the two-state solution collapses and we face a South African–style struggle for equal voting rights (also for the Palestin-ians in the territories), then, as soon as that happens, the State of Israel is finished."[56] Following in Sharon's footsteps, Olmert flew to Washington D.C. in May 2006 to propose a unilateral disengagement plan to Bush.[57]

As Olmert turned to unilateralism, clashes between special forces with loyalties to either Hamas or Fatah were an early indication that a Palestinian civil war was on the horizon. Taking a moderate line, Abbas attempted to reconcile his differ-ences with Hamas. To break the deadlock, Abbas gave Hamas a ten-day ultimatum to accept the idea of a Palestinian state along 1967 borders.[58] A rift within Fatah revealed a split between the "old guard," led by Ahmad Quria, which wanted to take a harder line against compromises with Hamas, and an emerging "young guard" led by Marwan Barghouti, which wanted to try to moderate Hamas. Abbas continued to side with the young guard and, against Israeli and U.S. desires, sought to bring Hamas into the political process.[59]

Within Hamas, a similar rift occurred between its exiled constituency, led by Khalid Meshal, which rejected moderation, and its indigenous leadership, represented by Ismael Haniyeh, which showed a willingness to moderate Hamas's extreme positions. In a significant move, more moderate elements within Hamas and Fatah signed the so-called "Prisoners Document" for national conciliation, initially drafted by imprisoned members of the two parties. Though Hamas's anti-Semitic charter calls for the destruction of Israel, the conciliation document essentially committed Hamas to a more moderate position that explicitly embraced a Palestinian state along the 1967 borders.[60] It declared:

> The Palestinian people in the homeland and in the Diaspora seek and struggle to liberate their land and remove the settlements and evacuate the settlers and remove the apartheid and annexation and separation wall and to achieve their right to freedom, return and independence and to exercise their right to self-determination, including the right to establish their independent state with al-Quds al-Shareef [Jerusalem] as its capital on all territories occupied in 1967, and to secure the right of return for refugees to their homes and properties from which they were evicted and to compensate them and to liberate all prisoners and detainees without any discrimination and all of this is based on the historical right of our people on the land of our forefathers and based on the UN Charter and international law and legitimacy in a way that does not affect the rights of our people.[61]

Additionally, the document sought to consolidate security forces, stating that "there is also a need to coordinate and organize the relationship between the security forces and the resistance and organize and protect their weapons."[62] Fatah's National Security Advisor, Mohammad Dahlan, and his Hamas counterparts reached an agreement to absorb Hamas's forces into the Palestinian Authority's security infrastructure.[63] Hamas's Prime Minister, Ismael Haniyeh, met with Jerome Segal of the University of Maryland, who in previous administrations had served as an informal conduit between the U.S. government and the PLO. Segal secured a signed letter from Haniyeh to Bush which stated, "We are so concerned about stability and security in the area that we don't mind having a Palestinian state in the 1967 borders and offering a truce for many years." Haniyeh's letter further declared, "We are not warmongers, we are peace makers and we call on the American government to have direct negotiations with the elected government."[64]

At that point, it seemed as if Bush had wagered correctly that the responsibilities of public office would moderate Hamas. But the United States was not interested in engagement and instead helped prepare Abbas's security forces for a military confrontation with Hamas. Olmert leaked information that Israel had allowed an arms shipment through from Jordan to Fatah which contained three thousand light firearms and millions of bullets. Hamas called for a probe and accused the United States and Israel of sparking "dissension among [the Palestinians] by arming and financing one side under the pretext of arming the presidential guard."[65]

Lacking a plan of action, the administration searched for other options. Olmert visited Washington and received a tentative green light from Bush to extend Sharon's Disengagement Plan to the West Bank. Olmert's "realignment" plan, like Sharon's, would be unilateral in nature and would look to remove settlers and soldiers from parts of the West Bank. In return, Israel would retain major settlement blocks and maintain a military presence in parts of the Jordan Valley without the consent of the Palestinian Authority.[66]

Without U.S. leadership in the peace process, Olmert was left to pursue his own plans. On June 9, 2006, Hamas called off a shaky sixteen-month ceasefire after the Israeli Navy killed seven and wounded twenty innocent civilians picnicking on the beach in Gaza. In the previous two months, Israel had fired six thousand shells into the Gaza Strip, which had killed fifteen civilians, five of whom were children. The Israeli Army indicated that it "regretted the strike on innocents" and was targeting areas where Palestinian militants launched homemade Qassam rockets that had injured several Israeli civilians. But the tragic beach incident was broadcast on television networks and inflamed great anger on the Palestinian street. Amid cries for revenge, Hamas unleashed a wave of Qassam rockets into Israel.[67]

Tensions between Israel and the Palestinians escalated further when Palestinian militants tunnelled into Israeli territory near the Israel Defense Forces (IDF) base at Kerem Shalom and abducted Corporal Gilad Shalit on June 25, 2006. In return for Shalit, Hamas demanded that Israel release Palestinian prisoners, mostly women and minors.[68] Days later, Israel responded by arresting 64 members of Hamas, including 23 legislators and a third of the Palestinian cabinet.[69] The G-8 Foreign Ministers condemned both actions.[70] Such growing tensions were a sign of worse things to come.

The Lebanon War

The capture of Shalit by Hamas was followed by the capture of two Israeli soldiers in Lebanon in July by Hezbollah. To accomplish its mission, Hezbollah militants shelled several Israeli towns with rocket fire, diverting attention away from its attack and subsequent abduction of two surviving Israeli soldiers across the border.[71] Annan condemned both the Hezbollah provocation for igniting a new round of violence and Israel's use of "excessive force" as it proceeded to launch war on Lebanon.[72] Similarly, the European Union condemned Israel's "disproportionate use of force" and indicated that Israel's "imposition of an air and sea blockade on Lebanon cannot be justified." Bush called Hezbollah's actions "pathetic" and supported Israel's "right to defend herself," while cautioning that the IDF "should not weaken the...government in Lebanon." Rice blamed Syria and called upon Israel to use caution so as not to compromise the democratically elected government of Lebanese Prime Minister Fuad Siniora. At the United Nations, the conservative U.S. agenda prevailed when U.S. Ambassador John Bolton exercised his veto power to prevent the Security Council from accusing Israel of using disproportionate force.[73]

Initially, the administration was united in its desire to see "Hezbollah knocked out" without destroying the democratically elected government in Beirut.[74] Because democracy promotion had unleashed a wave of anti-U.S. sentiment throughout the region, the administration now believed it needed to reestablish stability through force. The plan was to give Israel enough time to deliver a decisive blow against Hezbollah, and it was believed that a solid military victory would spark positive change throughout the region, diminishing the regional influence of Iran and Syria.[75] But other members of the Quartet thought differently. Opposing the position of the United States and the United Kingdom, Annan quickly worked toward a ceasefire. He understood that the war would not produce any winners, and that

Hezbollah had strategically set the bar low, defining victory as survival. Thus, Annan worked with Rice at the July 2006 G-8 Summit in St. Petersburg to issue a statement calling for a "cessation of violence."[76]

Ignoring Annan's words of caution, Bush continued to look for chances to regain the upper hand in the Middle East by defeating Hezbollah: "Our aim is to turn [the Middle East conflict] into a moment of opportunity and a chance for broader change in the region." Rice added, "A cessation of violence is crucial, but if that cessation of violence is hostage to Hezbollah's next decision to launch missiles into Israel or Hamas's next decision to abduct an Israeli citizen, then we will have gotten nowhere."[77] To aid Israel, the Bush administration authorized a delivery of precision-guided bombs to Israel, while it optimistically asked Egypt and the Saudis to use their influence to woo Syria away from Iran and Hezbollah.[78]

As the war in Lebanon continued, Bush presented Israel's actions as being part of the War on Terror. He stated, "The current crisis is part of a larger struggle between the forces of freedom and the forces of terror in the Middle East." Echoing the sequence principle, Bush reiterated that the antidote to terror was freedom: "When democracy spreads in the Middle East, the people of that troubled region will have a better future, the terrorists will lose their safe havens and their recruits, and the United States of America will be more secure."[79]

It would soon become apparent that the change Bush ushered in was not, as he had hoped, the defeat of Hezbollah and Hamas; neither was it the "creative chaos" Rice had spoken of. And it was certainly not—in Rice's ill-conceived phrase—the "birth pangs of a new Middle East."[80] The international community was "aghast" that the war was being conducted on the "backs of civilians," and Israel failed to articulate what strategic aims it could achieve.[81] Rice soon realized that Israel's "creative chaos" was actually chaotic destruction. If anything, democracy and force were ushering in a new era of unprecedented Iranian influence, the formation of a "Shiite crescent" across the Middle East.[82] This change was the unintended consequence of the Bush administration's policies.

As the chaos in Lebanon spread, conservatives and moderates presented two very different views of the war to Bush. Abrams tended to report a more optimistic assessment of the IDF's activities and wanted Israel to have a free hand against Lebanon. In what was taken as a statement of disinterest in restraining Israel,

Abrams then went to North Carolina for vacation.[83] By contrast, Welch understood that the war was not to be taken lightly and, contrary to Abrams's view, questioned the accuracy of IDF progress reports.[84] With massive civilian casualties and half a million internally displaced persons, it was very difficult to imagine how Israel could possibly be winning.[85] Israel tried to keep its war aims ambiguous and intentionally sought to inflict damage on Lebanon's civilian infrastructure, including bridges, roads, and airfields, so that refugees would flood the cities. Israeli leaders theorized that the angry Sunni and Christian populations would turn against Hezbollah in the south. Instead, the war achieved precisely the opposite result, uniting the Lebanese people against Israel.[86]

Wary of a mishap, Rice, Zelikow, and Welch urged Israel to be cautious in its use of force.[87] But on July 30, 2006, as Rice was meeting with Israeli Defense Minister Amir Peretz, she received a message from U.S. Ambassador to Lebanon Jeffrey Feltman saying that innocent civilians in Qana had once again been bombed. Israel had fired on a three-story building in which they sought shelter, killing at least twenty-eight people, including sixteen children. Thirteen people were left unaccounted for.[88] This may have evoked memories of the 1996 shelling of Qana, when the IDF shelled a UN compound and killed over one hundred civilians.[89] Rice was "sickened" by the loss of innocent life and angrily asked Peretz when he was planning on telling her about the incident. After Qana, she forcefully pushed for a cessation of aerial bombardment.[90]

As in Bush's first term, Rice tended to try and bridge the gaps between moderate diplomats in the State Department and conservatives in the Office of the Vice President, the Pentagon, and the White House. But as Israel's actions in Qana earned the condemnation of the international community and as victory in Lebanon looked ever more elusive, Rice pushed harder against Cheney and Abrams, even as they were eyeing Syria and Iran.[91] Conservatives were slowly losing more and more credibility with the president, and Rice's views were evolving.[92] As one senior official summarizes, administration conservatives "simply [had] no idea what they were talking about" because their "expertise is inversely correlated with experience."[93] Regardless of Rice's evolving views, she had little choice but to take a more moderate line. For one thing, she was no longer welcome in Lebanon and was instead forced to work through multilateral channels, namely the secretary general of the United Nations.[94]

Prominent moderate Republicans in Congress joined State Department diplomats in urging the president to protect U.S. interests. Senator John Warner observed, "This is a very critical time for the U.S. in the Middle East, and the Israeli actions will certainly have an impact beyond Lebanon and Gaza." Senator Chuck Hagel asserted that Israel's actions were "tearing Lebanon apart" and compromising U.S. interests.[95] The two statesmen were right. According to a poll conducted by the Beirut Center for Research and Information, support for Hezbollah in Lebanon had climbed dramatically to 87 percent, revealing "a national consensus identifying Israel as Lebanon's main enemy."[96]

As calls for a ceasefire continued, theoconservatives joined administration conservatives in mounting a campaign against moderation and demanded that Bush give Israel more time and weapons.[97] Pastor John Hagee, the founder of Christians United for Israel (who, ironically, was later accused of anti-Semitism), held a large gathering of 3,500 activists to pressure Bush and members of Congress to support Israel. He met with Abrams at the White House and warned, "Appeasement has never helped the Jewish people." Following their meeting, Abrams indicated that the two men were largely in agreement.[98] He had long advocated a union between theoconservatives and Zionist conservatives, and once advised, "Tomorrow's lobby for Israel has got to be conservative Christians, because there aren't going to be enough Jews to do it."[99]

After much indecision, Bush moved in a moderate direction and supported a UN Security Council Resolution of August 11, 2006, that called for a ceasefire. Annan achieved what he had worked toward and, though U.S. leadership was lacking, the secretary general was able to recruit a stabilizing force for South Lebanon with the help of the Europeans. In an attempt to reduce the damage to U.S. national security interests, Bush declared Hezbollah to be the loser of the war and noted that "most objective observers would give the United States credit for helping to lead the effort to get a resolution that addressed the root cause of the problem." But his words were overshadowed by Hezbollah's claim that it had achieved a "historic victory" over Israeli forces as they withdrew from Lebanon to make room for peacekeeping troops.[100] In a further show of defiance, Hezbollah boasted that it had not only survived the war, but also quickly rearmed itself with twenty thousand rockets.[101]

By most accounts, the Lebanon War was a strategic loss for Israel and the United States. To borrow a Kissingerian insight, "The guerilla wins if he does not lose. The conventional army loses if it does not win."[102] The Israeli Winograd Commission's Final Report ultimately accused Olmert's government of "serious failings and flaws" in its handling of the war. The report highlighted the fact that "Israel initiated a long war, which ended without its clear military victory. A semi-military organization of a few thousand men resisted, for a few weeks, the strongest army in the Middle East, which enjoyed full air superiority, and size and technology advantages."[103] In the end, Lebanese authorities reported 1,191 deaths, 4,409 injuries, and 900,000 internally displaced persons, with a third of deaths and casualties being children. Israeli authorities reported 43 civilian deaths, 997 injuries, and 300,000 internally displaced persons.[104]

Unable to learn the lessons of history, Olmert followed up the Lebanon War by calling on his people to make unilateral concessions in the West Bank, but the electorate greeted his words with great skepticism. A Likud member of the Knesset commented, "Olmert's remarks show that he is totally detached from reality. After his policy of unilateral retreats brought rockets to Haifa and Ashkelon, he stubbornly insists on continuing this wanton policy that will certainly bring rockets on every location in Israel." Under growing domestic pressure, Olmert announced that unilateral plans for the West Bank would be put on hold.[105] Left without a political plan, Olmert defied the Bush administration by refusing to tear down illegal outposts as promised by the Israelis in 2001, and instead, authorized more settlement expansion in the West Bank.[106]

Decline of the Conservatives

With failure in Iraq, failure in Palestine, and failure in Lebanon, conservatives lost major credibility with the president. Lewis Libby, the vice president's trusted advisor, was indicted by a grand jury and forced to step down.[107] Wolfowitz had already been transferred from the Pentagon to the World Bank. Undersecretary of Defense for Policy Douglas Feith had finally resigned amid scandal.[108] On top of that, a neoconservative split occurred within the administration.[109] Faced with failure, the conservative alliance outside the administration had already been showing signs of fracture. Even before the Lebanon War, prominent intellectual Francis Fukuyama set the tone by defecting from the neoconservative movement and denounced the "Leninism" of its leaders who believe "that history can be pushed along with the right application of power and will." He argued, "Neoconservatism, as both a political symbol and a body of thought, has evolved into something I can no longer support."[110]

Despite serious setbacks to their agenda, administration conservatives relentlessly pushed for unilateral military action against Iran. Conservatives in the U.S. Congress passed the Iranian Freedom Support Act, which imposed sanctions on governments or institutions "assisting the nuclear program of Iran or transferring advanced conventional weapons or missiles."[111] Similarly, conservatives worked to finalize legislation prohibiting all U.S. aid and contact with the Hamas-led Palestinian government. The Palestinian Anti-Terrorism Act of 2006, which was signed into law by the president, was enacted by Congress "to urge members of the international community to avoid contact with and refrain from supporting the terrorist organization Hamas until it agrees to recognize Israel, renounce violence, disarm, and accept prior agreements, including the Roadmap." This made it virtually impossible for members of the Bush administration to open negotiations with any part of the Palestinian Authority as long as Hamas was a part of it.[112]

A lack of cooperation from European allies, along with growing indignation among autocratic Arab allies, forced Rice to rethink the freedom agenda.[113] Cheney and his advisors continued to fall out of favor with Bush as Rice pushed for diplomacy and engagement with Iran. After meeting with Russian Foreign Minister Sergey Lavrov, Rice suggested to the president that it might be wise to keep open the possibility of direct negotiations with Iran.[114]

As the president moved in the direction of moderation, Abrams fought desperately to marginalize an idea that was gaining greater and greater traction within Rice's State Department: the Israeli-Palestinian peace process should be restarted in a serious way.[115] Zelikow, Rice's influential counselor, delivered a speech at the conservative Washington Institute for Near East Policy that reestablished the loathed link between the Israeli-Palestinian conflict and regional stability in the Middle East. He stated, "For the Arab moderates and for the Europeans, some sense of progress and momentum on the Arab-Israeli dispute is just a *sine qua non* for their ability to cooperate actively with the United States on a lot of other things that we care about." Zelikow also implicitly criticized the administration's handling of the war in Lebanon, and by extension, Rice's initial decision to side with conservatives by allowing the fighting to stretch out. He suggested that it did not win the United States any friends in the Muslim world.[116]

With an active peace process once again being seriously considered by the president, the conservative alliance was dealt another serious blow with the departure of Secretary of Defense Donald Rumsfeld from his post at the Pentagon. He was replaced by Robert Gates, a moderate realist and highly capable former director of the Central Intelligence Agency.[117] Additionally, Bush accepted Ambassador John Bolton's resignation in the face of great congressional opposition to his UN appointment.[118] The U.S. electorate expressed their grave dissatisfaction with the handling of the War on Terror in the November 2006 mid-term elections, and in a decisive victory, the Democrats took back Congress.[119] To make matters worse, the bipartisan Iraq Study Group Report left Rice defending the administration's policies as being "not at all utopian." The report advised that the administration abandon its attempts to turn Iraq into a Jeffersonian democracy and instead look to "Iraqi nationalists" and the Syrians for cooperation, while pursuing a two-state solution for the Israelis and Palestinians.[120]

Under the shadow of Abu Ghraib, a prison incident in which U.S. soldiers were captured on film torturing Iraqi prisoners, and a war gone terribly wrong, the conservative alliance, minus its key figures, was relegated to a back seat in the administration. As a second-term president without re-election concerns, Bush, once again, was faced with an opportunity to decide between parallelism or sequence.[121]

CHAPTER 7

⊕

A Requiem for Liberty

With six years of policy blowback, in 2007 George W. Bush looked to salvage his presidential legacy with a new team nearly cleansed of conservative figures. Democrats took over Congress, new Secretary of Defense Robert Gates took over the nation's defense infrastructure, General David Petraeus spearheaded a new way forward in Iraq, and John Negroponte joined Condoleezza Rice at the State Department as her deputy secretary of state. In a reorganized administration, utopian goals of democratically transforming the Middle East were noticeably subdued and replaced with a much more realistic vision of, in Rice's words, an "ongoing mutual effort to empower the moderates throughout the region in the struggle against extremism and terror."[1] Though the president embraced a more moderate approach, as championed by Rice, his dealings in the Israeli-Palestinian conflict were still tainted by the lingering residue of sequence. Only after Israel and Fatah failed to topple Hamas in Gaza pursuant to the sequence principle did the Bush administration finally return to square one, a negotiated peace process based on the principle of parallelism.

The Mecca Accords

At the start of 2007, the Palestinians looked more divided than ever before. The peace process was completely frozen, intra-Palestinian violence continued, and the humanitarian situation in the occupied territories looked bleaker than ever. With a green light to move forward with the peace process, Rice wanted a political victory, but the existence of the Hamas-led government hampered her plans.[2] Hamas was a "legally designated terrorist organization," and as such, the United States could not deal with it. State Department officials therefore found themselves in the ironic position of pressuring Palestinian President Mahmoud Abbas to dissolve the elected government.[3] In particular, Rice sought to keep Abbas separated from Hamas so that he could be legally dealt with, equipped, and funded.[4] The State Department secretly helped facilitate the movement of arms to Abbas's special forces, but the shipment was leaked to the press by Israel and vehemently denied by Fatah.[5] Because of the way Israel handled their information about the secret weapons shipments, it appeared as if the Israeli government did not necessarily want Fatah to have the upper hand.[6]

As the peace process stagnated and factional Palestinian violence erupted, Iran opportunistically extended more and more regional influence *vis-à-vis* Israeli-Palestinian affairs, much to the chagrin of Saudi Arabia. Backed by Iran, Hamas established its own Executive Force to counter Fatah's Presidential Force, which was supported by the United States and its allies. Keen to counter Iran's influence in Arab affairs, Saudi King Abdullah invited Abbas and Prime Minister Ismael Haniyeh to resolve their differences at a meeting in Saudi Arabia.

With Hamas and Fatah simultaneously pursuing military superiority, both parties knew that a civil war would yield no winners. After several rounds of bloodshed, they decided to accept King Abdullah's invitation to travel to Mecca for national unity negotiations. Much to the surprise of their Saudi hosts and the international community, the two sides agreed to form a National Unity Government with Hamas gaining nine posts, Fatah six, and other parties four. Independents were appointed to the most sensitive positions. However, Hamas agreed only to "respect," not to "commit itself," to previous agreements, thus falling short of explicitly recognizing Israel and renouncing violence. Abbas stated that the purpose of the accords was "to save Palestinian blood. If they succeed in this, it's a successful meeting. But in the long run, if they can't end the economic and political siege, there is no guarantee that the government will last very long."[7]

The Saudi king pledged a billion dollars in aid to the Palestinians as an incentive, the Russians refused the U.S. idea of boycotting the Palestinians, the French welcomed the deal, and the European Union offered cautious optimism, indicating that it would "open a dialogue with" the unity government. Seizing the moment, the European Union's Javier Solana urged the Bush administration to quickly enter "final status talks." He stated, "The crisis-management approach to the Israeli-Palestinian conflict is over. We need to enter the conflict-resolution stage and try to end the occupation of 1967."[8]

UN Special Envoy Alvaro de Soto went a step further, making his views on the matter abundantly clear: the international community should attempt to moderate Hamas rather than wasting precious diplomatic capital. As he later put it, "A good case can and has been made by the peace camp in Israel that the whole idea of requiring the Palestinians to recognize up front, as a precondition to talks, that Israel has a right to exist is bogus. Israel has never been asked to recognize up front that the Palestinians have a right to a State.... When Hamas members are asked about the recognition demand, they respond with a rhetorical question: 'What are the borders of this Israel you would have us recognize?'"[9]

Unlike the other Quartet partners, the United States was extremely unhappy with the Mecca Accords because the agreement did not sufficiently bring Hamas in line with U.S. requirements and conditions. Though Rice was eager to restart peace negotiations, she was at once hindered by mediocre support from the White House and by being placed in a position where she could no longer legally deal with the Palestinian Authority as long as Hamas was part of it.[10] Thus, her immediate goal became the dissolution of the National Unity Government.[11] While she committed the United States to work with moderate leaders, including Abbas, Rice was intent on seeing Hamas fail. For her, the National Unity Government was not simply about Palestine; it was part of a much larger effort to defeat extremism throughout the Middle East.[12] Because Iran and Syria were undermining U.S. efforts in Iraq and its proxies, Hezbollah and Hamas, had recently prevailed in Lebanon and Palestine respectively, it was believed that radical Islamism, if left unchecked, would seriously damage U.S. interests and lives.[13]

Dismissing Hamas's gestures of moderation, Rice pressed forward with a bold plan to catalyze peace talks, suddenly moving to "accelerate the Road Map and to move towards the establishment of a Palestinian state." In order to gain credibility among the Arabs, she spoke of establishing a political horizon to provide the Palestinians with a vision of the ultimate goal. Though democracy promotion would still remain a part of the administration's rhetoric, her vision "to empower moderates throughout the region in the struggle against extremism and terror" defined the administration's new foreign policy.[14]

Because Bush wanted support from Arab nations for his "New Way Forward" in Iraq, he offered his support for Rice's efforts to deliver a political victory in Palestine. Though Rice realized that the United States had to undo tremendous damage caused by years of wavering and neglect, she also realized that it was possible to get the two sides to talk if the United States was willing to pledge its political support. Following Rice's visit to the region, both Abbas and Israeli Prime Minister Ehud Olmert agreed to three-way talks.[15] But the conditions on the ground were not in Rice's favor. Olmert's approval ratings were barely in double digits, Bush was viewed as a lame-duck president, and Abbas was just barely hanging on to power.[16]

Rice warned that while the United States would shun a National Unity Government, it would still proceed with negotiations between Abbas and the Israelis. Determined to move the peace process forward, she intensified her shuttle diplomacy in the region and in a defiant shot at administration conservatives, Rice asserted, "As long as I'm secretary of state, that's what I'm going to do."[17] Knowing that time was running out, she decided that talks between the two sides could only be initiated in the context of a major international summit.[18]

As a consequence of the new tone of compromise in Washington, Jordan's King Abdullah II was invited to deliver an address before a newly moderated Congress. The king called upon the United States to have "courage and vision" in leading the peace process. "Sixty years of Palestinian dispossession, forty years under occupation, a stop-and-go peace process," he argued, "has left a bitter legacy of disappointment and despair, on all sides." The United States could transform this moment of crisis into a moment of opportunity that would "restore hope to [the] region's people."[19]

Though moderates in Congress welcomed the speech, foreign policy conservatives predictably expressed skepticism. Powerful California Congressman Tom Lantos warned that restarting peace talks "is sort of unrealistic at a time when the dominant element in the Palestinian area does not recognize the existence of Israel."[20] From within the administration, the few remaining conservatives also rejected a return to the peace process.[21] Vice President Dick Cheney conveyed the president's vision for peace, based "on the foundation of security, not surrender."[22]

As before, theoconservatives followed Cheney's lead in opposing Rice's attempts to restart a peace process. Pastor John Hagee delivered a speech at the annual American Israel Public Affairs Committee (AIPAC) dinner in which he decried attempts to force Israel to concede land. To a cheering crowd of Zionist conservatives, Hagee bellowed, "The sleeping giant of Christian Zionism has awakened; there are 50 million Christians standing up and applauding the State of Israel. If a line has to be drawn," he declared, "draw the line around both Christians and Jews; we are united; we are indivisible; we are bound together by the Torah—the roots of Christianity are Jewish."[23]

But in a new climate of moderation, theoconservatives faced opposition from other Christian leaders. In a July 29, 2007, *New York Times* letter to Bush rebutting Hagee's extremism, prominent moderate and liberal evangelical Christian leaders offered support for peace negotiations:

> Historical honesty compels us to recognize that both Israelis and Palestinians have legitimate rights stretching back for millennia to the lands of Israel/Palestine. Both Israelis and Palestinians have committed violence and injustice against each other. The only way to bring the tragic cycle of violence to an end is for Israelis and Palestinians to negotiate a just, lasting agreement that guarantees both sides viable, independent, secure states.[24]

With the backing of moderates, Rice redoubled her efforts to restart the peace process, but not without cost. Conservatives accused her of turning into Bill Clinton, and former allies accused her of chasing a Nobel Peace Prize.[25] Because she had spoken to Bush about the peace process prior to her acceptance of the secretary of state post, conservatives suspected that she was a closet peace-process proponent all along. By contrast, moderates saw Rice's gradual transformation into a voice of moderation as a reasoned response to the continuous failure of conservative policies to secure more favored outcomes in Afghanistan, Iraq, North Korea, Lebanon, Syria, and Palestine. As Aaron David Miller wryly noted, Rice was not turning into Clinton; she was "becoming Colin Powell."[26]

Clothed in Powell's mantle, Rice became the champion of the peace process. When newly elected Speaker of the House of Representatives Nancy Pelosi visited Syria to meet with President Bashar Al-Assad in April 2007, Cheney described it as "bad behavior," but Rice herself ended up briefly meeting with Syrian Foreign Minister Walid al-Moallem the following month to discuss ways to secure its porous border with Iraq and exchanged informal "pleasantries" with the Iranians at a luncheon.[27]

In what seemed like another victory for moderation, Israeli and Palestinian leaders met on April 15, 2007, for the first of several biweekly talks where they discussed low-level issues like border crossings and Abbas's plan to reorder his security forces in coordination with U.S. Security Coordinator for Israel-Palestinian Authority Lt. General Keith Dayton.[28] But while Rice was pushing for negotiations, she was also preparing Abbas's forces for a showdown with Hamas. Fatah had recruited approximately 1,400 fighters to join its Special Force, but its soldiers lacked sufficient resources due to congressional restrictions. By contrast, the Executive Force of Hamas was estimated to be somewhere between 6,000 and 10,000 men.[2]

The War Among Brothers

On June 14, 2007, the situation in the occupied Palestinian territories again moved into crisis mode. Masked Hamas gunmen seized control of the Gaza Strip in twenty-four hours, taking over Fatah's Preventive Security headquarters, including its weapons and offices. Hamas used its newly found power to repay the notorious Palestinian Authority's Preventative Security forces for years of torture and crackdowns ordered by senior Fatah security figures, notably Mohammad Dahlan, the U.S.-backed national security advisor.

When Fatah forces fell in Gaza, Dahlan was out of the country receiving medical treatment abroad.[30] His fellow security chiefs, General Rashid Abu Shabak, Samir Masharawi, and Yussef Issa, were nowhere to be found.[31] Though the U.S. State Department was preparing Fatah for a confrontation with Hamas, its Middle East team did not expect it to come so soon. Deputy Assistant Secretary of State J. Scott Carpenter was sitting in his office watching Al Jazeera when all of a sudden images of Hamas and Fatah fighters were broadcasted. Immediately, he and his colleague

Robert Danin called Dayton and told him what they saw on the news. Dayton said, "That's not possible," to which Danin replied, "Well, General, we're looking at it right now." According to Carpenter, the State Department fully believed Dahlan's reassurances that he "had things in hand," when in reality, Hamas was waiting for him to leave the country to "spring a coup."[32]

Fatah's embarrassing performance in Gaza was due to several important factors. First, they were not fully trained or prepared for a confrontation with Hamas. What little aid did come was too little, too late. Second, after the election of Hamas, Palestinian Authority employees, including security personnel, had not been paid full salaries and were severely demoralized.[33] Third, while Hamas obtained weapons through secret channels, Israel had refused to allow Fatah to access sufficient supplies of weapons and equipment. Though the United States had worked out a deal with the Egyptians, Jordanians, and donors from the Gulf to equip Abbas's forces, Israel prevented items such as bulletproof vests, vehicles, helmets, night vision goggles, and other essential equipment from reaching Fatah's forces.[34]

Fourth, U.S. funds for non-lethal aid were held up in Congress by conservatives such as House Majority Leader Tom DeLay, who did not agree with the administration's efforts to arm Fatah.[35] Fifth, what funds and supplies did make it through to the Palestinian Authority were siphoned off by corrupt members of the organization. It was later revealed that Salam Fayyad confiscated $7 million from Mohammad Dahlan's bank account; these funds were supposed to be used to defeat Hamas in Gaza.[36] Finally, the pro-Abbas Palestinian security chiefs shamefully abandoned their troops before the battle. Though Rice understood that Dahlan and his forces lacked training and equipment, she expected them to at least fight "to a draw," not just "leave."[37]

Abbas, the Israelis, and the Bush administration characterized the Hamas takeover of the Gaza Strip as a "coup" executed by Hamas. But in reality, things were a bit more complicated. As David Wurmser recalls, prior to the Hamas takeover a fissure had emerged within the U.S. conservative alliance. While some neoconservatives remained absolutely opposed to arming Fatah against Hamas, Elliott Abrams reluctantly chose to follow the State Department's lead and agreed to support the secret program. Abrams believed that eventually Fatah was going to have to "violently and forcibly" challenge Hamas. Because conservatives in the Office of the

Vice President were staunchly opposed to arming the Palestinians in the first place, they felt vindicated by the violence in Gaza. In their view, not only had arming the Palestinian Authority done little for Israeli security, but with Fatah's defeat, the arms and supplies were now in the hands of Hamas terrorists.[38] Wurmser's feeling, therefore, was not so much that the Hamas "coup" had come out of the blue but that Hamas was reacting to Fatah's plans to take out Hamas first. Former Quartet envoy James Wolfensohn offers further confirmation of this narrative, noting that prior to Hamas's takeover of Gaza, the State Department, anticipating a Fatah-Hamas showdown, asked him to close the Quartet's office in Gaza.[39]

Rice candidly recalls that the decision to turn the train-and-equip program against Hamas was made well before Hamas's takeover of the Gaza Strip. Early on, everyone knew that "Hamas was clearly being armed, and they were being armed quite effectively by Iran in particular." But the administration saw an opportunity to act because "Hamas had started to split" internally—between exiled Hamas leader Khaled Meshal, who lived in Syria, and the "poor, hapless" Ismael Haniyeh sitting among the "really bad boys in Gaza." Rice warned members of Congress, "The other guys are being armed; do you want the good guys not to be armed?" Though a military confrontation was on the horizon, Rice believed that "Hamas pre-empted before the Palestinian forces were completely ready." Hamas knew that the Palestinian Authority was getting stronger, and with international economic sanctions causing real trouble for them, they decided "to upset the apple cart" and launch a "coup."[40]

Though the president's freedom agenda for the Middle East had collapsed both in theory and in practice, the Hamas takeover of the Gaza Strip only sharpened the binary way in which he approached the conflict. He understood the "bad guys," whom he would not deal with, to be the terrorists living in the Gaza Strip, and the "good guys," whom he would deal with, to be those living in the West Bank. He stated, "We're at the beginning stages of a great ideological conflict between those who yearn for peace and those who want their children to grow up in a normal, decent society—and radicals and extremists who want to impose their dark vision on people throughout the world."[41]

From the administration's perspective, Hamas's takeover of the Gaza Strip was "the best thing that could have happened," in the sense that it resolved the major problem of moral categories. Abbas used his presidential powers to declare a state of emergency and immediately dissolved the National Unity Government. Although Hamas characterized Abbas as a "collaborator" and claimed that "Prime Minister Haniyeh remains the head of the government," Abbas appointed his former Finance Minister Salam Fayyad as Prime Minister with a mandate to build state institutions in the West Bank. Ostensibly, the Bush administration and the Israelis now had a Palestinian partner—the good guys—whom they were willing and able to deal with. Once Fatah and Hamas governments were clearly defined and differentiated, Rice pushed harder than ever for negotiations.[42]

However optimistically Rice and the rest of Bush's national security team looked upon the violence, one thing was certain. Should the U.S. peace negotiations between Fatah and Israel be successfully completed, the democratically elected government in Gaza could not be ignored. Although Rice believed that an eventual peace agreement could go to a referendum, in order for a referendum to actually work, and for its terms to be respected by the entire Palestinian community, Hamas would have to allow the Palestinians in the Gaza Strip to participate.[43] At some point, sooner or later, negotiations would have to include Hamas.

Unlike the Bush administration, the average Palestinian viewed the Hamas takeover of Gaza as the worst thing that could have happened. The Palestinian Independent Commission for Citizens' Rights estimated that between 2006 and 2007, factional fighting resulted in the death of over six hundred Palestinians.[44] Beyond the death toll, the Hamas-Fatah split essentially established two authorities on the ground—one in Gaza and one in the West Bank—making the Palestinian right to self-determination ever more elusive. As one Palestinian commentator noted, "We Palestinians are writing the final chapters of our national enterprise."[45]

Following Hamas's takeover of Gaza, the United States and the European Union ended their embargo of aid to the Palestinian Authority in the West Bank. The administration agreed to unfreeze $86 million that was intended to bolster Fatah's security forces and encouraged Abbas to replace the democratically elected government with an appointed emergency government. While Hamas decried the international community's double standard on freedom and democracy, the United States developed a "West Bank–first" strategy that would improve life by reducing checkpoints and increasing aid for those living under Abbas's Palestinian Authority.[46]

Annapolis

With the West Bank–first strategy in hand, Bush looked for ways to improve the lives of Palestinians living under the rule of the Palestinian Authority. Since his good friend, former UK Prime Minister Tony Blair, was a longstanding supporter of peace talks, the president supported his appointment as the Quartet's Middle East envoy, where he was charged with economic development. Wolfensohn had resigned from the post in frustration after being treated disrespectfully by conservative members of the administration. Although Rice had offered to renew his term, he essentially said, "thanks, but no thanks."[47] Blair, like Wolfensohn, would bring tremendous political capital to the peace talks; however, as the *New York Times* editorial board observed, given his apparent inability to speak "unwelcomed truths to people in power," his nomination may not have been ideal.[48]

As they had done with Powell, conservatives launched an all-out assault on the newly moderate secretary of state. With Gaza in grave turmoil, conservatives argued that the root of the Hamas problem was located outside the Palestinian territories in Iran. What was needed was action guided by the sequence principle, not a political process based on the Road Map's principle of parallelism. Former UN Ambassador John Bolton indicated that "regime change or the use of force are the only available options to prevent Iran from getting a nuclear weapons capability, if they want it." Prominent neoconservative commentator Norman Podhoretz laid out an argument for action against Iran in clear terms: "the plain and brutal truth is that if Iran is to be prevented from developing a nuclear arsenal, there is no alternative to the actual use of military force." Similarly, Wurmser believed that Rice's diplomatic approach was failing.[49] In an effort to counter moderation, Senator Joseph Lieberman solicited the support of theoconservatives and spoke before Pastor John Hagee's extremist Christians United for Israel Conference, praising him as a "man of God." Lieberman declared, "I know the support of Christian Zionists today is critical to Israel's security and strength, and to America's security and strength."[50]

Most significantly, Abrams made the case within the administration that a peace process was in fundamental opposition to the sequence principle outlined in the June 2002 Rose Garden Speech. As he saw it, no peace process should commence until terrorist infrastructure was dismantled and "entirely new" Palestinian leadership was democratically elected.[51] Abrams believed that Rice was chasing a legacy and that in doing so, she had abandoned her principles.[52] He had a lot of face time with the president and, along with Cheney, presented the "cons" to Bush, but their words fell on deaf ears. Rice presented the "pros," and eventually the president made the decision to move forward with the peace process.[53] As far as Stephen Hadley was concerned, Bush, Rice, and he "were as close as a president and national security advisor and secretary of state have ever been. There was no daylight between the three" on Middle East policy. Hadley disagreed with Abrams's criticism of Rice and believed that Abrams had "a little bit of his own agenda" when it came to Middle East policy. But, in looking back, he asserts, "the agenda that mattered was the president's, and Condi and I were locked at the hip and with the president in carrying out that agenda."[54]

With his national security advisor and secretary of state in complete agreement to proceed, the president called for an international conference, offering significant credibility to Rice's peacemaking efforts. The logic of the proposed Annapolis Conference was explicitly based on the parallelism of the Road Map. As Hadley recalls, the president's vision was premised on the notion that one needed to press forward on four fronts in parallel. First, Israelis and Palestinians had to engage in direct negotiations. Second, Israeli-Palestinian peace needed to be an extension of Arab-Israeli peace. This is the reason why Bush extended an Annapolis invitation to the Syrians and convinced the Saudis to renew their support for the Saudi Peace Initiative. The Saudis wanted form, not substance. They urged the United States to address final-status issues and wanted Israel to cease construction on the separation wall as a gesture of good faith.[55] Third, newly appointed Palestinian Prime Minister Fayyad was empowered and given support for his efforts to build transparent institutions that would support a Palestinian state with law, governance, and order, and that would also be able to coexist in peace and stability next to Israel. Finally, by improving movement and access for the Palestinians, the president sought to reduce the level of cynicism surrounding the conference.[56] Yet the conference was criticized not only by Hamas extremists, but also by administration conservatives. Abrams refused to call it a conference, and around the White House would refer to it as the "Annapolis meeting."[57]

With the peace process suddenly moved from the bottom to the top of the list of priorities, Rice and Hadley agreed to divide up the relevant tasks. The State Department took the lead on peace negotiations, and the National Security Council concerned itself with institution-building and ensuring that peace could be sustained once an agreement was signed. Hadley delegated the task of interagency coordination to Abrams, but could not get his otherwise exceptionally skilled deputy "to pay attention"; he questioned what Abrams and "his office did" to support institution-building in the West Bank.[58]

Without Abrams supporting him, Hadley eventually took over his work and every other week held a secure video call or a meeting in the situation room with Dayton, Danin, and others to get everyone coordinated. Once the process started moving, Hadley was able to coordinate a list of things that Fayyad needed in order to achieve progress in the West Bank. Eventually, Hadley felt as if he was "pushing on an open door" because the Israelis were getting "excited for what Fayyad was doing." But for Fayyad to succeed, "he not only needed support in the institution-building, he needed the prospect of a negotiation, or it wasn't going to work."[59]

By this time, Hadley, like Rice, had completely signed on to the moderate agenda for Palestine. As Hadley had learned from years of setbacks, progress in the West Bank depended on a realistic political horizon. He and Rice asked the president to demand parallel rather than sequential concessions from Israel. Olmert agreed to strengthen Abbas's hand by releasing 250 of the approximately 10,000 Palestinian prisoners in Israeli jails. Bush once again promised to release aid to Abbas's security forces.[60] Rice met with Fayyad but also found herself defending the administration's perceived double standard on democracy promotion. She indicated that the United States believed "strongly in the right of people to express themselves…in elections" but emphasized that elected governments have the "obligation to govern responsibly."[61] In late August, Olmert and Abbas met again to discuss more substantive issues, but the Palestinians still complained that core final-status issues needed to be addressed with an exchange of documents.[62]

Even as Rice's version of moderation clearly dominated the administration on Israeli-Palestinian issues, Bush continued to waver on how to address the Iranian nuclear issue. Rice urged a continuation of diplomacy, and in a blow to conservatives, disbanded the hawkish Iran Syria Policy and Operations Group headed by

Abrams and Elizabeth Cheney.[63] But Dick Cheney pushed to have Iran's Revolutionary Guard Corps designated as a terrorist organization.[64] Bush moved in the direction of conservatives on this issue and decided to label the group a terrorist organization in August 2007.[65]

As part of Bush's new strategy to support Arab Sunni moderates against Iranian influence, the United States announced plans to sell precision-guided weapons to Gulf states. In an attempt to prevent the multi-billion dollar sale, Israel dispatched Defense Minister Shaul Mofaz to Washington.[66] Along with the Israelis, conservatives in Congress expressed concern that the precision-guided weapons could be used by the Arabs against Israel instead of Iran. In an effort to gain congressional approval of its $20 billion arms sale to the Gulf states, the administration approved an arms deal to Israel valued at $30 billion.[67]

But just when the region seemed to be settling down for peace talks, on September 6, 2007, Israel sent a message to Iran by striking a Syrian site suspected of being a North Korean–equipped nuclear facility in its early stages. Prior to the strike, Olmert tried to convince Bush to attack Syria, but Bush refused and did not comment on the attacks.[68] For fear of starting a regional war, Bush delayed releasing more detailed photographs of what appeared to be the makings of a secret nuclear reactor.[69] The strike sparked an internal debate about whether the administration should oppose Israel's action in order to protect its diplomatic overtures to Syria and North Korea. While Vice President Cheney argued that preemption was justified, Rice and Gates expressed concern about the negative fallout over the strike, especially since the Syrian site was not an immediate threat to Israel.[70] Thus, as a conciliatory gesture following the attacks, the United States formally invited Syria to the Annapolis Conference in November 2007.[71]

Having averted a potentially explosive situation, Rice refocused the administration's efforts on the ultimate prize—peace—and made her seventh trip to the region in 2007. But something appeared to be changing in the way Rice viewed and understood the Palestinians. She seemed to connect with Palestine as the birthplace of Christ on a spiritual and emotional level. Rice, a devout Christian and the daughter and granddaughter of Presbyterian ministers, visited Bethlehem and disclosed that "she could spell Bethlehem before she could spell her name."[72] She was seriously disturbed by what she saw when she visited the birthplace of Christianity and, recalling her childhood in segregated Birmingham, Alabama, she later remarked, "I know what it's like to hear that you can't use a certain road, or pass through a checkpoint because you are a Palestinian. I know what it is like to feel discriminated against and powerless."[73] One could only wonder if these words were not among the few in politics spoken sincerely from the heart.

More Missed Opportunities

It was clear to all concerned that the secretary of state would spend her last days in office relentlessly pursuing an Israeli-Palestinian deal.[74] In an attempt to woo Arab states to Annapolis, the administration pushed Israel to pursue final-status negotiations. The United States promised to "be assiduously fair, and very tough, and if necessary... public." Because both Israelis and Palestinians claimed the other side was not living up to its end of the Road Map, the administration continued to reject the notion of sequence and pushed for parallel steps to be taken by both Israelis and Palestinians in keeping with the Road Map. In a further move toward moderation, Rice promised that the Golan Heights would be on the agenda.[75]

The Annapolis Conference was a significant event, and though Hamas was excluded from the negotiations, the effort was nevertheless a serious attempt to make peace between the Israelis and the Palestinians.[76] At the conference, Bush outlined the same vision of a political process that Colin Powell had called for five years before. Reading the conference statement, Bush rejected the sequence principle, called upon both parties to fulfill their parallel obligations under the Road Map, and indicated that progress would be "judged" by the United States. He called upon the Palestinians to "govern justly and dismantle the infrastructure of terror." He argued that they "must show the world they understand that, while the borders of a Palestinian state are important, the nature of a Palestinian state is just as important."[77]

As for the Israelis, Bush offered unusually demanding guidelines: "They must show the world that they are ready to begin to bring an end to the occupation that began in 1967, through a negotiated settlement." Such an agreement would, according to Bush, require that Israel dismantle settlements and "establish Palestine as the Palestinian homeland, just as Israel is the homeland for the Jewish people." Though a significant proportion of the Palestinian people were living under a Hamas government in Gaza and Abbas had just dismantled a democratically elected government, Bush ignored the elephant in the room and called for a "democratic, viable Palestinian state." In a characteristically optimistic tone, Bush declared that the "day is coming when freedom will yield the peace we desire and the land that is holy to so many will see the light of peace."[78]

In her prepared remarks, Rice avoided platitudes about freedom and democracy altogether. Instead, she called for parallelism, urging both parties to fulfill their obligations under the Road Map and to complete final negotiations in one year's time. Rice described Annapolis as "the beginning, not the end, of a renewed effort to realize the two-state vision of peace and security." Though the administration, until then, had offered next-to-no support for a peace process, she charged the international audience to "be prepared to commit to the work of tomorrow with equal energy and urgency as we approach the work of today."[79]

Abbas described Olmert as being serious about peace and, quoting Abraham Lincoln, stated, "Let us strive on to finish the work we are in, to do all that we may achieve and cherish a just and lasting peace among ourselves and with all nations." In an attempt to relate to Bush's concept of liberty, Abbas spoke about the beauty of Annapolis as a symbol of "liberty, the most exalted value of all." Citing Israel's parallel obligations under the Road Map, he called on Israel to take concrete steps: "freez[ing] all settlement activities including natural growth, reopening institutions in Jerusalem, removing settlement outposts, removing checkpoints, releasing prisoners and facilitating the mission of the Palestinian Authority in restoring law and order." In what was clearly a personal appeal to Bush, Abbas stated, "Freedom, for Palestinians, is perhaps the most evocative word—the word that captures the collective hope of Palestinians and their aspiration for future generations."[80]

Olmert offered a similar conciliatory tone. Speaking to Abbas and the Palestinian people, he stated, "We no longer, and you no longer, have the privilege of clinging to dreams which are disconnected from the sufferings of our peoples, the hardships they experience daily and the burden of living under ongoing uncertainty, with no chance for change or hope." Olmert stated his goal as two independent democratic states living side by side in peace.[81]

The hope generated by the Annapolis Conference was followed up with a donors' conference in Paris on December 17, 2007, where $7.5 billion was pledged to Abbas's Palestinian Authority. The United States committed itself to $555 million, although part of that sum had already been promised but was held up in Congress. Major contributions from France, Germany, Norway, Spain, Sweden, and the United Kingdom ensured that the Palestinian Authority would finally have some of the money necessary to reform its security infrastructure and build the institutions of a state under Fayyad's direction.[82]

Although there was fresh momentum from the meetings in Annapolis and Paris, it did not take long for the energy to dissipate. Olmert rejected Hamas's December 2007 offer for a ceasefire, and instead, Israel's Housing and Construction Ministry indicated that its 2008 budget proposal included plans to build five hundred housing units in one of the West Bank's largest settlement blocks.[83] The prospects for a peaceful resolution in 2008 were off to a rocky start, but unlike in previous years, the Bush administration was inclined to respond.

Because the conservatives had very little influence over Bush in his final days in office, he pressed Israel on its obligation to freeze settlements—but not hard enough. He indicated that he was expecting the Israeli government "to get rid of unauthorized settlements." Sharon had promised Bush that he would dismantle more than twenty tiny settlements built after 2001 in the West Bank, but almost none of them were removed. Furthermore, following the Annapolis Conference, Olmert implicitly cited the sequence principle and the letters between Sharon and Bush as rendering "flexible what is written in the Road Map." He argued that because the Palestinians had not met their obligations, Israel did not have to either. But Olmert also conceded that in refusing to freeze settlements and natural growth, Israel was not fully meeting its obligations. He stated, "There is a certain contradiction in this between what we're actually seeing and what we ourselves promised."[84]

To move both parties in the direction of peace, Bush made a high-profile visit to both Israel and Palestine in January 2008. In an attempt to build credibility among the Palestinians, he visited Bethlehem's Church of the Nativity and drove through the checkpoint in Ramallah, commenting that checkpoints "create massive frustrations for the Palestinians."[85] He hoped "as a result of a formation of a Palestinian state" that "walls and checkpoints" would be removed and "people will be able to move freely in a democratic state." In a characteristic statement of religious conviction, Bush expressed his vision for peace, "greatly inspired by my belief that there is an Almighty, and a gift of that Almighty to each man, woman and child on the face of the earth is freedom."[86]

On January 10, 2008, at the King David Hotel in Jerusalem, Bush reiterated his call for a "viable, contiguous, sovereign, and independent" Palestinian state, which would serve as the homeland for the Palestinian people, including compensated refugees. Echoing the principle of parallelism, he ended his statement by reasserting the centrality of Israeli-Palestinian peace to regional security. Six years after severing that link, he stated, "The establishment of the state of Palestine is long overdue. The Palestinian people deserve it. And it will *enhance the stability of the region*, and it will contribute to the security of the people of Israel. The peace agreement should happen, and can happen, by the end of this year."[87] As Bush left on an optimistic note, his departure was overshadowed by comments from Hamas's Ismael Haniyeh, who declared, "The problem of Palestine will remain alive." In a further blow to Bush's mission, the publication of the Winograd Commission's report slammed Olmert's performance in the Lebanon War and undermined his ability to deliver politically.[88]

Choosing to deliver his keynote address in the United Arab Emirates on January 13, 2008, Bush offered a theological defense of his freedom agenda, while simultaneously embracing the moderate vision of a peace process. Showing slightly more philosophical nuance, he emphasized "freedom and justice," not simply freedom and democracy. He declared that "a great new era is unfolding before us... founded on the equality of all people before God. This new era is being built with the understanding that power is a trust that must be exercised with the consent of the governed—and deliver equal justice under the law." Glossing over the increased social strife and inequality in the region since the Iraq War, Bush hailed social progress in the Middle East carried out by moderate monarchs, not democrats. He stated, "In my country, we speak of these developments as the advance of freedom. Others may call it the advance of justice. Yet whatever term we use, the ideal is the same. In a free and just society, every person is treated with dignity."[89]

Ignoring Hamas's rise to power, Bush declared that the "fight against the forces of extremism is the great ideological struggle of our time. And in this fight, our nations have a weapon more powerful than bombs or bullets. It is the desire for freedom and justice written into our hearts by Almighty God—and no terrorist or tyrant can take that away," as evidenced in the Lebanese and Iraqi elections, as well as the Palestinian presidential election. Though Bush acknowledged that elections do not guarantee freedom, he indicated that it was the "declared policy of the United States to support [the people of the region] as they claim their freedom—as a matter of natural right and national interest." Much to the conservatives' annoyance, Bush once again cited a link between regional peace and Palestinian self-determination: "an independent, viable, democratic, and peaceful Palestinian state is more than the dream of the Palestinians. It's also the best guarantee for peace for all its neighbors." Never abandoning his theology of history, Bush told his audience, "a future of liberty stands before you. It is your right. It is your dream. And it is your *destiny*."[90]

If Bush declared freedom to be the destiny of the region, no group seemed to want it more than the 1.5 million Palestinians trapped in Gaza, described as the largest open-air prison in the world. In a form of collective punishment, Israel had cut off all non-emergency supply shipments into Gaza to pressure the Palestinians to stop rocket fire into Israel. Hamas responded by destroying the Egyptian-Gazan barrier at Rafah, and an estimated 700,000 Palestinians made their way into Egypt to secure supplies such as food, fuel, medicine, and cigarettes. But after twelve days of free movement, and after Hamas continued to break down more parts of the barrier, the Islamist movement agreed to allow Egypt to once again secure the crossing.[91]

With the people of Gaza suffering, prospects for peace looked bleak at the beginning of 2008. Israelis launched an assault against Hamas, injuring forty-five Palestinians and killing eight members of Hamas, including the son of a Hamas leader and two civilians. Palestinians sent more rockets into Israel and injured five civilians, including a five-year-old girl.[92] Israeli Deputy Defense Minister Matan Vilnai warned the Palestinians of a "*shoah*" or holocaust.[93] In March 2008, Israel launched an incursion into Gaza which claimed more than one hundred lives, including dozens of civilians, over a five-day period. Abbas responded by suspending peace talks.[94]

In the face of collapsing peace talks, the determined Rice once again headed to the region in March 2008 to push peace negotiations forward. But skeptics cast a long shadow over her trip. As former State Department official Aaron David Miller noted, "You cannot make peace with half of the Palestinian polity and go to war with the other half."[95] Though the administration shunned any communication with Hamas, they eventually realized, as former Israeli Foreign Minister Shlomo Ben-Ami observed, that a ceasefire was the only hope for obtaining an agreement by the end of the year. Egypt was called upon by the United States to open up an indirect channel of negotiations to stop Israeli incursions in Gaza in exchange for a cessation of rocket fire.[96] In an effort to bolster peace talks further, Bush dispatched Vice President Cheney to the region to meet with Olmert and Abbas. In Israel, Cheney conspicuously betrayed his lack of enthusiasm for peace negotiations by emphasizing the preeminence of the Iranian threat before turning to the topic of the peace process.[97] He spoke of the "darkening shadows" in Gaza, and as he met with Abbas in Ramallah, the vice president warned that terrorism could "kill the legitimate hopes and aspirations of the Palestinian people."[98]

Following Cheney's visit, Rice made yet another visit to the region to forward the president's goal of securing a peace agreement by the year's end. She indicated that the rockets from Gaza needed to stop, but did not offer a U.S. plan to mediate between Israel and Hamas.[99] In early April 2008, Olmert and Abbas met in Jerusalem after Abbas agreed to resume negotiations. In defiance of the Road Map, Olmert refused to freeze settlements completely for fear of losing key parts of his shaky coalition government. But as Palestinian negotiator Saeb Erekat pointed out, Israel's actions, while preserving what little popularity Olmert enjoyed, seriously undermined the credibility of Abbas.[100]

As Israel celebrated its sixtieth birthday, Olmert hailed Bush as "an unusual friend of the people of Israel." Before the Knesset, Bush delivered an impassioned speech decrying compromise with extremist groups. Offering an implicit criticism of former U.S. President Jimmy Carter, who had previously met with Hamas, Bush stated, "Some seem to believe we should negotiate with terrorists and radicals, as if some ingenious argument will persuade them they have been wrong all along.... We have an obligation to call this what it is—the false comfort of appeasement, which has been repeatedly discredited by history." Once again reaffirming his theology of history, Bush said:

Ultimately, to prevail in this struggle, we must offer an alternative to the ideology of the extremists by extending our vision of justice and tolerance, freedom and hope. These values are the self-evident right of all people, of all religions, in all of the world because they are a gift from Almighty God. Securing these rights is also the surest way to secure peace. Leaders who are accountable to their people will not pursue endless confrontation and bloodshed.[101]

Following his trip to Israel, Bush delivered a second speech directed toward an Arab audience in Egypt. He once again spoke in theological terms of liberty's providential spread:

Freedom is also the basis for a democratic system of government, which is the only fair and just ordering of society and the only way to guarantee the God-given rights of all people. Democracies do not take the same shape; they develop at different speeds and in different ways, and they reflect the unique cultures and traditions of their people. There are skeptics about democracy in this part of the world, I understand that. But as more people in the Middle East gain firsthand experience from freedom, many of the arguments against democracy are being discredited.

He condemned Middle Eastern leaders for jailing opposition leaders (most of whom were Islamists), despite the fact that a significant portion of the democratically elected Hamas politicians remained in Israeli prisons. He concluded his speech by declaring his theology of history to be "a universal vision, based on the timeless principles of dignity and tolerance and justice—and it unites all who yearn for freedom and peace in this ancient land."[102]

Regardless of Bush's lofty language of liberty, Carter's peacemaking efforts and Rice's twenty-three trips to the region were yielding favorable results. In mid-June 2008, the Egyptians brokered a six-month truce between Hamas and Israel. The Carter Center helped break the impasse by convincing Hamas to accept a ceasefire that was limited to Gaza alone. According to Hrair Balian, who assisted Carter, hundreds of rockets were sent into Israel before the ceasefire. After the truce, that number was limited to a few per month. The few rockets that were fired came from other fringe groups, criminals who were running tunnels, disgruntled members of Hamas, or others looking to see Hamas fail. Hamas kept its word and did not violate its truce with Israel.[103]

Meanwhile, Olmert privately made what Rice considered "a very, very generous offer to Abbas."[104] The offer was based on the 1967 borders, with near one-to-one land swaps and agreement on a passageway between Gaza and the West Bank. As for Jerusalem, it was to be a shared capital for both states, and was to be administered by a city council that would be half-Palestinian and half-Israeli. Jewish neighborhoods would go to the Israelis, and Palestinian neighborhoods would go to the Palestinians. As for sovereignty of the Temple Mount, both sides would claim sovereignty, but they would agree to disagree by not challenging each other's sovereignty.[105]

A symbolic number of Palestinian refugees would be allowed to exercise their "right of return" inside of Israel, while Israelis would call it "family reunification." It was agreed that "major compensation" would be given to the Palestinian refugees. Though both Israel and Palestine would have looked geographically "ugly," the Palestinian state would have been "pretty contiguous." Rice maintains that Olmert's offer was better than what was discussed at Camp David in 2000. According to Rice, one of the main problems with Olmert's offer was that Abbas could not accept it because Olmert would not give him anything to study. The prime minister "would only show him a map and then take it back, because Olmert was, by this time, desperately afraid that he was going to be" in real legal trouble; corruption charges were pending against him in Israel.[106]

Then all hope was lost. As Rice recalls, Olmert did indeed run into "real trouble," and he indicated that he would resign after corruption charges were brought against him. Already lacking credibility among his people for mishandling the Lebanon War, Olmert could not hang on to power any longer. The Palestinians were ready for a deal, but they knew "Olmert was too weak to actually deliver."[107] Referring to the peace agreement, Hadley wincingly speculates, "we would have gotten it except that Olmert [got] into trouble politically with his investigation."[108] Similarly, Rice recalls, if "Olmert [did not] get into trouble he might actually [have gotten] a deal."[109] Six years after Bush had refused to deal with the Palestinians until they restored integrity to corrupt institutions, his internationally supported peace initiative was torpedoed by alleged Israeli corruption. Rice continued to look for opportunities, saying, "we don't give up," but Olmert lacked a popular mandate to deliver.[110] Tzipi Livni, his potential successor, failed to put together a government and instead called for early elections.[11]

"Blind in Gaza"[112]

Having failed at peace, Olmert turned to war. Though Hamas had respected the Egyptian-brokered ceasefire with Israel that was concluded on June 19, 2008, Israel violated its terms in two ways.[113] According to Balian, Israel was to relax its siege and allow hundreds of truckloads of food and humanitarian supplies into the Gaza Strip each day. This did not happen. Also, though Hamas was willing to extend the ceasefire, Israel launched a major incursion into Gaza on November 4, 2008, with the stated intention of destroying a tunnel that the movement was digging within Palestinian territory. Given Israel's knowledge of the tunnel's existence, it is hard to imagine how it could have been deemed a threat, much less an immediate threat. Six Hamas fighters were killed during the incursion, and the group responded by unleashing a barrage of rockets and mortars.[114]

With prime ministerial candidates Tzipi Livni and Benjamin Netanyahu issuing bellicose election statements about toppling Hamas, Olmert, not wanting to be outshined, returned as a fool to his folly.[115] December 2008 was his last chance to redeem his legacy, and he chose to do so by launching a war dubbed Operation Cast Lead, just weeks before U.S. President-elect Barack Obama was about to assume office. The stated aim of the multiphase mission, which included aerial bombardment and a ground invasion, was made abundantly clear by the prime minister's deputy, Haim Ramon: "The goal of the operation is to topple Hamas."[116] Given this objective, Olmert will unfortunately be remembered not only as the first Israeli prime minister to face criminal indictment for corruption, but also as the first to have failed in two successive wars.

Determined not to repeat the mistakes of the Lebanon War, Rice prepared a UN resolution calling for a ceasefire. She had been sickened by the surprise bombing of Qana during the summer of 2006, and this time around, did not want to watch from the sidelines as more innocent civilians needlessly perished. But she lacked the support of the president.[117] According to Olmert's account of events, once he learned of her intentions, he called Bush's line while Rice was delivering a speech and said, "Get me President Bush on the phone." Olmert then asked him to instruct Rice to abstain from the vote on the resolution; Rice ultimately abstained. Though Olmert had a lukewarm relationship with Rice, his public recollection of the events was unusually disrespectful. He stated, "She was left shamed [by a] resolution that she prepared and arranged, and in the end she did not vote in favor [of]."[118] Olmert was right. Rice was indeed humiliated by the indecisive president, who once again moved away from parallelism and supported Israel's last bungled attempt at sequence.

The Report of the United Nations Fact Finding Mission on the Gaza Conflict, headed by Justice Richard Goldstone, accused Israel of perpetrating war crimes, and with meticulous detail documented its grave breaches of international law. In a particularly disturbing case study, the report described how the Israeli army ordered approximately one hundred men, women, and children from the al-Samouni family into a house, which was bombed the next day, killing twenty-one and wounding nineteen. Those who survived the explosions sought permission to leave, but were told by the soldiers to "go back to death." It should be noted here that Hamas also perpetrated war crimes and that its low-tech rockets directed at civilian areas dealt a heavy psychological blow to Israeli communities in the south of Israel, causing children to suffer from severe post-traumatic stress disorder.[119]

Beyond the human toll, the three-week war damaged and destroyed $2 billion worth of Palestinian assets, including over 4,000 homes and 1,500 factories and workshops, and created a homeless population of 50,000.[120] Approximately 773 non-combatants, 320 minors, and 109 women were killed on the Palestinian side, along with 13 Israelis (3 civilians, and 10 combatants, 4 of whom were killed by friendly fire).[121] In the end, the real winners were extremist groups like Hamas and Hezbollah, who bolstered their credibility throughout the Middle East by portraying helpless Palestinian civilians being slaughtered by a U.S.-funded army.[122] The utter devastation in Gaza marked the denouement of an eight-year drama in which the world's strongest nation sought to democratize the Middle East, and to do so through force. One finds clarity in the words of Tacitus, who in days of old recorded, "they make a desolation and call it peace."[123]

CHAPTER 8

Conclusion

God grant me the serenity
to accept the things I cannot change;
courage to change the things I can;
and wisdom to know the difference.[1]

Whatever may come of the twenty-first century, September 11, 2001, will be marked as a day unlike any other. A seemingly stable world order was thrown into convulsions, transformed and transfixed in an instant by a stunning display of force executed not at the behest of a sovereign nation, but by a handful of deluded men seeking to disrupt U.S. global hegemony. In the drama that unfolded, the Al Qaeda provocation succeeded in drawing the world's sole superpower into a fateful campaign that at first blush could have been mistaken for a religious crusade. In what came to be known by modest estimates as the "three trillion dollar war," the United States attempted to defeat an idea by force while its budget surplus in 2000 became a $1.5 trillion deficit by 2008.[2] If Osama bin Laden and his fanatical followers set about to change the world, history will judge that they succeeded in their cause.

Instead of strategically targeting an elusive enemy using the full energies of the capable women and men serving in the U.S. armed forces, clandestine services, and diplomatic corps, President George W. Bush instead commissioned a clumsy "shock and awe" mission to destroy one utopian idea and replace it with another.

His freedom agenda came at the heavy cost of U.S. blood and treasure and fared not much better than Hercules's instinctive strategy against the Hydra. As each threat was removed, a bigger one appeared in its place. In Afghanistan and Pakistan, corrupt Western-backed leaders faced a rising tide of religious extremism. In Iran, the guardians tightened their grip on power *vis-à-vis* a covert nuclear program, the repression of its citizens, and deeper penetration into the Gulf states, Iraq, Syria, Lebanon, and the occupied Palestinian territories. Consequently, regional security was severely disrupted, thousands of innocents perished, and U.S. stature and significance diminished.

The aim of this book has been to explain the contested ideas and assumptions behind Bush's unsuccessful Middle East policy, with a particular focus on the Israeli-Palestinian conflict. It has been argued that in a world transformed, two competing visions of U.S. statecraft emerged, each one presupposing diametrically opposed views of human nature and destiny. Even during the final moments of his presidency, Bush never truly made a decision as to which view should guide U.S. foreign policy toward the Israeli-Palestinian conflict.

On the one hand, a conservative alliance, consisting of theoconservatives, neo-conservatives, and conservative nationalists, sought to transform the world "as it is" into the world "as it should be." After 9/11, neoconservatives and conservative nationalists understood the menace of terrorism to be rooted in an endemic pathology of "un-freedom" sweeping the lands of Islam. Borrowing from the Christian idea that history is a linear process directed at an absolute goal of social redemption, they discerned that history was inevitably moving toward its ultimate end or *goal*, the spread of liberal democracy. For these optimistic utopians, humanity would enter into a more perfect epoch of liberty once the Middle East was forcefully brought under the "rational" sovereignty of modernity. The War on Terror was thus conceived by one apologetic historian as a fight "for the very notion of the Enlightenment."[3]

Like their optimistic counterparts, theoconservatives also held utopian views, only in a pessimistic and less secularized sense. For them, that same redemptive work of history, the inauguration of a golden age of peace, would be accomplished by the forceful end or *termination* of history precipitated by the battle of Armageddon located in modern Israel. Because both utopian systems shared a common mission of ending history, be it in its goal or termination, optimistic and pessimistic conservatives were wholly united in their policy recommendations.

In practical terms, the unified policy platform of conservative utopians has been referred to throughout this book as the principle of *sequence*. According to this position, the preeminent U.S. foreign policy objective should be to promote democracy throughout the Middle East, and if necessary to do so by shocking force. Instead of pursuing a negotiated settlement to the Israeli-Palestinian conflict, sequentialism provided staunch support for Israel's preemptive strategies while promoting regime change in states that sponsor terrorism, notably Iraq, Iran, and Syria. According to the sequence principle, until a dramatic sociopolitical transformation takes place in Palestine, during which democratically elected leaders completely dismantle all terrorist institutions, no political process should be undertaken by the United States. This policy was most clearly stated in Bush's June 2002 Rose Garden speech.

On the other hand, moderate realists advocated for an approach that dealt with the world "as it is." They argued that it is not realistic to conform entire human communities to abstract moral precepts that govern individual conduct, for the depravity of human nature is a fact of life at the most basic level. For them, positive social change had to develop organically within societies. Grand ideas about replacing dictatorial regimes across the Middle East with U.S.-imposed liberal democracies were deemed by realists to be little more than fantasies.[4] With a heavy dose of skepticism and a fair bit of cynicism, they decried utopian plans to redeem humanity by liberating the people of the Middle East.

Instead, realists saw the problem of terrorism as stemming primarily from grievances and feelings of dishonor. For them, a notable example was the continued persistence of the Palestinian question. Decades had gone by in which the plight of the Palestinians had been used and abused by Arab, Muslim, and Israeli leaders to serve their own ends. In a post-9/11 world, they argued, the United States could no longer afford to be seen by Arabs and Muslims as sponsoring heavy-handed measures taken by Israel against Palestinian populations. Instead, the United States needed to emerge as a more even-handed arbiter in Israeli-Palestinian affairs, extracting *parallel* concessions from both sides. In opposition to the conservative principle of sequence, moderate realists endorsed this principle of parallelism as adumbrated in the Quartet's Road Map policy of 2003.

Caught in the middle of these two schools, the president's closest foreign policy advisor, Condoleezza Rice, unsuccessfully sought to resolve the inherent tensions between realist and utopian positions and their corollary policies of parallelism and sequence. More important, it was not always clear that Bush fully understood the distinction between the two incompatible views, and consequently, he wavered indecisively between them. Thus, at times, one could be forgiven for asking whether Bush was a devoted Palestinian nationalist or more Likud than Likud. Upon assuming office, he instinctively disliked Yasser Arafat, Ariel Sharon, and the very idea of intervening in the conflict. On several occasions he directed these ill feelings toward Sharon in what were considered highly embarrassing episodes in the U.S.-Israeli "special relationship." Yet under the counsel of sober-minded moderates like Colin Powell, he became the first U.S. president to recognize the Palestinian right to self-determination in unambiguous terms and at no less conspicuous a forum than the United Nations.

Then everything changed. With the traumatic events of 9/11, Bush appeared to have assumed a messianic complex as the leader of the free world with a theologically informed mandate to spread liberty. In yet another bold move that contradicted previous policies, Bush undertook an audacious project to free Palestine, not from its occupiers, but from its democratically elected leader, Yasser Arafat. Embracing the principle of sequence as proposed by conservative utopians, Bush sought to resolve the Israeli-Palestinian conflict by creating "new men" in Palestine, uncorrupted democrats untainted by terror who would be accountable to their people, to democratic institutions, and to their democratic neighbors in Israel. As he stated in his June 2002 Rose Garden speech, only once this dramatic sociopolitical transformation was complete would he support a political process between Israelis and Palestinians.

But as the Iraq War loomed on the horizon, Bush once again lacked decisiveness and moved back in the direction of the moderates. Ignoring the principle of sequence, he embraced the Quartet's Road Map and its stated principle of parallelism, which sought reciprocal concessions from Palestinians and Israelis within the context of an established political process. Endorsed by the international community, the plan was dismissed out of hand by Sharon. Lacking a deep understanding of what was at stake, Bush reversed course, shelved the Road Map, and instead accepted Sharon's version of sequence as defined by his Disengagement Plan for Gaza.

After winning a solid reelection victory in 2004, Bush renewed his commitment to the conservative vision of sequence and the "freedom agenda." But his record of indecisiveness persisted into the second term. Under the guidance of his trusted Secretary of State, Condoleezza Rice, "realism" and "utopianism" were being comingled in a new approach to statecraft, one in which interests and values were viewed as being "one and the same." The aim of this freedom agenda was not simply stability, but, as summarized in that contradictory phrase, a "balance of power that favors freedom."[5]

Declaring liberty to be the means and ends of Middle East policy, Bush continued to move indecisively as he mixed and matched conservative and moderate policy prescriptions. He resolved to transform the Middle East into something new, but also hinted that he might move forward with a political process in Palestine. With successful elections being undertaken in Iraq, Lebanon, and Palestine, it seemed as if the progress of liberty would create peace and stability in a new Middle East after all. Instead, as Bush soon learned, the freedom agenda unleashed a destabilizing wave of fundamentalism that fed the fires of religious extremism and challenged U.S. values and interests perhaps more than ever before. Notably, with the electoral successes of Hezbollah in Lebanon and Hamas in Palestine, Iran solidified its regional influence through proxy militias.

After the Palestinian elections of 2006, Bush all but abandoned the democracy component of the sequence principle and instead turned to military force. But it was only after U.S.-backed Israeli forces failed to defeat Hezbollah and U.S.-backed Fatah forces failed to defeat Hamas that Bush once again turned away from sequence and moved toward the Road Map's vision of parallelism. Consequently, he launched the Annapolis Conference, empowering his able secretary of state to pursue serious negotiations. With a remarkable show of eleventh-hour diplomacy, Rice shuttled back and forth to the region, but alas, her efforts were torpedoed by the corruption and political incompetence of Israeli Prime Minister Ehud Olmert.

In a last-ditch attempt to topple Hamas, Olmert broke his truce with the militant organization and launched a devastating war in which both Israel and Hamas perpetrated war crimes. Rather than supporting his secretary of state's efforts to bring about a ceasefire, Bush humiliated her and once again changed his mind, moved back to a policy of sequence, and backed Olmert's devastating war in Gaza.

Together with an erratic eight-year record of Middle East policy failures, Bush's response to the war in Gaza demonstrated that he was, in the words of Machiavelli, an "irresolute prince"—inconsistent and utterly incompetent when it came to leading U.S. foreign policy in the Middle East. By virtue of rank and duty, Bush was undoubtedly the "decider-in-chief," but his decisively indecisive record in Israeli-Palestinian affairs was a fateful landmark in the struggle for peace.

NOTES

⊞

CHAPTER 1

1. Condoleezza Rice, *No Higher Honor: A Memoir of My Years in Washington* (New York: Crown, 2011), pp. 415–419; interview with Condoleezza Rice, December 2009; Glenn Kessler, *The Confidante: Condoleezza Rice and the Creation of the Bush Legacy* (New York: Macmillan, 2007), pp. 135–140; and interviews with David Welch, November and December 2009.

2. Karen Hughes, *Ten Minutes from Normal* (New York: Penguin, 2004), pp. 279–282.

3. Interview with Condoleezza Rice, December 2009.

4. George W. Bush, *Decision Points* (New York: Crown, 2010).

5. Fareed R. Zakaria, "The Arrogant Empire," *Newsweek*, March 23, 2003; and Fareed R. Zakaria, *The Post-American World* (New York: W.W. Norton and Co., 2008).

6. Scott Horton, "This is Starting to Get Dangerous," *Harper's*, March 15, 2010.

7. Kanan M. Makiya, "The Arab Spring Started in Iraq," *New York Times*, April 6, 2013; and Peter Maass, "Did the Iraq War Bring the Arab Spring?" *New Yorker*, April 9, 2013.

8. George W. Bush, Second Inaugural Address, January 20, 2005, http://www.npr.org/templates/story/story.php?storyId=4460172; and Condoleezza Rice, Remarks at the American University of Cairo, June 20, 2005, http://2001-2009.state.gov/secretary/rm/2005/48328.htm.

CHAPTER 2

1. Interview with Christopher Meyer, September 2009.

2. John Quincy Adams, Address to the U.S. House of Representatives, July 4, 1821, http://millercenter.org/president/speeches/detail/3484.

3. The Second Gore-Bush Presidential Debate, The Commission on Presidential Debates, October 11, 2000, http://www.debates.org/index.php?page=october-11-2000-debate-transcript.

4. Christina Lamb and David Wastell, "Assad death plunges the Middle East into turmoil," *Telegraph*, June 11, 2000; and "Why is Israel Pulling Out?" BBCnews.co.uk, May 23, 2000.

5. George Mitchell et al., Sharm El-Sheikh Fact-Finding Committee Report (The Mitchell Report), May 4, 2001, http://2001-2009.state.gov/p/nea/rls/rpt/3060.htm.

6. Report of the Commission of Inquiry into the Events at the Refugee Camps in Beirut, Israel Ministry of Foreign Affairs, February 8, 1983, http://mfa.gov.il/.

7. Interviews with Shlomo Ben-Ami, December 2009.

8. Marwan Muasher, *The Arab Center* (New Haven, Conn.: Yale University Press, 2008), p. 294.

9. Or Commission, "The Or Commission Report," September 2, 2003; Yair Ettinger, "92 Hearings, 377 Witnesses, 4,289 Exhibits," *Ha'aretz*, September 3, 2003; and Jack Khoury, "Israeli Arabs prepare for month to commemorate October 2000 riots," *Ha'aretz*, September 23, 2010.

10. In the author's interview with Shlomo Ben-Ami, the latter described Sharon's visit as a "trigger" or "ignition" rather than the root cause. For more commentary, see Ariel Sharon, Letter to Secretary of State Madeleine Albright, October 2, 2000; George Mitchell et al., "The Mitchell Report," May 4, 2001; and Or Commission, "The Or Commission Report."

11. Interview with Condoleezza Rice, December 2009.

12. Or Commission Report.

13. Mitchell Report.

14. Interview with Daniel Kurtzer, December 2009. Hamas leader Mahmoud Zahar contradicted this conclusion, noting that "President Arafat instructed Hamas to carry out a number of military operations in the heart of the Jewish state after he felt that his negotiations with the Israeli government then had failed." Zahar, a political rival of Arafat, did not provide evidence to support his claim. For more information, see Khaled Abu Toameh, "Arafat ordered Hamas attacks against Israeli in 2000," *Jerusalem Post*, September 29, 2010.

15. Interview with Elias Zananiri, December 2009.

16. Interview with Hussein Agha, September 2009; interview with Elias Zananiri, December 2009; interview with Fayaz Tarawneh, September 2009; and interview with Salam Majali, September 2009.

17. Interview with Condoleezza Rice, December 2009; interview with Colin Powell, January 2010; interview with Richard Armitage, February 2010; interview with Anthony

Zinni, December 2009; interview with William Inboden, September 2009; and Bill Clinton, *My Life: The Presidential Years* (New York: Random House, 2004) pp. 633–635.

18. Interview with Daniel Kurtzer, December 2009.

19. Interview with Colin Powell, January 2010; and interview with Daniel Kurtzer, December 2009.

20. Dennis Ross, *The Missing Peace: The Inside Story of the Fight for Middle East Peace* (New York: Farrar, Straus and Giroux, 2004).

21. Hussein Agha and Robert Malley, "Camp David: The Tragedy of Errors," *New York Review of Books*, August 9, 2001. Other accounts include: Shlomo Ben-Ami, *Scars of War, Wounds of Peace: The Israeli-Arab Tragedy* (Oxford: Oxford University Press, 2006); Itamar Rabinovich, *Waging Peace: Israel and the Arabs, 1948–2003* (Princeton, N.J.: Princeton University Press, 2004); Yossi Beilin, *The Path to Geneva: The Quest for a Permanent Agreement, 1996–2004* (New York: RDV/Akashik Books, 2004); and Clayton Swisher, *The Truth About Camp David: The Untold Story About the Collapse of the Middle East Peace Process* (New York: Nation Books, 2004).

22. Interview with Norman Finkelstein and Shlomo Ben-Ami, *Democracy Now: The War and Peace Report,* February 14, 2006.

23. Aaron David Miller, "Israel's Lawyer," *Washington Post*, May 23, 2005.

24. As Shlomo Ben-Ami recalls, a fundamental problem was that Israelis came to Egypt to translate the Clinton parameters into an agreement, while the Palestinians believed that they needed to be changed. The latter felt that the Clinton parameters were untenable on fundamental issues, namely refugees, Jerusalem, and territory. Moreover, the summit did not have the backing of the U.S. government. On the resignation of Prime Minister Ehud Barak, see "PM Barak Announces Intention to Resign," Press Release from the Prime Minister's Media Advisor, December 10, 2000.

25. "Mideast talks to end as hopes fade," CNN.com, January 27, 2006; Interview with Norman Finkelstein and Shlomo Ben-Ami, *Democracy Now*; and Deborah Sontag, "A Special Report: Quest for the Middle East Peace: How and Why it Failed," *New York Times*, July 26, 2001.

26. Interview with Hussein Agha, September 2009; interviews with Shlomo Ben-Ami, December 2009; and Miguel Moratinos, "Moratinos Non-Paper," January 2001, http://unispal.un.org/.

27. Joint Israeli-Palestinian Statement, *Jerusalem Post*, January 27, 2000.

28. Interview with Christopher Patten, September 2009.

29. William A. Orme Jr., "The World: The Middle East; Disillusionment With a Friend," *New York Times*, March 25, 2001; interview with Daniel Kurtzer, December 2009; interview with Richard Armitage, February 2010; and interview with Condoleezza Rice, December 2009.

30. Interview with Richard Haass, November 2009.

31. Interview with Marwan Muasher, February 2010; and interviews with David Wurmser, March 2010.

32. Oliver Burkeman, "Rumsfeld's Progress," *Guardian*, November 10, 2006; and Sidney Blumenthal, *How Bush Rules: Chronicles of a Radical Regime* (Princeton, N.J.: Princeton University Press, 2006), pp. 302–304.

33. Donald Rumsfeld, *Known and Unknown: A Memoir* (New York: Penguin, 2011), p. 500.

34. Tony Blair, *A Journey: My Political Life* (New York: Knopf, 2010), p. 407; emphasis added.

35. Interview with Richard Haass, November 2009; and interview with former senior U.S. official, 2010.

36. Interviews with David Wurmser, March 2010.

37. Interview with former senior U.S. official; "Letter to President Bush on the War on Terrorism," Project For a New American Century, September 20, 2001; William Kristol, Editorial, *Weekly Standard*, November 19, 2001; and William Kristol, "Bush vs. Powell," *Washington Post*, September 25, 2001.

38. Many rulers, including the Iranian-backed Hassan Nasrallah, leader of Hezbollah, claim to be descendants of the Prophet of Islam.

39. Richard Perle et al., "A Clean Break: A New Strategy for Securing the Realm," Institute for Advanced Strategic and Political Studies, July 1996, http://www.iasps.org/strat1.htm.

40. Interview with Richard Armitage, February 2010.

41. Ron Suskind, "Faith, Certainty, and the Presidency of George W. Bush," *New York Times,* October 17, 2004.

42. Interview with Colin Powell, January 2010; interview with former senior U.S. official; interview with Daniel Kurtzer, December 2009; and interview with Richard Armitage, February 2010.

43. Interview with Daniel Kurtzer, December 2009; and interview with Richard Armitage, February 2010.

44. Jane Perlez, "Bush and Sharon Find Much in Common," *New York Times*, March 21, 2001.

45. Interview with Richard Armitage, February 2010.

46. Michel Foucault, *Society must be defended: Lectures at the Collège de France, 1975–76* (New York: Macmillan, 2003); and Avi Shlaim, "Ariel Sharon's War Against the Palestinians," *Logos*, Vol. 3, No. 3 (Summer 2004).

47. William A. Orme Jr., "The World: The Middle East; Disillusionment With a Friend"; and Remarks by Secretary of State Colin L. Powell at the American Israel Public Affairs Committee, Washington, D.C., March 19, 2001.

48. Jane Perlez, "Powell Assails Israel for Gaza Incursion," *New York Times*, April 18, 2001; and Jane Perlez, "Bush and Sharon Find Much in Common."

49. Interview with Colin Powell, January 2010.

50. Jane Perlez, "C.I.A. Chief Going to Israel In Effort to Maintain Calm," *New York Times*, June 6, 2001; George Tenet, *At the Center of the Storm: My Years at the CIA* (New York: HarperCollins, 2008), pp. 93–97; and interview with Hussein Agha, September 2009.

51. Interviews with David Wurmser, March 2010.

52. Interview with Anthony Zinni, December 2009.

53. Aaron David Miller, *The Much Too Promised Land: America's Elusive Search for Arab-Israeli Peace* (New York: Bantam, 2008), p. 332.

54. William Safire, "Ariel Makes His Point to George," *New York Times*, June 28, 2001.

55. William A. Orme Jr., "Shock Wave in Israel Over Bush's Comment," *New York Times*, June 28, 2001.

56. Interview with Christopher Meyer, September 2009.

57. "Bush calls for Mid-East restraint," BBCNews.com, August 11, 2001.

58. Catherine Bertini, United Nations Mission Report, August 11–19, 2002, http://domino.un.org/bertini_rpt.htm.

59. Miller, *The Much Too Promised Land*, p. 333.

60. "ZOA Criticizes President Bush For Again Refusing To Move U.S. Embassy To Jerusalem—Reneging On Campaign Promise," ZOA.org, December 22, 2006. The promise to move the U.S. embassy to Jerusalem has been delivered with some regularity in Washington, D.C., without action being taken by the U.S. State Department.

61. Patrick E. Tyler, "Shock of Sept. 11 Is Making Americans More Supportive of Israel, Polls Suggest," *New York Times*, May 13, 2002.

62. Toby Harnden, "Israeli Attacks Expose Divisions in Bush Cabinet," *Telegraph*, August 4, 2001.

63. Jane Perlez and Patrick E. Tyler, "Before Attacks, U.S. Was Ready To Say It Backed Palestinian State," *New York Times*, October 2, 2001.

64. Interview with Christopher Meyer, September 2009.

65. Manuel Perez-Rivas, "Bush Vows to Rid the World Of Evil-Doers," CNN.com, September 16, 2001.

66. George W. Bush, "Act of War Statement," September 12, 2001, http://news.bbc.co.uk/2/hi/americas/1540544.stm.

67. Interviews with David Wurmser, March 2010.

68. Bernard Lewis, "The Roots of Muslim Rage," *Atlantic Monthly*, September 1990; and Bernard Lewis, "What Went Wrong," *Atlantic Monthly*, January 2002.

69. Interview with Christopher Patten, September 2009; and interviews with David Wurmser, March 2010.

70. Dick Cheney, Address to the Commonwealth Club, San Francisco, Calif., August 7, 2002.

71. Interviews with David Wurmser, March 2010.

72. Jim Mann, *Rise of the Vulcans: The History of Bush's War Cabinet* (New York: Viking, 2004), p. 266.

73. Interview with Richard Armitage, February 2010.

74. Interview with Colin Powell, January 2010; and interviews with David Wurmser, March 2010.

75. Interviews with David Wurmser, March 2010.

76. Ibid.

77. Interview with Elliott Abrams, November 2009; interview with William Inboden, September 2009; and interview with Stephen Hadley, January 2010.

78. William Kristol, "The Axis of Appeasement," *Weekly Standard*, August 26–September 2, 2002.

79. Interviews with David Wurmser, March 2010; and interview with Richard Armitage, February 2010.

80. Interview with Richard Armitage, February 2010; and interviews with David Wurmser, March 2010.

81. Muasher, *The Arab Center*, p. 112.

82. Ibid.

83. Rueven Koret, "Sharon Warns West Against Appeasement," *Israel Insider*, October 4, 2001.

84. Jane Perlez and Katharine Q. Seelye, "U.S. Strongly Rebukes Sharon for Criticism of Bush, Calling It 'Unacceptable'," *New York Times*, October 6, 2001.

85. James Bennet, "Sharon Apologizes Over Dispute With U.S.," *New York Times*, October 7, 2001.

86. Perlez and Seelye, "U.S. Strongly Rebukes Sharon for Criticism of Bush, Calling It 'Unacceptable'."

87. Interview with Condoleezza Rice, December 2009; interview with Salam Fayyad, December 2009; and George W. Bush, Speech at the United Nations General Assembly, November 10, 2001.

88. Interview with Condoleezza Rice, December 2009; and interview with Michael Gerson, December 2009.

89. Serge Schmemann, "Arafat Thankful for Bush Remark about 'Palestine'," *New York Times*, November 12, 2001; Douglas Jehl, "Saudi Says Bush's Words May Soothe Arab Feelings," *New York Times*, November 23, 2001; and David Graves, "Britons on Alert Against More Suicide Bomb Blasts," *Telegraph*, October 7, 2001.

90. Muasher, *The Arab Center*, p. 113.

91. Interview with Richard Perle, November 2009; and James Bennet, "Sharon Apologizes Over Dispute With U.S." *New York Times*, October 7, 2001.

92. "Arafat Horrified by Attacks, but Thousands of Palestinians Celebrate; Rest of World Outraged," FOXNews.com, September 12, 2001; William Bennett, "Where Bush Rewards Terror," *Washington Post*, March 20, 2002.

93. Chris Mitchell, "Remembering 9/11," CBNNews.com, September 11, 2008.

94. Elaine Sciolino, "Senators Urge Bush Not to Hamper Israel," *New York Times*, November 17, 2001.

95. Susan Rosenbluth, "VP Candidate Joseph Biden: 'Tehran's Favorite Senator'," *Jewish Voice and Opinion*, September 2008; and interview with Chuck Hagel, November 2009.

96. Interview with Richard Armitage, February 2010; and interview with Marwan Muasher, February 2010.

97. The Madrid Conference and the Oslo Accords were diplomatic efforts undertaken by the George H. W. Bush and Bill Clinton administrations, respectively, to advance peace among the Israelis, Palestinians, and Arabs.

98. Colin Powell, Speech at McConnell Center for Political Leadership, University of Louisville, Kentucky, November 19, 2001, http://www.theguardian.com/world/2001/nov/20/afghanistan.israel.

99. Interview with Michael Doran, November 2009; interview with Richard Perle, November 2009; interview with Elliott Abrams, November 2009; and interview with Douglas Feith, November 2009.

100. Interview with Anthony Zinni, December 2009; and interview with Richard Armitage, February 2010.

101. Interview with Stephen Hadley, January 2010; interview with Elliott Abrams, November 2009; and interview with Michael Doran, November 2009.

102. Judith Miller, "U.S. to Block Assets It Says Help Finance Hamas Killers," *New York Times*, December 4, 2001; Mike Allen, "Bush Freezes Suspected Terror Assets," *Washington Post*, December 4, 2001.

103. Elaine Sciolino, "U.S. Jewish Leaders Say Bush Was Blunt In Assailing Arafat," *New York Times*, December 14, 2001.

104. "Arafat: End Suicide Bombings," *Associated Press*, December 16, 2001; and Suzanne Goldenberg, "Killing of Militant Undermines Arafat's Ceasefire Appeal," *Guardian*, December 18, 2001.

105. Written correspondence with Mohammad Dahlan, January 2010.

106. Interview with Condoleezza Rice, December 2009.

107. The President's International Affairs Budget Request for FY 2003, Hearing Before the Committee on International Relations, House of Representatives, February 6, 2002, http://commdocs.house.gov/committees/intlrel/hfa77532.000/hfa77532_0f.htm.

108. Hanan Greenberg, "Karine-A Organizer Convicted," YNetnews.com, July 29, 2009. For other views see: Trita Parsi, *Treacherous Alliance: The Secret Dealings of Israel, Iran, and the United States* (New Haven, Conn.: Yale University Press, 2007), p. 234; and Brian Whitaker, "The Strange Affair of Karine-A," *Guardian*, January 21, 2002.

109. Interview with Condoleezza Rice, December 2009.

110. Interview with Christopher Patten, September 2009.

111. Arafat's regime should in no way be taken as a model of democracy.

112. Jimmy Carter, "America Can Persuade Israel to Make a Just Peace," *New York Times*, April 21, 2002; and Interview with Hrair Balian, February 2010.

113. Karma Nabulsi, "Arafat the Obstacle Has Been Exposed as a Myth," *Guardian*, November 15, 2005.

114. Interview with Stephen Hadley, January 2010; interview with Douglas Feith, November 2009; and interview with Elliott Abrams, November 2009.

115. Interview with Elias Zananiri, December 2009; interview with Marwan Muasher, February 2006; and Muasher, *The Arab Center*, p. 118.

116. "Powell Says Arafat Takes Responsibility," *New York Times*, February 14, 2002.

117. Bob Woodward, *Bush at War: Inside the Bush White House* (New York: Simon and Schuster, 2002), p. 297.

118. Interview with Michael Gerson, December 2009; and David Frum, *The Right Man: The Surprise Presidency of George W. Bush* (New York: Random House, 2003), p. 238.

119. George W. Bush, State of the Union Address, January 29, 2002, http://georgewbush-whitehouse.archives.gov/stateoftheunion/2002/.

120. Geoffrey Aronson, "Settlement Monitor," *Journal of Palestine Studies*, Vol. 26, No. 4 (Summer 1997), pp. 138–148; and Geoffrey Aronson, "Settlement Monitor," *Journal of Palestine Studies*, Vol. 35, No. 4 (Summer 2006), p. 132.

121. Yasser Arafat, "The Palestinian Vision of Peace," *New York Times*, February 3, 2002.

122. Muasher, *The Arab Center*, p. 118; and interview with Marwan Muasher, February 2010.

123. Elisabeth Bumiller and Thom Shanker, "Sharon Tells Bush He Expects Creation of Palestinian State," *New York Times*, February 8, 2002.

124. Seymour Hersh, "The Debate Within," *New Yorker*, March 11, 2002.

125. Ewen MacAskill, "Isolated Powell disowns Arafat," *Guardian*, July 2, 2002.

126. David E. Sanger, "Bush Officials End Support Of Sharon's Tough Stance," *New York Times*, March 7, 2002.

127. Robert Kagan and William Kristol, "Cheney Trips Up," *Weekly Standard*, April 1, 2002.

128. Interview with Anthony Zinni, December 2009.

129. Press Release, Office of the Secretary General, United Nations, March 28, 2002; and Muasher, *The Arab Center*, p. 123.

130. Muasher, *The Arab Center,* p. 134; and interview with Marwan Muasher, February 2010.

131. George W. Bush, "Speech on Middle East Violence," White House Rose Garden, April 4, 2002.

132. Serge Schmemann with Todd S. Purdum, "U.S. Says Powell Demanded Pullout by Israeli Forces," *New York Times*, March 15, 2002; and interview with Marwan Muasher, February 2010. The Saudi peace plan, "proposed by Saudi Arabia's crown prince Abdullah, offered a "normalization" of relations with Israel if it withdrew from all occupied Arab land, accepted a Palestinian state with Jerusalem as its capital and agreed to the return of Palestinian refugees"; "Arab League Endorses Saudi Peace Plan, *Guardian*, March 28, 2002.

133. Interview with Richard Armitage, February 2010; and Ed Vulliamy, "Israel: We have nothing to hide in Jenin," *Guardian*, April 21, 2002.

134. "Jenin: IDF Military Operations," *Human Rights Watch*, Vol. 14, No. 3 (E) (May 2002); and Report of the Secretary-General Prepared Pursuant to General Assembly Resolution ES-10/10 adopted on May 7, 2002, July 30, 2002.

135. David E. Sanger, "As Fighting Rages, Bush Demands Israeli Withdrawal," *New York Times*, April 7, 2002.

136. Interview with Christopher Meyer, September 2009.

137. Memo from David Manning to Tony Blair, March 14, 2002.

138. Interview with Christopher Meyer, September 2009.

139. Interview with Jonathan Powell, September 2009; interview with Colin Powell, January 2010; and interview with Christopher Meyer, September 2009.

140. Interview with Colin Powell, January 2010.

141. Interview with Christopher Meyer, September 2009.

142. Interview with Richard Armitage, February 2010.

143. Woodward, *Bush at War*, pp. 323–325.

144. Interview with Colin Powell, January 2010.

145. Interview with Richard Armitage, February 2010.

146. Interview with Colin Powell, January 2010.

147. Ibid.

148. Interview with Anthony Zinni, December 2009; and interview with Chuck Hagel, November 2009.

149. Interview with Anthony Zinni, December 2009.

150. Interview with Colin Powell, January 2010.

151. Interview with Richard Haass, November 2009.

CHAPTER 3

1. Bob Woodward, *State of Denial* (New York: Simon and Schuster, 2004), pp. 45–47; and Eric Rouleau, "Trouble in the Kingdom," *Foreign Affairs*, Vol. 84, No. 4 (July/August 2002).

2. Interview with Chuck Hagel, November 2009; and interview with Jonathan Powell, September 2009.

3. The Road Map, initially developed by the Jordanians and the European Union, outlined a parallel process of peace negotiations with reciprocal concessions to be made by both Israelis and Palestinians. After receiving the backing of the United States, the Quartet (the European Union, United Nations, United States, and Russia) proposed the document as the basis for renewed negotiations.

4. Morton Klein, "ZOA Strongly Praises Defense Secretary Rumsfeld For Distancing Himself From The Term 'Occupied Territory,'" zoa.org, August 7, 2002.

5. Interview with Elliott Abrams, November 2009; interviews with David Wurmser, March 2010; interview with Michael Doran, November 2009; interviews with David Welch, November and December 2009; interview with Richard Perle, November 2009; and interview with Douglas Feith, November 2009.

6. Richard Perle et al., "A Clean Break: A New Strategy for Securing the Realm," Institute for Advanced Strategic and Political Studies, Washington, D.C., July 1996, http://www.iasps.org/strat1htm.

7. Bernard Lewis and James Woolsey, "King and Country," *Wall Street Journal*, October 29, 2003.

8. The "Jordanian option" was the idea that Jordan would take control over the West Bank. Interview with Fayaz Tarawneh, September 2009; interview with Jawad Annani, September 2009; and interview with Ayman Safadi, September 2009.

9. Interview with Richard Armitage, February 2010.

10. Meyrav Wurmser et al., "An Emerging Palestinian Alternative: Can Peace Be Achieved Through Democracy?" Hudson Institute, June 6, 2002; Sharon Sadeh, "Arafat's Opposition in New York," *Ha'aretz*, May 20, 2002; and Robert Pollock, "We Need A Palestinian Mandela," *Wall Street Journal*, May 17, 2002.

11. Interview with Chuck Hagel, November 2009.

12. The Eagle Forum, March 3, 2010, accessed April 4, 2010, http://www.eagleforum.org/Scoreboard/#.

13. Interview with Chuck Hagel, November 2009.

14. Interview with Tom DeLay, May 2010; Tom DeLay, "The Imperative for Action," Houston Forum, August 21, 2002; and William Kristol, "Memorandum: Iraq and the War on Terror," Project for a New American Century, August 21, 2002.

15. Interview with Christopher Meyer, September 2009.

16. Interview with Richard Perle, November 2009.

17. Interview with Christopher Patten, September 2009.

18. Frank Rich, "The Booing of Wolfowitz," *New York Times*, May 11, 2002; and Dick Armey, *Hardball* with Chris Matthews, MSNBC Transcript, May 1, 2002.

19. Jack Tapper, "Retiring, Not Shy," *New York Times*, September 1, 2002.

20. Interview with Tom DeLay, May 2010; and Barbara Slavin, "Don't give up 1967 lands, DeLay tells Israel lobby," *USA Today*, April 23, 2002.

21. Interview with Tom DeLay, May 2010.

22. James Inhofe, "America's Stake in the War on Terrorism," U.S. Senate, December 4, 2001; David Brooks, "Bill Frist's New South," *Weekly Standard*, January 27, 2003; Bill Frist, Interview with American Friends of Likud, accessed February 12, 2009: http://www.thelikud.org/channels/features/feature_02.html; David Kirkpatrick, "Frist Draws Criticism From Some Church Leaders," *New York Times*, April 22, 2005; W. Gregory Pope, Sermon on the Eighth Sunday After Pentecost, "How is it all going to end?" Crescent Hill Baptist Church, Louisville, Kentucky, July 22, 2007; and "PM Sharon met with US Senator Mitch McConnell," Press Release from the Prime Minister's Office, Israel, November 16, 2004.

23. Inhofe, "America's Stake in the War on Terrorism."

24. Sam Brownback, Address to the Israeli Knesset, July 19, 2004; Marissa Brostoff, "Far Right Israelis Get Boost From Senator," *Forward*, October 10, 2007; and Binyamin

Elon et al., "Rehabilitation of the Palestinian Refugees," The Israel Initiative, January 2008, http://www.israelinitiative.org/.

25. Interview with Tom DeLay, May 2010; and Andrew Kohut, "American Views of the Mideast Conflict," *New York Times*, May 14, 2002.

26. Interview with Christopher Meyer, September 2009; interview with Jonathan Powell, September 2009; interview with Christopher Patten, September 2009; interview with Chuck Hagel, November 2009; and interview with Fayaz Tarawneh, September 2009.

27. Interviews with David Wurmser, March 2010.

28. Elisabeth Bumiller, "Seeking to Stem Growing Political Fury, Bush Sends Conservative to Pro-Israel Rally," *New York Times*, April 16, 2002; and Transcript, National Solidarity Rally With Israel, Washington, D.C., April 15, 2002.

29. Robert Kagan and William Kristol, "Cheney Trips Up," *Weekly Standard*, April 1, 2002.

30. Charles Krauthammer, "Arafat's Harvest of Hate," *Washington Post*, March 26, 2002.

31. Editorial, "Redrawing the Map," *Wall Street Journal*, March 7, 2002.

32. William Safire, "Ending the War Process," *New York Times*, March 11, 2002.

33. Fouad Ajami, "Arafat's War," *Wall Street Journal*, March 29, 2002.

34. John Derbyshire, "Why don't I care about the Palestinians?" *National Review*, May 9, 2002.

35. Transcript, National Solidarity Rally With Israel.

36. Benjamin Netanyahu, Speech to the U.S. Senate, Washington, D.C., April 11, 2002.

37. Interview with Paul Wolfowitz, February 2010.

38. Transcript, National Solidarity Rally With Israel.

39. Interview with Paul Wolfowitz, February 2010; Abraham McLaughlin and Gail Russell Chaddock, "Christian right steps in on Mideast," *Christian Science Monitor*, April 16, 2002; and "Press Release: Bauer Calls Attacks on Israel 'Moral Outrage,'" Our American Values, Merrifield, Va., April 1, 2002, http://www.ouramericanvalues.org.

40. Elisabeth Bumiller, "Seeking to Stem Growing Political Fury, Bush Sends Conservative to Pro-Israel Rally"; Richard L. Berke and David E. Sanger, "Some in Administration Grumble As Aide's Role Seems to Expand," *New York Times*, May 13, 2002; and Todd S. Purdum, "Bush to Set Out Broad Approach on Mideast Soon, Powell Says," *New York Times*,

June 12, 2002.

41. Craig Horowitz, "Israel's Christian Soldiers," *New York*, September 22, 2003.

42. Interview with Marwan Muasher, February 2010.

43. Interview with Jonathan Powell, September 2009.

44. Bob Woodward, *Bush at War: Inside the Bush White House* (New York: Simon and Schuster, 2002), p. 282.

45. Interview with Elliott Abrams, November 2009; and George W. Bush, State of the Union Address, January 28, 2003.

46. Interview with Stephen Hadley, January 2010; and interview with Condoleezza Rice, December 2009.

47. Interview with Condoleezza Rice, December 2009.

48. Interview with Elliott Abrams, November 2009; and George W. Bush, *Decision Points* (New York: Crown, 2010), p. 397.

49. Interview with Stephen Hadley, January 2010. Emphasis added.

50. Interview with Tim Goeglein, November 2009.

51. David E. Sanger, "Back to Earth; War Was Easy," *New York Times*, April 21, 2002.

52. Bush, *Decision Points*, p. 145; interview with Michael Gerson, December 2009; and interview with William Inboden, September 2009.

53. Interview with Condoleezza Rice, December 2009; interviews with David Wurmser, March 2010; and interview with Elliott Abrams, November 2009.

54. Interview with Jonathan Powell, September 2009; and Efraim Halevy, *Man in the Shadows: Inside the Middle East Crisis With the Man Who Led the Mossad* (New York: St. Martin's Press, 2006), p. 244.

55. Bush, *Decision Points*, p. 403; interview with Stephen Hadley, January 2010; interview with Elliott Abrams, November 2009; and interview with William Inboden, September 2009.

56. Interview with Douglas Feith, November 2009.

57. Charles Krauthammer, "Peace Through Democracy," *Washington Post*, June 28, 2002.

58. Interview with Rowan Williams, September 2009.

59. Natan Sharansky with Shira Wolosky Weiss, *Defending Identity: Its Indispensable Role in Protecting Democracy* (New York: Public Affairs, 2009); and Jean-Jacques Rousseau (trans. Maurice Cranston), *The Social Contract* (London: Penguin Books, 1968), p. 64.

60. Christopher Patten; interview with former senior U.S. official; interview with Richard Armitage, February 2010; and Donald Rumsfeld, *Known and Unknown: A Memoir* (New York: Penguin, 2011), p. 500.

61. Sharansky, "Where do we go from here?" *Jerusalem Post*, May 3, 2002; and George W. Bush, Speech, June 24, 2002.

62. Interview with Condoleezza Rice, December 2009; interview with Colin Powell, January 2010; Miller, *The Much Too Promised Land*, p. 348; Bush, *Decision Points*, pp. 398, 404; Elliott Abrams, *Tested By Zion: The Bush Administration and the Israeli-Palestinian Conflict* (Cambridge: Cambridge University Press, 2013), pp. 40–43.

63. Interview and correspondence with Douglas Feith, November 2009.

64. Interviews with David Wurmser, March 2010; interview with Richard Armitage, February 2010; and interview with Colin Powell, January 2010.

65. Interview with Richard Armitage, February 2010.

66. Interview with Condoleezza Rice, December 2009; and Ewen MacAskill, "Isolated Powell disowns Arafat," *Guardian*, July 2, 2002.

67. Interview with Colin Powell, January 2010; interview with Condoleezza Rice, December 2009; and Miller, *The Much Too Promised Land*, p. 348.

68. Bush, *Decision Points*, p. 404.

69. Natan Sharansky and Ron Dermer, *The Case for Democracy: The Power of Freedom to Overcome Tyranny and Terror* (New York: Public Affairs, 2004), p. 234; and interview with Richard Armitage, February 2010.

70. Interview with Condoleezza Rice, December 2009.

71. Interview with Condoleezza Rice, December 2009; interview with Michael Gerson, December 2009; and interview with Douglas Feith, November 2009.

72. Interview with Condoleezza Rice, December 2009; Karen Hughes, *Ten Minutes from Normal* (New York: Penguin, 2004), pp. 279–282.

73. "Bush says its time for action," CNN.com, November 6, 2001.

74. Bush, *Decision Points*, p. 146.

75. Interview with Condoleezza Rice, December 2009; and William Kristol, "Getting Serious," *Weekly Standard*, November 19, 2001.

76. Natan Sharansky, "Where do we go from here?"; Natan Sharansky, "Democracy for Peace," American Enterprise Institute World Forum, Beaver, Colo., June 20, 2002; and interview with Richard Perle, November 2009.

77. Sharansky, *The Case for Democracy*, pp. 240–241.

78. Dan Ephron and Tamara Lipper, "Sharansky's Quiet Role," *Newsweek,* July 15, 2002.

79. Interview with Elliott Abrams, November 2009; interview with Richard Perle, November 2009; and interview with Colin Powell, January 2010.

80. Interview with Richard Perle, November 2009.

81. Interview with Marwan Muasher, February 2010.

82. Sharansky, "Where do we go from here?"; and George W. Bush, Speech, June 24, 2002.

83. Ibid.

84. Ariel Sharon, Speech, Herzliya Conference, December 4, 2002.

85. Interview with Tom DeLay, May 2010.

86. Alison Mitchell, "Pro-Israel Voices of 2 Parties Praise Bush Mideast Speech," *New York Times*, June 26, 2002.

87. "In Israel—Bauer Presents Prime Minister Sharon with Letter of Support," Press Release, Our American Values, Merrifield, Va., July 1, 2002.

88. Halevy, *Man in the Shadows*, pp. 234–235.

89. Sharansky, *The Case for Democracy*, p. 244.

90. George W. Bush, "Speech," June 24, 2002.

91. Interviews with David Welch, November and December 2009; and interview with Salam Fayyad, December 2009.

92. Sharansky, "Democracy for Peace."

93. Interview with Salam Fayyad, December 2009.

94. Hanan Ashrawi, "The Case for Democracy in the Palestinian National Narrative," Baker Institute for Public Policy, Rice University, Houston, Texas, October 20, 2009, pp. 9, 8, 21.

95. Interview with Richard Armitage, February 2010.

96. "Iran-Contra Figure to Lead Democracy Efforts Abroad," *Washington Post*, February 3, 2005.

97. Peter Goodman, "Ending Battle, Wolfowitz Resigns From World Bank," *Washington Post*, May 18, 2007.

98. "Report: Cheney 'Furious' That Bush Wouldn't Pardon Scooter Libby," *Washington Post*, February 17, 2009.

99. Ian Urbina, "24 States' Laws Open to Attack After Campaign Finance Ruling," *New York Times*, January 22, 2010; and James C. McKinley, Jr., "DeLay is Convicted in Texas Donation Case," *New York Times*, November 24, 2010.

100. "Security and Reform in Israel and the Palestinian Territories," World Economic Forum, Dead Sea, Israel, May 22, 2005; Inigo Gilmore, "Israelis warn Blair not to 'interfere' in Palestinian process," *Telegraph*, December 19, 2004; Jeremy Bowen, "Arafat Investigated," Transcript, BBC.com, November 9, 2003; and Phoebe Greenwood, "Ehud Olmert convicted in corruption case," *Guardian,* July 10, 2012. Ultimately, Olmert was cleared of two of the three corruption charges but found guilty of the third.

101. Interview with Condoleezza Rice, December 2010.

102. Vita Bekker, "Israeli Leaders Hit With Wave of Scandals," *Forward*, August 25, 2006; and Ofra Edelman, "Former president Moshe Katsav begins testimony on rape charge," *Ha'aretz*, January 10, 2010.

103. Marc Perlman, "Olmert Corruption Probe Exposes Murky Role of US Money in Elections," *Forward*, May 23, 2008.

104. Interviews with David Wurmser, March 2010.

105. Interview with senior U.S. official; and Patrick Cockburn, "Ministers quizzed on links to Russian Mafia," *Independent*, June 17, 1997.

106. Bekker, "Israeli Leaders Hit With Wave of Scandals."

107. Alexander Solzhenitsyn, *The Gulag Archipelago* (New York: Harper and Row, 1973), pp. 313–314.

108. Muasher, *The Arab Center*, pp. 161–163; and interview with Marwan Muasher, February 2010.

109. Julia Preston and James Bennet, "At U.N., US Calls for End to the Siege of Arafat," *New York Times*, September 24, 2002; United Nations, Security Council: Draft Resolution, S/2002/1061, September 23, 2002; and United Nations, Security Council Resolution, SC/2001/7158, September 9, 2001.

110. Steven R. Weisman, "US Still Trying to Unfold Mideast Road Map" *New York Times*, November 15, 2002.

111. Ariel Sharon, Speech, Herzliya Conference, December 4, 2002.

112. Interview with Marwan Muasher, February 2010.

113. Interview with Richard Armitage, February 2010.

114. Flynt Leverett and Hillary Mann Leverett, "Road Map to Nowhere," *Foreign Policy*, July 1, 2009.

115. Muasher, *The Arab Center*, pp. 174–175; and interview with Marwan Muasher, February 2010.

116. Interview with Christopher Patten, September 1, 2009.

117. Interview with Kofi Annan, November 2010.

118. Interview with Marwan Muasher, February 2010; and interview with David Wurmser, March 2010.

119. Interview with Colin Powell, January 2010; and Tony Karon, "What to Do First: Israel or Iraq?" *Time*, August 30, 2002.

120. Bob Simon, "Zion's Christian Soldiers," *60 Minutes*, October 6, 2002, http://www.cbsnews.com/8301-18560_162-524268.html.

121. Maureen Dowd, "Rapture and Rupture," *New York Times*, October 6, 2002.

122. Laurie Goodstein, "Evangelical Figures Oppose Religious Leaders' Broad Antiwar Sentiment," *New York Times*, October 5, 2002.

123. Serge Schmemann, "Sharon Postpones a Trip to Florida Next Month," *New York Times*, August 23, 2002.

124. Interview with Tom DeLay, May 2010; interview with Richard Armitage, February 2010; interview with Marwan Muasher, February 2010; interview with Christopher Patten, September 2009; and interview with Jonathan Powell, September 2009.

125. Interviews with David Wurmser, March 2010.

126. Elliott Abrams, ed., *The Influence of Faith: Religious Groups and U.S. Foreign Policy* (Lanham, Md.: Rowman and Littlefield, 2001); Elliott Abrams and David G. Dalin, eds., *Secularism, Spirituality, and the Future of American Jewry* (Washington, D.C.: Ethics and Public Policy Center, 1999); and Elliott Abrams, *Faith or Fear: How Jews Can Survive in a Christian America* (New York: Free Press, 1997).

127. Interview with Jean Geran, September 2009; and interview with senior U.S. official.

128. Interview with senior U.S. official.

129. Interview with Stephen Hadley, January 2010.

130. Interviews with David Welch, November and December 2009; and interview with John Bellinger III, February 2010.

131. Interview with Philip Zelikow, January 2010.

CHAPTER 4

1. This quote from George W. Bush's First Inaugural Address on January 20, 2001, was originally inspired by Nahum 1:3 (King James Version).

2. The latter phrase was drawn from Psalm 35: 4 (King James Version).

3. Revelation 5: 9–12, (King James Version); and Lewis E. Jones, "There is Power in the Blood," 1899.

4. George W. Bush, State of the Union Address, January 29, 2003.

5. Interview with Condoleezza Rice, December 2009.

6. Interview with Colin Powell, January 2010.

7. Interviews with David Wurmser, March 2010.

8. Interview with Richard Perle, November 2009; Richard Perle et al., "A Clean Break: A New Strategy for Securing the Realm," Institute for Advanced Strategic and Political Studies, Washington, D.C., July 1996, http://www.iasps.org/strat1.htm; interviews with David Wurmser, March 2010; and interview with Douglas Feith, November 2009.

9. Interview with Colin Powell, January 2010.

10. Interview with Richard Armitage, February 2010.

11. Interview with Paul Wolfowitz, February 2010; interview with Colin Powell, January 2010; interview with Douglas Feith, November 2009; and Douglas Feith, *War and Decision* (New York: HarperCollins, 2008), pp. 207–208.

12. Interview with Richard Armitage, February 2010.

13. Interview with Fayaz Tarawneh, September 2009; interview with Christopher Meyer, September 2009; and interview with Jonathan Powell, September 2009.

14. Interview with Douglas Feith, November 2009.

15. Interviews with David Wurmser, March 2010; and interview with Richard Armitage, February 2010.

16. Interview with Fayaz Tarawneh, September 2009; interview with Christopher Meyer, September 2009; and interview with Jonathan Powell, September 2009.

17. Feith, *War and Decision*, p. 511; and interview with Christopher Meyer, September 2009.

18. Interview with Douglas Feith, November 2009; and interview with Paul Wolfowitz, February 2010.

19. Yitzhak Benhorin, "Doug Feith: Israel didn't push for Iraq War," YNews.com, May 13, 2008.

20. Interview with Chuck Hagel, November 2009.

21. Philip Zelikow denied the substance of this statement in an interview with the author and also in an exchange of letters with John Mearsheimer and Stephen Walt in the *London Review of Books*, May 25, 2006, http://www.lrb.co.uk/v28/n10/letters. The public record, however, suggests otherwise.

22. "Transcript: Special Report/Analysis: Latest on War in Iraq," National Public Radio (NPR), *Talk of the Nation*, March 24, 2003; Tim Ripley, "Special forces western shadow," *Scotsman*, March 28, 2003; and Aluf Benn, "PM intimates will only respond to Iraq attack if population hit," *Ha'aretz*, September 26, 2010.

23. Dan Collins, "Israel to U.S.: Don't Delay Iraq Attack," CBSnews.com, August 16, 2002.

24. James Bennet, "Israel says Iraq War Would Benefit the Region," *New York Times*, February 27, 2003; and Ephraim Halevy, "Future Developments in the Middle East and the Persian Gulf," Munich Conference on Security Policy, February 9, 2003.

25. Aluf Benn, "Enthusiastic IDF Awaits War in Iraq," *Ha'aretz*, February 17, 2003.

26. Robert Fisk, "The wartime deceptions: Saddam is Hitler and it's not about oil," *Independent*, January 27, 2003.

27. Stephen Farrell et al., "Attack Iran the Day Iraq War Ends, Demands Israel," *London Times*, November 5, 2002.

28. Interviews with David Wurmser, March 2010.

29. Interview with Colin Powell, January 2010; and Colin Powell, Speech before the United Nations, New York, February 5, 2003.

30. Matthew Rycroft, Memorandum to David Manning, July 23, 2002.

31. David E. Rosenbaum, "Bush and Pentagon Wrangle Over War Budget Request," *New York Times*, February 27, 2003.

32. Bob Woodward, *Plan of Attack* (New York: Simon and Schuster, 2004), p. 260.

33. George W. Bush, Speech, American Enterprise Institute, Washington, D.C., February 26, 2003.

34. During an interview, a former senior U.S. official detailed examples of Abbas's corruption but did not supply any documentation.

35. Interview with Jonathan Powell, September 2009.

36. Ze'ev Schiff, "U.S.-EU crisis is death blow to 'road map,'" *Ha'aretz*, February 12, 2003. The Quartet was a body representing the European Union, the United Nations, the United States, and Russia which was charged with the task of mediating the Israeli-Palestinian conflict.

37. James Bennet, "Sharon Says Europe Is Biased In Favor of the Palestinians," *New York Times*, January 20, 2003.

38. Isaiah 49: 6–9 (King James Version).

39. George W. Bush, Commencement Address to the U.S. Coast Guard, New London, Conn., May 21, 2003, http://www.presidency.ucsb.edu/ws/?pid+915#axzz2gAaCjMzU.

40. Trita Parsi, *Treacherous Alliance: The Secret Dealings of Israel, Iran, and the United States* (New Haven, Conn.: Yale University Press, 2007), pp. 245–257.

41. The Middle East Road Map, April 30, 2003.

42. Hanan Ashrawi, "The Case for Democracy in the Palestinian National Narrative," James A. Baker III Institute for Public Policy, Rice University, Houston, Texas, October 20, 2009; Marwan Muasher, *The Arab Center* (New Haven, Conn.: Yale University Press, 2008), p. 195; and interview with Marwan Muasher, February 2010.

43. Ashrawi, "The Case for Democracy in the Palestinian National Narrative."

44. Interview with Douglas Feith, November 2009.

45. Interview with Condoleezza Rice, December 2009.

46. Interview with Richard Perle, November 2009.

47. Steven R. Weisman, "White House Is Pressing Israelis To Take Initiatives in Peace Talks," *New York Times*, April 17, 2003.

48. Steven R. Weisman, "April 20–26; The Battle Lines Start in Washington," *New York Times*, April 27, 2003.

49. Newt Gingrich, "Transforming the State Department," Address, American Enterprise Institute, Washington, D.C., April 22, 2003.

50. Steven R. Weisman, "Bush's Goal: Balancing a Host of Opposing Forces," *New York Times*, May 1, 2003; and Charles Krauthammer, "Shades of Oslo," *Washington Post*, June 6, 2003.

51. Interview with Douglas Feith, November 2009.

52. James Bennet, "The World: Crossing Jordan; The Exit That Isn't On Bush's 'Road Map,'" *New York Times*, May 18, 2003.

53. Steven R. Weisman, "Bush Insists Mideast Peace Plan Will Move Forward, Despite Bombings," *New York Times*, May 20, 2003.

54. Ami Eden, "Bush's Maneuvers Bewilder Jerusalem and Activists," *Forward*, June 6, 2003.

55. Israeli Cabinet Statement on Road Map and 14 Reservations, May 25, 2003.

56. Interview with Elias Zananiri, December 2009; interview with Mohammad Dahlan, January 2010; and interview with Hussein Agha, September 2009.

57. "News Summary A12," *New York Times*, May 27, 2003.

58. Interview with Marwan Muasher, February 2010.

59. George W. Bush, Statement, Sharm El-Sheikh, Egypt, June 3, 2003; and interview with Jonathan Powell, September 2009.

60. Ariel Sharon, Statement, The Aqaba Summit, Aqaba, Jordan, CNN.com, June 4, 2003; Mahmoud Abbas, Statement, The Aqaba Summit, Aqaba, Jordan, CNN.com, June 4, 2003; and George W. Bush, Statement, The Aqaba Summit, Aqaba, Jordan, CNN.com, June 4, 2003.

61. Muasher, *The Arab Center*, p. 192; and interview with Marwan Muasher, February 2010.

62. Ira Stoll, "Sharansky: More Harm Than Good," *New York Sun*, June 4, 2003.

63. Interview with Stephen Hadley, January 2010; and interview with Condoleezza Rice, December 2009.

64. Interview with Douglas Feith, November 2009; interview with Elliott Abrams, November 2009; interview with Richard Perle, November 2009; and interview with Michael Doran, November 2009.

65. Greg Myre, "Israel to Begin Controversial Phase of Barrier Construction," *New York Times*, June 14, 2004.

66. "Five Years After the International Court of Justice Advisory Opinion: A Summary of the Humanitarian Impact of the Barrier," UN Office for the Coordination of Humanitarian Affairs, Occupied Palestinian Territory, July 2009, http://www.ochaopt.org/. On July 9, 2004, the International Court of Justice ruled that the wall was illegal, noting that its path affected about 80 percent of settlers living in the occupied Palestinian territories. Furthermore, the Court argued that "the construction of the wall and its associated regime 'create a "fait accompli' on the ground that could well become permanent, in which case…[it] would be tantamount to *de facto* annexation." The court further concluded that the wall prohibits

the Palestinian people from exercising their right to self-determination. "Legal Consequences of the Construction of a Wall in the Occupied Palestinian Territory," Advisory Opinion, International Court of Justice, 2004/28, http://icj-cij.org/.

67. Interview with Michael Gerson, December 2009.

68. Glenn Kessler, "Scowcroft is Critical of Bush," *Washington Post*, October 16, 2004; and interview with Richard Armitage, February 2010.

69. Interview with Jawad Anani, September 2009; interview with Abdelsalam Majali, September 2009; interview with Fayaz Tarawneh, September 2009; interview with Ayman Safadi, September 2009; written correspondence with Mohammad Dahlan, January 2010; interview with Salam Fayyad, December 2009; and interview with Elias Zananiri, December 2009.

70. Moshe Arens, "The fence, revisited," *Ha'aretz*, October 28, 2008.

71. Amos Harel, "Shin Bet: Palestinian truce main cause for reduced terror," *Ha'aretz*, January 2, 2006.

72. "Christian Zionists Criticized for Opposition to 'Road Map,'" *Associated Press*, July 24, 2003.

73. Interview with Tom DeLay, May 2010; and Steven R. Weisman, "U.S. Plans Fast Aid for Gaza Projects," *New York Times,* July 10, 2003.

74. David Firestone, "DeLay Is to Carry Dissenting Message On a Mideast Tour," *New York Times*, July 25, 2003.

75. James Bennet, "Palestinians Must Bear Burden of Peace, DeLay Tells Israelis," *New York Times,* July 31, 2003.

76. "Nurturing a Fragile Mideast Peace," *New York Times*, July 30, 2003; and interview with Tom DeLay, May 2010.

77. "News Summary A2-8," *New York Times*, July 30, 2003; and interview with Tom DeLay, May 2010.

78. James Morrison, "Israel Gives Thanks," *Washington Times*, November 27, 2003.

79. Sheryl Gay Stolberg, "Democrats Put On Defensive By G.O.P.'s Israel Policy," *New York Times*, August 2, 2003.

80. Steven R. Weisman, "U.S. May Reduce Aid Plan to Get Israel to Halt Barrier," *New York Times,* August 5, 2003.

81. David Stout, "Bush and Powell Try to Quell Exit Rumors," *New York Times*, August 6, 2003.

82. Richard W. Stevenson and Edmund L. Andrews, "Bush Orders Move to Freeze Assets of Hamas Charities," *New York Times*, August 23, 2003.

83. Muasher, *The Arab Center,* p. 196; and interview with Marwan Muasher, February 2010.

84. James Bennet, "Israel Announces Official Decision to Remove Arafat," *New York Times*, September 12, 2003.

85. Elisabeth Bumiller, "Bush Blames Arafat for Undercutting Peace Efforts," *New York Times,* September 18, 2003.

86. David Stout, "Bush Reaffirms That Israel Has Right to Defend 'Homeland,'" *New York Times*, October 6, 2003.

87. Syria Accountability and Lebanese Sovereignty Restoration Act of 2003, http://gpo.gov/; and interview with Tom DeLay, May 2010.

88. Interview with Paul Wolfowitz, February 2010; and interviews with David Wurmser, March 2010.

89. Brian Knowlton, "House Panel Votes to Impose Sanctions on Syria," *New York Times,* October 8, 2003.

90. "Pat Robertson's 'nuke' idea draws protest," CNN.com, October 10, 2003.

91. Steven R. Weisman, "A Bush Aide Criticizes Israel for Not Doing More to Foster Peace," *New York Times*, December 12, 2003; and Steven R. Weisman, "U.S. Rescinds Part of Loan Guarantees to Israel," *New York Times*, November 26, 2003.

92. Richard Bernstein, "Sharon Threatens to Impose Split on Palestinians," *New York Times*, December 19, 2003.

93. Ariel Sharon, Speech, Herzliya Conference, Herzliya, Israel, December 18, 2003.

94. Ibid.

95. Richard Bernstein, "Sharon Threatens to Impose Split on Palestinians"; and Steven R. Weisman, "U.S. May Support Israeli Approach on Leaving Gaza," *New York Times*, February 13, 2004.

96. Steven R. Weisman, "U.S. Urges Israel to Work With Arabs in Any Pullout," *New York Times*, February 26, 2004.

97. Interview with Elliott Abrams, November 2009; interview with Condoleezza Rice, December 2009; and interview with James Wolfensohn, November 2009.

98. George W. Bush, Address to the AIPAC Policy Conference, Washington, D.C., May 18, 2004; Greg Myre, "Sharon Says He Expects Cabinet to Approve Gaza Pullout,"

New York Times, June 2, 2004.

99. James Bennet, "Sharon Tells U.S. That Pullback Will Not Replace Peace Plan," *New York Times*, February 20, 2004.

100. Interviews with David Wurmser, March 2010.

101. Interview with Richard Armitage, February 2010.

102. Interview with Chuck Hagel, November 2009; and interview with Anthony Zinni, December 2009.

103. Interview with Daniel Kurtzer, December 2009.

104. Interview with Condoleezza Rice, December 2009.

105. Baruch Kimmerling, *Politicide: Ariel Sharon's War Against the Palestinians* (London: Verso, 2003).

106. Ariel Sharon, Letter to George W. Bush and appended Disengagement Plan, April 14, 2004.

107. Interview with Dov Weisglass, *Ha'aretz*, October 8, 2004.

108. Steven R. Weisman, "Israel Pushes White House to Accept Its Withdrawal Plan," *New York Times*, March 27, 2004.

109. Brian Knowlton, "Bush Supports Sharon's Plan to Withdraw From the Gaza Strip," *New York Times*, April 14, 2004.

110. Interviews with David Wurmser, March 2010.

111. Interview with Daniel Kurtzer, December 2009.

112. Ibid.

113. Ibid.

114. George W. Bush, Letter to Ariel Sharon, April 14, 2004.

115. Ibid.; Dov Weisglass, Letter to Condoleezza Rice, April 18, 2004; Daniel Kurtzer, "The Settlements Facts," *Washington Post*, June 14, 2009; interview with Daniel Kurtzer, December 2009; and Glenn Kessler, "Israelis Claim Secret Agreement With U.S.," *Washington Post*, April 24, 2008.

116. George W. Bush, Letter to Ariel Sharon, April 14, 2004; Dov Weisglass, Letter to Condoleezza Rice, April 18, 2004; interview with Elliott Abrams, November 2009; Elliott Abrams, "Hillary is Wrong About Settlements," *Wall Street Journal*, June 26, 2009; and Glenn Kessler, "Israelis Claim Secret Agreement With U.S.," *Washington Post*, April 24, 2008.

117. Interviews with David Wurmser, March 2010.

118. Elissa Gootman, "Sharon Says His Pledge Not to Harm Arafat No Longer Holds," *New York Times*, April 24, 2004.

119. Greg Myre, "Sharon Says He Expects Cabinet to Approve Gaza Pullout," *New York Times,* June 2, 2004.

120. James Bennet, "Israel Says Demolition Of Homes Will Proceed," *New York Times*, May 17, 2004.

121. Steven Erlanger, "Sharon Issues Bids for New Housing Units for Settlers," *New York Times*, August 18, 2004.

122. Steven R. Weisman, "U.S. Now Said to Support Growth for Some West Bank Settlements," *New York Times,* August 21, 2004.

123. Erlanger, "Sharon Issues Bids for New Housing Units for Settlers."

124. Richard W. Stevenson, "Bush Campaign Plays Up Pro-Israel Stance," *New York Times*, May 15, 2004.

125. Elisabeth Bumiller, "Bush Cites Doubt America Can Win War on Terror," *New York Times*, August 31, 2004.

126. Ron Suskind, "Faith, Certainty and the Presidency of George W. Bush," *New York Times*, October 17, 2004.

127. Steven R. Weisman, "Kerry and Bush Compete for the Role of Israel's Best Friend," *New York Times*, August 31, 2004.

128. Roger Cohen, "Linked Fates; Israel, the U.S. and the Age of Terror," *New York Times,* November 7, 2004.

CHAPTER 5

1. Interview with J. Scott Carpenter, November 2009; interview with Michael Gerson, December 2009; interviews with David Wurmser, March 2010; Joel C. Rosenberg, "Two Great Dissidents: Natan Sharansky's Vision, and President Bush's," *National Review*, November 19, 2004; William Kristol, "Honoring Democracy," *Weekly Standard*, January 24, 2005; Elisabeth Bumiller, "Bush's Book Club Picks a New Favorite," *New York Times*, January 31, 2005; and John F. Dickerson, "What the President Reads," CNN.com, January 10, 2005.

2. George W. Bush, Second Inaugural Address, January 20, 2005.

3. Interview with Jonathan Powell, September 2009; Dan Balz and Jim VandeHei, "Bush Speech Not a Sign of Policy Shift, Officials Say," *Washington Post*, January 22, 2005; Natan Sharansky and Ron Dermer, *The Case for Democracy: The Power of Freedom to Overcome Tyranny and Terror* (New York: Public Affairs, 2004); and Charles Krauthammer, "Democratic Realism: An American Foreign Policy for a Unipolar World," Irving Kristol Lecture, American Enterprise Institute, Washington, D.C., February 2004.

4. Sharansky and Dermer, *The Case for Democracy*, xxxi, 72, 278; George W. Bush, Second Inaugural Address; and Elisabeth Bumiller, "Bush's Book Club Picks a New Favorite," *New York Times*, January 31, 2005, http://www.nytimes.com/2005/01/31/politics/31letter.html.

5. George W. Bush, State of the Union Address, February 2, 2005.

6. Interview with Michael Gerson, December 2009.

7. Interview with Condoleezza Rice, December 2009; and Condoleezza Rice, Opening Statement, U.S. Senate Foreign Relations Committee, January 18, 2005.

8. Interview with Condoleezza Rice, December 2009; interviews with David Wurmser, March 2010; and interview with Hussein Agha, September 2009.

9. Condoleezza Rice, "A Balance of Power that Favors Freedom," Wriston Lecture, New York City, New York, October 1, 2002, http://www.manhattaninstitute.org/html/wl2002.htm.

10. Interviews with David Wurmser, March 2010.

11. Interviews with David Welch, November and December 2009; and interview with J. Scott Carpenter, November 2009.

12. Bob Woodward, *The War Within* (New York: Simon and Schuster, 2008), p. 8; and interview with Stephen Hadley, January 2010.

13. Personnel Announcement, The White House Office of the Press Secretary, February 2, 2005.

14. Interviews with David Welch, November and December 2009; and interview with Philip Zelikow, January 2010.

15. Interview with Elliot Abrams, November 2009.

16. Glenn Kessler, *The Confidante: Condoleezza Rice and the Creation of the Bush Legacy* (New York: St. Martin's, 2007), pp. 128–129.

17. Interviews with David Wurmser, March 2010; and interview with Tom DeLay, May 2010.

18. Dick Cheney, Inauguration Day Interview With Don Imus, Transcript Excerpt, NBCnews.com, January 20, 2005.

19. Edwin Black, "Spat Erupts Between Neocons, Intelligence Community," *Forward*, December 31, 2004; David Johnston, "Pentagon Analyst Gets 12 Years for Disclosing Data," *New York Times*, January 20, 2006.

20. Eric Schmitt, "Senior Official Behind Many of the Pentagon's Most Contentious Policies is Stepping Down," *New York Times*, January 27, 2005.

21. "Review of Pre-Iraqi War Intelligence Activities of the Office of the Undersecretary of Defense for Policy," Inspector General's Report, Department of Defense, Washington, D.C., February 9, 2007, p. 4.

22. "Report on Intelligence Activities Relating to Iraq Conducted by the Policy Counterterrorism Evaluation Group and the Office of Special Plans Within the Office of the Undersecretary of Defense for Policy," Select Committee On Intelligence, U.S. Senate, June 2008.

23. Hearing before the Committee on Foreign Relations, U.S. Senate, April 12, 2005; and Dafna Linzer and Charles Babington, "Former Colleague Says Bolton Abused Power at State Department," *New York Times*, April 13, 2005.

24. Interview with Condoleezza Rice, December 2009; interviews with David Wurmser, March 2010; and interviews with David Welch, November and December 2009.

25. France opened an inquiry into the death of Arafat after a Swiss lab found elevated levels of radioactive material on Arafat's clothing. Sarah DiLorenzo, "France Opens Murder Inquiry into Arafat's Death," *Associated Press*, August 28, 2012.

26. Interview with Salam Fayyad, December 2009; and Steven Erlanger, "Israel Lauds New Palestinian Leader For Moves to Stop Attacks," *New York Times*, January 23, 2005.

27. Ariel Sharon, Speech, Sharm El-Sheikh Summit, Egypt, CNN.com, February 8, 2005; and Mahmoud Abbas, Speech, Sharm El-Sheikh Summit, Egypt, CNN.com, February 8, 2005.

28. Interviews with David Welch, November and December 2009.

29. George W. Bush, Second Inaugural Address; and Steven Erlanger, "Israel Cuts Back Military Action to Answer Abbas," *New York Times*, January 29, 2005.

30. Steven Weisman, "Bush Praises Choice of Abbas as New Palestinian President," *New York Times*, January 10, 2005.

31. Interview with Condoleezza Rice, December 2009; interviews with David Welch,

November and December 2009; interview with Philip Zelikow, January 2010; and Steven R. Weisman and Steven Erlanger, "U.S. Prods Israel For Hard Choices On Palestinians," *New York Times*, February 7, 2005.

32. United Nations Security Resolution, SC/2005/1559, September 2, 2004.

33. Transcript of interview with Condoleezza Rice, *Washington Post*, December 15, 2006; Steven R. Weisman and Hassan M. Fattah, "U.S. Recalls Its Envoy In Syria, Linking Nation to Beirut Blast," *New York Times*, February 16, 2005; United Nations Security Resolution, SC/2005/1559, September 2, 2004; and Flynt Leverett, "Don't Rush on the Road to Damascus," *New York Times*, March 2, 2005.

34. Hassan M. Fattah, "Hezbollah Backs Syria, Challenging Lebanese Opposition," *New York Times*, March 7, 2005; and Steven R. Weisman, "Lebanon Needs to Act First for Syria to Exit, Envoy Says," *New York Times*, March 14, 2005.

35. George W. Bush, Remarks at Concert Noble, Brussels, Belgium, February 21, 2005, http://online.wsj.com/article/SB110899882887960041.html.

36. Chris McGreal, "Blair Presses Reluctant Abbas into London Conference," *Guardian*, February 28, 2005.

37. Condoleezza Rice, Opening Remarks, Conference on Palestinian Reform, London, March 1, 2005.

38. Interview with Hussein Agha, September 2009; interview with Elias Zananiri, December 2009; interview with Fayaz Tarawneh, September 2009; and interviews with David Welch, November and December 2009.

39. Barbara Starr, "Four-star general faces demotion over misspending allegations," CNN.com, August 15, 2012.

40. Greg Myre, "Israel to Expand Largest West Bank Settlement," *New York Times*, March 22, 2005.

41. Interview with Condoleezza Rice, December 2009; Greg Myre, "Israel Rejects Referendum on Gaza Plan," *New York Times*, March 29, 2005.

42. Interview with Daniel Kurtzer, December 2009; and Steven Erlanger, "Rice Says U.S. Opposes Israeli Plan For Settlement Expansion," *New York Times*, March 26, 2005.

43. Greg Myre, "Israel Hints at Possible Delay in Gaza Withdrawal," *New York Times*, April 18, 2005.

44. George W. Bush and Ariel Sharon, Press Conference, Crawford, Texas, April 11, 2005, http://www.presidency.ucsb.edu/ws/?pid=73672; emphasis added.

45. Ibid.

46. Ibid.

47. Interview with former senior U.S. official; and Steven R. Weisman, "Bush Agrees to Give Envoy Bigger Role in Mideast Talks," *New York Times*, May 28, 2005.

48. Interview with Tom DeLay, May 2010; interview with Elias Zananiri, December 2009; written correspondence with Mohammed Dahlan, January 2010; and Steven Weisman, "Palestinians to Get Aid, With Strings, In House Plan," *New York Times*, May 6, 2005.

49. Steven Erlanger, "It's Official: Gaza Pullout is Delayed," *New York Times*, May 10, 2005.

50. The President's News Conference with President Mahmoud Abbas of the Palestinian Authority, May 26, 2005.

51. Interview with James Wolfensohn, November 2009; and Alvaro de Soto, End of Mission Report, May 2007, http://image.guardian.co.uk/sys-files/Guardian/documents/2007/06/12/DeSotoReport.pdf.

52. Interview with Christopher Patten, September 2009.

53. Greg Myre, "Palestinian Factions Agreed to Extend Truce With Israel," *New York Times*, March 18, 2005.

54. Jeremy Sharp, "Egypt: 2005 Presidential and Parliamentary Elections," CRS Report for Congress, Congressional Research Service, Washington, D.C., September 21, 2005; Robin Wright, "Iraq Winners Allied With Iran Are the Opposite of U.S. Vision," *Washington Post*, February 14, 2005; Report on Palestinian Elections for Local Councils: Round One, National Democratic Institute for International Affairs, Washington, D.C., 2005, ndi.org; and Hussein Dakroub, "Hezbollah Wins Easy Victory in Elections in Southern Lebanon," *Washington Post*, June 6, 2005.

55. Condoleezza Rice, Remarks at the American University of Cairo, Egypt, June 20, 2005; emphasis added.

56. John Kifner, "Hezbollah-led Lebanese Slate Celebrates," *New York Times*, June 7, 2005; Dakroub, "Hezbollah Wins Easy Victory in Elections in Southern Lebanon"; Christine Hausner, "Abbas Postpones Elections in Move Rejected By Hamas," *New York Times*, June 5, 2005; and Steven R. Weisman, "U.S. Ready to See Hezbollah in Lebanon Role," *New York Times*, March 10, 2005.

57. Report on Palestinian Elections for Local Councils: Round One; and Steven Erlanger, "Hamas Wins Key Elections in West Bank," *New York Times*, December 16, 2005.

58. Interview with Elias Zananiri, December 2009; interview with Hussein Agha, September 2009; interview with Fayaz Tarawneh, September 2009; and written correspondence with Mohammad Dahlan, January 2010.

59. Interview with Elliot Abrams, November 2009.

60. Report on Palestinian Elections for Local Councils: Round One; and Erlanger, "Hamas Wins Key Elections in West Bank."

61. Written correspondence with Mohammad Dahlan, January 2010; interview with Elias Zananiri, December 2009; and interview with Fayaz Tarawneh, September 2009.

62. De Soto, End of Mission Report.

63. Ariel Sharon, Letter to George W. Bush and appended Disengagement Plan, April 14, 2004, http://www.mfa.gov.il/mfa/foreignpolicy/peace/mfadocuments/pages/exchange%20of%20letters%20sharon-bush%2014-apr-2004.aspx.

64. Yoram Dinstein, *The International Law of Belligerent Occupation* (Cambridge: Cambridge University Press, 2009) pp. 309–312; and Fourth Geneva Convention, Article 33, August 12, 1949, http://www.icrc.org/ihl/COM/380-600038?OpenDocument.

65. Ibid.

66. "Abbas Voices Joy At Gaza Pullout," BBCnews.com, August 19, 2005; "Abbas: Pullout a 'great moment,'" BBCnews.com, September 13, 2005; and Kessler, *The Confidante*, p. 131.

67. Address by Prime Minister Ariel Sharon to the High Level Plenary Meeting of the 60th Session of the United Nations, New York City, New York, September 15, 2005; emphasis added.

68. Joel Brinkley, "Rice Urges Israel to Aid Palestinian Election," *New York Times*, September 21, 2005.

69. Steven R. Weisman, "Estimate Revised on When Iran Could Make Nuclear Bomb," *New York Times*, August 3, 2005.

70. Seymour Hersh, "The Iran Plans," *New Yorker*, April 17, 2006.

71. Interviews with David Wurmser, March 2010; David Wurmser, *Tyranny's Ally: America's Failure to Defeat Saddam Hussein* (Washington, D.C.: AEI Press, 1999); and Jeffrey Goldberg, "The Point of No Return," *Atlantic*, September 2010.

72. Wurmser, *Tyranny's Ally*, pp. 74, 109.

73. "28 Religious Leaders Appeal to Bush For Special Envoy to Push for Middle East Peace," *New York Times*, January 13, 2005.

74. Ron Kampeas, "On Somber Day, DeLay's Spirits Raised by Pro-Israel's Group's Support," *Jewish Telegraphic Agency*, October 3, 2005; E.J. Kessler, "Houston Jews Feeling Mixed On Indictment of Tom DeLay," *Forward*, October 7, 2005; and Bill of Indictment, District Court of Travis County, Texas, 147th Judicial District, September 28, 2005.

75. Schmitt, "Senior Official Behind Many of the Pentagon's Most Contentious Policies Is Stepping Down."

76. Interview with Elliot Abrams, November 2009.

77. Steven Erlanger, "Abbas Raises Questions About His Meeting With Sharon," *New York Times*, October 6, 2005.

78. Brinkley, "Rice Urges Israel to Aid Palestinian Election."

79. Kessler, *The Confidante*, pp. 130–131.

80. Richard Perle, "Why Did Bush Blink on Iran? (Ask Condi)," *Washington Post*, June 25, 2006.

81. De Soto, End of Mission Report, pp. 7–9.

82. Kessler, *The Confidante*, pp. 122, 131–133; interview with James Wolfensohn, November 2009; interview with Elliot Abrams, November 2009; and interview with Michael Doran, November 2009.

83. De Soto, End of Mission Report, p. 7.

84. Joint Press Conference with Condoleezza Rice, Javier Solana, and James Wolfensohn, Jerusalem, November 15, 2005; and The Agreement on Movement and Access, State of Palestine Permanent Observer Mission to the United States, November 15, 2005, http://www.un.int/wcm/content/site/palestine/cache/offonce/pid/12018.

85. Arnon Regular, "Palestinian Militants Ransack Former Gush Katif Greenhouses," *Ha'aretz*, February 10, 2006; interview with Condoleezza Rice, December 2009; interview with James Wolfensohn, November 2009; Kessler, *The Confidante*, p. 134; and De Soto, End of Mission Report.

86. Steven Weisman, "Rice Again Asks Israel and Palestinians to Bridge Divide," *New York Times*, November 14, 2005.

87. The Agreement on Movement and Access One Year On, United Nations Office for the Coordination of Humanitarian Affairs, Jerusalem, November 2006, ochaopt.org.

88. Kessler, *The Confidante*, p. 131.

89. Weisman, "Rice Again Asks Israel and Palestinians to Bridge Divide."

90. Interviews with David Wurmser, March 2010; and interview with Richard Armitage, February 2010.

91. Steven Erlanger, "Mideast Knot: One Map, Many Paths," *New York Times*, October 14, 2005.

92. De Soto, End of Mission Report.

93. Condoleezza Rice, "The Promise of Democratic Peace," *Washington Post*, December 11, 2005.

94. Ibid.

CHAPTER 6

1. Condoleezza Rice, "Transformational Diplomacy: Shaping U.S. Diplomatic Posture in the 21st Century," School of Foreign Service, Georgetown University, Washington, D.C., January 18, 2006, http://2001-2009.state.gov/secretary/rm/2006/5936.htm.

2. Steven Erlanger, "Sharon in Coma; New Party Faces a Crucial Test," *New York Times*, January 6, 2006.

3. Interviews with David Welch, November and December 2009; interview with J. Scott Carpenter, November 2009; written correspondence with Mohammad Dahlan, January 2010; interview with Fayaz Tarawneh, September 2009; and Martin Indyk, *Innocent Abroad: An Intimate Account of American Peace Diplomacy in the Middle East* (New York: Simon and Schuster, 2009), pp. 282–283.

4. Quartet Statement on Palestinian Legislative Council Elections, London, England, December 28, 2005, http://2001-2009.state.gov/r/pa/prs/ps/2005/58532.htm.

5. Alvaro de Soto, End of Mission Report, May 2007, pp. 15–16, http://image. guardian.co.uk/sys-files/Guardian/documents/2007/06/12/DeSotoReport.pdf.

6. Glenn Kessler, *The Confidante: Condoleezza Rice and the Creation of the Bush Legacy* (New York: St. Martin's, 2007), pp. 138–139; Final Report on the Palestinian Legislative Council Elections, National Democratic Institute, Washington, D.C., January 25, 2006, http://www.ndi.org/files/2068_ps_elect_012506.pdf; Scott Wilson, "Hamas Sweeps Palestinian Elections, Complicating Peace Efforts in Mideast," *Washington Post*, January 27, 2006; and interview with Hrair Balian, February 2010.

7. George W. Bush, Press Conference Transcript, *Washington Post*, January 26, 2006; and Glenn Kessler, "Bush Is Conciliatory in Accepting Vote of Hamas," *Washington Post*, January 27, 2006.

8. Condoleezza Rice, Remarks at the World Economic Forum, Davos, Switzerland, January 26, 2006.

9. Steven R. Weisman, "Bush Leaving Door Open for a Change By Hamas," *New York Times*, January 26, 2006.

10. Interview with J. Scott Carpenter, November 2009.

11. Ibid.

12. Steven Erlanger, "Egypt Insists that Hamas Stop Violence," *New York Times*, February 2, 2006.

13. De Soto, End of Mission Report, p. 12.

14. Greg Myre, "Putin Considers Inviting Hamas Leaders to Moscow," *New York Times*, February 10, 2006.

15. Steven Weisman, "U.S. Digs in on Withholding Aid to Hamas Government," *New York Times*, February 17, 2006.

16. Joel Brinkley, "Saudis Reject U.S. Request to Cut Off Aid to Hamas," *New York Times*, February 23, 2006.

17. Quartet Statement on Palestinian Legislative Council Elections, January 30, 2006; interview with Kofi Annan, November 2010; and De Soto, End of Mission Report.

18. Khaled Abu Toameh, "Regime Change in Palestine?" *Wall Street Journal*, January 24, 2006; Arnon Regular, "Hamas Captures Control of Student Council at Nablus University," *Ha'aretz*, November 29, 2005; "Hamas Wins Student Elections at Hebron University," *Ha'aretz*, March 16, 2005; Associated Press, "Mainstream Fateh Edges Ahead of Rival Hamas in W. Bank Student Council Elections," *Ha'aretz*, April 14, 2005; Khaled Abu Toameh, "Hamas, Islamic Jihad Win Birzeit Student Elections," *Jerusalem Post*, December 11, 2003; and Aaron Pina, "Palestinian Elections," Congressional Research Service, Washington, D.C., February 9, 2006.

19. Kessler, *The Confidante*, p. 131.

20. Shaul Mishal and Avraham Sela, *The Palestinian Hamas: Vision, Violence, and Coexistence* (New York: Columbia University Press, 2000), p. vii; and Thomas L. Friedman, "Let Hamas Sink or Swim on Its Own," *New York Times*, February 17, 2006.

21. State Department, "U.S. Assistance to the Palestinians," Press Release, Jerusalem,

February 7, 2005, http://2001-2009.state.gov/r/pa/prs/ps/2005/41870.htm; interview with Tom DeLay, May 2010; and interview with Elias Zananiri, January 2010.

22. Omran Risheq, "Why Palestinians Will Not Hold Elections, At Least for Now," *Arab Reform Bulletin*, July 21, 2010; and Khalil Shikaki, "With Hamas In Power: Impact of Palestinian Domestic Developments on Options for the Peace Process," Working Paper 1, Crown Center for Middle East Studies, Brandeis University, Waltham, Mass., February 2007, pp. 5–6.

23. Interview with Condoleezza Rice, December 2009; interview with Stephen Hadley, January 2010; and Steven R. Weisman, "Rice Admits U.S. Underestimated Hamas Strength," *New York Times*, January 30, 2006.

24. Ibid.

25. Written correspondence with Mohammad Dahlan, January 2010; and interview with former senior U.S. official.

26. Interview with J. Scott Carpenter, November 2009.

27. De Soto, End of Mission Report, p. 21.

28. As with Arafat's government, Hamas's approach should not be regarded as a model of democratic politics.

29. Interview with former senior U.S. official; and interview with J. Scott Carpenter, November 2009.

30. Interview with former senior U.S. official; and interviews with David Wurmser, March 2010.

31. Interview with Condoleezza Rice, December 2009.

32. Written correspondence with Mohammad Dahlan, January 2010.

33. Interview with former senior U.S. official.

34. Interview with former senior U.S. official; interviews with David Wurmser, March 2010; and Ali Waked, "Fayyad Confiscates $7 Million from Dahlan," Ynetnews.com, July 8, 2007.

35. George W. Bush, State of the Union Address, January 31, 2006.

36. Ibid.

37. James Wolfensohn, "Office of the Special Envoy for Disengagement," *Washington Post*, February 25, 2006.

38. Steven Erlanger, "Europeans Offer $144 Million Aid to Palestinians," *New York Times*, February 28, 2006.

39. Michael Slackman, "As Syria's Influence in Lebanon Wanes, Iran Moves In," *New York Times*, March 13, 2006.

40. Richard Perle et al., "A Clean Break: A New Strategy for Securing the Realm," Institute for Advanced Strategic and Political Studies, Washington, D.C., July 1996, http://www.iasps.org/strat1.htm; interviews with David Wurmser, March 2010; and Dick Cheney, Remarks to the American Israel Public Affairs Committee, washingtonpost.com, March 7, 2006.

41. Interview with John Bellinger, February 2010.

42. George W. Bush, "Democracy and the Future of Iraq: Address to Freedom House," Washington, D.C., March 29, 2006.

43. Steven Weisman, "U.S. May Shift Aid From Palestinian Authority to Relief Agencies," *New York Times*, March 13, 2006; interview with Larry Garber, July 2007; and Acquisition & Assistance Policy Directive, U.S. Agency for International Development, Washington, D.C., March 24, 2004.

44. George W. Bush, Speech before the Foundation for Defense of Democracies, Washington, D.C., NYTimes.com, March 14, 2006.

45. Interview with Philip Zelikow, January 2010.

46. Bush, "Democracy and the Future of Iraq: Address to Freedom House."

47. Conal Urquhart, "Gaza on the Brink of Implosion as Aid Cut-off Starts to Bite," *Guardian*, April 16, 2006.

48. "Assessment of the Future Security Risks in the Occupied Palestinian Territory," United Nations, April 11, 2006, http://unispal.un.org/unispal.nsf/eed216406b50bf648525 6ce10072f637/5f45b9f386865ccb8525715a0068823b?OpenDocument.

49. Steven R. Weisman, "U.S. Softens Position on Palestinian Aid," *New York Times*, May 10, 2006.

50. Steven Erlanger and Greg Myre, "Israel Will Buy Supplies for Gaza Hospitals, Premier Says," *New York Times*, May 19, 2006.

51. Temporary International Mechanism Progress Report, European Commission, January 18, 2008, http://eeas.europa.eu/palestine/tim/index_en.htm; and Steven Erlanger, "Israeli Leader Promises Jordan He Will Meet Abbas Soon," *New York Times*, June 8, 2006.

52. Steven Weisman, "Aid Plan for Palestinians Hits U.S. Roadblock," *New York Times*, June 14, 2006; and Steven Weisman, "Europe Plan to Aid Palestinians Stalls Over U.S. Salary Sanctions," *New York Times*, June 15, 2006.

53. Steven Weisman, "U.S. Agrees to Plan for Stipends for Some Palestinians," *New York Times*, June 17, 2006.

54. Mahmoud Ahmadinejad, Letter to George W. Bush, washingtonpost.com, May 9, 2006.

55. Interview with Tom DeLay, May 2010; and Steven Erlanger, "Abbas Enlists Prisoners to Unsettle Hamas," *New York Times*, May 27, 2006.

56. Barak Ravid et al., "Olmert to Haaretz: Two State Solution, or Israel is Done For," *Ha'aretz*, November 29, 2007; and "Olmert Suspends Withdrawal Plan," BBCnews.com, August 18, 2006.

57. Greg Myre, "Israeli Foreign Minister and Abbas Meet at Economic Forum," *New York Times*, May 22, 2006.

58. Erlanger, "Abbas Enlists Prisoners to Unsettle Hamas."

59. Shikaki, "With Hamas In Power."

60. Ibid.

61. The National Conciliation Document of the Prisoners, Jerusalem Media and Communication Centre, June 28, 2006, http://unispal.un.org/unispal.nsf/0/7ccbf1fc97fe8bb98525719b005efcf2.

62. Ibid.

63. Avi Issacharoff and Shlomi Shamir, "Fateh, Hamas Reach Agreement on Division of Security Forces," *Ha'aretz*, June 18, 2006.

64. Barak Ravid, "In 2006 Letter to Bush, Haniyeh Offered Compromise with Israel," *Ha'aretz*, November 14, 2008.

65. Khaled Abu Toameh, "Hamas: Probe Arms Transfer to Abbas," *Jerusalem Post*, July 17, 2006.

66. Ehud Olmert, Address to Joint Meeting of the U.S. Congress, washingtonpost.com, May 24, 2006; and "A Viable Palestinian State," Editorial, *New York Times*, May 25, 2006.

67. "Beach Strike Shakes Hamas Ceasefire," CNN.com, June 9, 2006; Chris McGreal, "Death on the Beach: Seven Palestinians Killed as Israeli Shells Hit Family Picnic," *Guardian*, June 10, 2006; and Steven Erlanger, "Hamas Fires Rockets Into Israel, Ending 16-month Truce," *New York Times*, June 11, 2006.

68. "Q & A: Gilad Shalit," BBCnews.com, November 30, 2009; and Steven Erlanger, "Tensions Rise After Israeli is Kidnapped," *New York Times*, June 26, 2006.

69. Steven Erlanger, "Seizures Show New Israel Line Against Hamas," *New York Times*, June 30, 2006.

70. Helen Cooper, "G-8 Leaders Set Deadline For Iranian Response," *New York Times*, June 29, 2006.

71. Greg Myre and Steven Erlanger, "Clashes spread to Lebanon as Hezbollah raids Israel—Africa & Middle East—International Herald Tribune," *New York Times,* July 12, 2006.

72. "Annan demands Lebanon ceasefire," BBCnews.com, July 20, 2006.

73. "EU: Israeli Use of Force 'Disproportionate,'" *Ha'aretz*, July 14, 2006; and Jim Rutenberg, "Bush Gives Qualified Support for Israel's Strikes," *New York Times*, July 14, 2006.

74. Interview with Stephen Krasner, November 2009.

75. Interview with former U.S. official; and interview with Kofi Annan, November 2010.

76. Interview with Kofi Annan, November 2010; "G8 Press Release," July 16, 2006; and Press Release, United Nations, un.org, July 20, 2006.

77. Jim Rutenberg et al., "Despite Joint Statement on Mideast, Strains Emerge as U.S. Supports Israel's Campaign," *New York Times*, July 17, 2006; and David Stout and Christine Hauser, "Bush Sees a Chance for Change to Sweep Middle East," *New York Times*, July 28, 2006.

78. David Cloud and Helen Cooper, "U.S. Speeds Up Bomb Delivery for Israel," *New York Times*, July 22, 2006; and Helen Cooper and David Sanger, "U.S. Plan Seeks to Wedge Syria Away from Iran," *New York Times*, July 23, 2006.

79. David Stout, "Bush Ties Battle With Hezbollah to War on Terror," *New York Times*, July 31, 2006.

80. Interviews with David Welch, November and December 2009; interview with Richard Armitage, February 2010; interview with former senior U.S. official; and interview with Philip Zelikow, January 2010. The phrase "birth pangs" is drawn from an apocalyptic verse: Matthew 24: 8 (King James Version).

81. Interviews with David Welch, November and December 2009.

82. Tony Karon, "Condi in Diplomatic Disneyland," *Time*, July 26, 2006; Edward Wong and Michael Slackman, "In Break With Bush, Iraqi Leader Assails Israel," *New York Times*, July 19, 2006.

83. Interviews with David Welch, November and December 2009; and interview with Condoleezza Rice, December 2009.

84. Interviews with David Welch, November and December 2009.

85. Karon, "Condi in Diplomatic Disneyland"; and interviews with David Welch, November and December 2009.

86. Interview with former senior U.S. official.

87. Interview with former senior U.S. official.

88. "Fatal Strikes: Israel's Indiscriminate Attacks Against Civilians," *Human Rights Watch*, Vol. 18, No. 3 (August 2006).

89. "Israel/Lebanon: Israel Responsible for Qana Attack," hrw.org, July 30, 2006.

90. Helen Cooper, "From Carnage in Lebanon, A Concession," *New York Times*, July 31, 2006; and interview with former senior U.S. official.

91. Seymour Hersh, "Watching Lebanon," *New Yorker*, August 21, 2006.

92. Helen Cooper and David Sanger, "A Talk at Lunch that Shifted the Stance on Iran," *New York Times*, June 4, 2006.

93. Interview with former senior U.S. official.

94. Interview with Kofi Annan, November 2010; and Steven Erlanger and Hassan M. Fattah, "Israel Halts Bombing After Deadly Strike," *New York Times*, July 30, 2006.

95. "Key Republicans Break With President Bush On Mideast," CNN.com, July 31, 2006.

96. Editorial, "Poll Finds Support for Hizbullah's Retaliation," Beirut Center for Research and Information, Lebanon, July 29, 2006.

97. David Cloud, "Israel Asks U.S. to Ship Rockets With Wide Blast," *New York Times*, August 11, 2006.

98. David Kirkpatrick, "For Evangelicals, Supporting Israel is 'God's Foreign Policy,'" *New York Times*, November 14, 2006; and Max Blumenthal, "Hagee: Pro-Israel, Anti-Semitic?" *Nation*, May 23, 2008.

99. Sidney Blumenthal, "How Bush Rules," *New York Times,* September 24, 2006.

100. Jim Rutenberg, "Bush Defends U.S. Handling of Lebanese Conflict, Asserting that Hezbollah is the Loser," *New York Times*, August 15, 2006; Steven Erlanger, "Israel Begins to Pull Its Troops Out of Lebanon," *New York Times*, August 15, 2006; and United Nations, Security Council Resolution, SC/2006/1701, August 11, 2006.

101. Michael Slackman and John O'Neil, "Hezbollah Chief Leads Huge Rally," *New York Times*, September 22, 2006.

102. Glen P. Hastedt, *Encyclopedia of American Foreign Policy* (New York: Facts on File, 2004), p. 201.

103. Winograd Commission, "Winograd Commission Final Report," cfr.org, January 30, 2008, http://www.cfr.org/israel/winograd-commission-final-report/p15385.

104. Report of the Commission of Inquiry on Lebanon pursuant to Human Rights Council Resolution S-2/1, Human Rights Council, United Nations General Assembly, November 23, 2006, p. 26, http://www2.ohchr.org/english/bodies/hrcouncil/docs/specialsession/A.HRC.3.2.pdf.

105. Hillel Fendel, "Olmert: War in Lebanon Promotes Withdrawal Plan," Israel-NationalNews.com, August 2, 2006; and "Olmert Suspends 'Withdrawal Plan,'" BBC-News.com, August 18, 2006.

106. Steven Erlanger, "Israeli Leader Allows West Bank Construction Bids," *New York Times*, September 4, 2006.

107. David Stout, "Libby Resigns His Post; Rove's Fate Remains Unresolved," *New York Times*, October 28, 2005.

108. Steven R. Weisman, "Wolfowitz Resigns, Ending Long Fight at World Bank," *New York Times*, May 18, 2007; and David S. Cloud and Mark Mazzetti, "Prewar Intelligence Unit at Pentagon is Criticized," *New York Times*, February 9, 2007.

109. Interviews with David Wurmser, March 2010.

110. Francis Fukuyama, "After Neoconservatism," *New York Times Magazine*, February 19, 2006.

111. *Iran Freedom Support Act*, Pub. L. No. 109-203, 109th Cong., 2nd. Sess. (September 28, 2006).

112. Interview with Elliot Abrams, November 2009; interview with Stephen Krasner, November 2009; interview with John Bellinger, February 2010; and *Palestinian Anti-Terrorism Act of 2006*, Pub. L. No. 109-446, 109th Cong., 2nd. Sess. (December 21, 2006).

113. David Sanger and Eric Schmitt, "Cheney's Power No Longer Goes Unquestioned," *New York Times*, September 10, 2006.

114. Helen Cooper and David Sanger, "A Talk at Lunch that Shifted the Stance on Iran."

115. Interview with Philip Zelikow, January 2010.

116. Ibid.; Philip Zelikow, Keynote Address, Weinberg Founders Conference, Washington, D.C., washingtoninstitute.org, September 15, 2006; and Helen Cooper and David Sanger, "Rice Counselor Gives Advice Others May Not Want to Hear," *New York Times*, October 28, 2006.

117. Zbigniew Brzezinski, "Robert Gates," *Time*, April 30, 2009.

118. Peter Baker and Glen Kessler, "UN Ambassador Bolton Won't Stay," *Washington Post*, December 5, 2006.

119. Jim Kuhnhenn, "Democrats Win Control of Congress," *Washington Post*, November 9, 2006.

120. David Sanger, "Duelling Views Pit Baker Against Rice," *New York Times*, December 8, 2006; and The Iraq Study Group Report, United States Institute of Peace, Washington, D.C., December 6, 2006.

121. Seymour Hersh, "Torture at Abu Ghraib," *New Yorker*, May 10, 2004.

CHAPTER 7

1. Thom Shanker and Greg Myre, "Rice, In Israel, Backs Mideast Moderates, But Offers No Plan," *New York Times*, January 14, 2007.

2. Interview with Condoleezza Rice, December 2009.

3. Interview with Stephen Krasner, November 2009.

4. Interview with Condoleezza Rice, December 2009.

5. Helen Cooper, "U.S. Scolds Israel on Plan for West Bank Settlement," *New York Times*, December 28, 2006; and Steven Erlanger, "Israel Says Egypt Sends Weapons to Abbas' Forces, With Israeli and U.S. Approval," *New York Times*, December 29, 2006.

6. Interview with former senior U.S. official.

7. Steven Erlanger, "In Palestinian Peace Deal, Hope and a Political Snare," *New York Times*, February 10, 2007; Roger Hardy, "Analysis: What Was Achieved At Mecca," BBC-news.com, February 9, 2007; and Steven Erlanger, "A Hamas Leader Tries to Halt Spiralling Violence," *New York Times*, January 5, 2007.

8. Steven Erlanger, "U.S. Picks an Inauspicious Time to Restart Peace Talks," *New York Times*, January 25, 2007; Erlanger, "In Palestinian Peace Deal, Hope and a Political Snare"; Roger Hardy, "Analysis: What Was Achieved At Mecca"; and Erlanger, "A Hamas Leader Tries to Halt Spiralling Violence."

9. Alvaro de Soto, End of Mission Report, May 2007.

10. Ibid.; and interview with former senior U.S. official.

11. Interview with Condoleezza Rice, December 2009; interviews with David Welch, November and December 2009; and interview with Stephen Krasner, November 2009.

12. Interview with former senior U.S. official.

13. Shanker and Myre, "Rice, in Israel, Backs Mideast Moderates, but Offers No Plan"; and interview with former senior U.S. official. Focusing on the Israeli-Palestinian conflict, U.S. Central Command staff later warned that it was endangering U.S. interests. See Mark Perry, "The Petraeus Briefing: Biden's Embarrassment is Not the Whole Story," Foreign-policy.com, March 13, 2010.

14. Thom Shanker and Greg Myre, "Rice Plans Meeting With Mideast Leaders," *New York Times*, January 16, 2007.

15. Thom Shanker, "Perhaps Thinking of His Legacy, Bush Has Rice on the Move," *New York Times,* January 19, 2007; and Michael Oren, "What if Syria and Israel Find Common Ground," *New York Times*, January 24, 2007.

16. Erlanger, "U.S. Picks an Inauspicious Time to Restart Peace Talks."

17. In a November 2009 interview with the author, Elliott Abrams stated his belief that Rice took Middle East policy away from the Rose Garden speech policy of June 24, 2002. See also Helene Cooper, "Rice Struggles to Restart Peace Talks," *New York Times*, February 18, 2007.

18. Helene Cooper, "Rice Faces an Uphill Battle for Middle East Breakthrough," *New York Times*, February 16, 2007.

19. King Abdullah II, Address to Joint Meeting of U.S. Congress, Washington, D.C., March 7, 2007.

20. Helene Cooper, "Jordan's King Seeks Greater U.S. Role In Peace Effort," *New York Times*, March 8, 2007.

21. Interviews with David Wurmser, March 2010; and interview with Elliott Abrams, November 2009.

22. Brian Knowlton, "Cheney Assails Those Favoring Iraq Drawdown," *New York Times*, March 12, 2007; and Dick Cheney, Remarks to the American Israel Public Affairs Committee, washingtonpost.com, March 7, 2006.

23. John Hagee, Speech to the AIPAC Policy Conference, March 11, 2007.

24. Letter to President Bush from Evangelical Leaders, *New York Times*, July 29, 2007.

25. Interview with former senior U.S. official.

26. Helene Cooper, "Look Who's Reboarding That Clinton Shuttle," *New York Times*, April 1, 2007.

27. Helene Cooper and Michael Slackman, "Rice Meets Syrian Foreign Minister," *New York Times*, May 3, 2007.

28. Isabel Kershner, "Israeli and Palestinian Leaders Open Regular Peace Talks," *New York Times*, April 16, 2007.

29. Isabel Kershner, "Palestinian Faction Aims to Unite Its Militias," *New York Times*, April 1, 2007.

30. Interview with J. Scott Carpenter, November 2009.

31. Avi Issacharoff and Amos Harel, "Civil War/Hamastan and Fatahstan," *Ha'aretz*, June 13, 2007.

32. Interview with J. Scott Carpenter, November 2009.

33. Interview with Elias Zananiri, December 2009. It is possible that funds for salaries were embezzled by corrupt members of the Palestinian Authority.

34. Interview with J. Scott Carpenter, November 2009; and interview with former senior U.S. official.

35. Interview with Tom DeLay, May 2010.

36. Ali Waked, "Fayyad Confiscates $7 million from Dahlan," *Israel News*, August 7, 2007.

37. Interview with Condoleezza Rice, December 2009.

38. Interviews with David Wurmser, March 2010.

39. Interview with James Wolfensohn, November 2009.

40. Interview with Condoleezza Rice, December 2009.

41. Transcript of George W. Bush's Comments on Iraq, *New York Times*, July 12, 2007.

42. Interview with Condoleezza Rice, December 2009; interview with Salam Fayyad, December 2009; interviews with David Welch, November and December 2009; and Isabel Kershner and Steven Erlanger, "Palestinian Split Deepens; Government in Chaos," *New York Times*, June 15, 2007.

43. Interview with Condoleezza Rice, December 2009.

44. Mohammed Assadi, "Factional Battles Kill 616 Palestinians Since 2006," *Reuters*, June 6, 2007.

45. Kershner and Erlanger, "Palestinian Split Deepens; Government in Chaos."

46. Helene Cooper, "U.S. Unfreezes Millions in Aid to Palestinians," *New York Times*, June 19, 2007.

47. Interview with Jonathan Powell, September 2009; and interview with James Wolfensohn, November 2009.

48. Helene Cooper, "U.S. is Urging Blair to Be Lead Envoy," *New York Times*, June 21, 2007; and "A New Job For Tony Blair," *New York Times*, June 25, 2007.

49. Helene Cooper and David Sanger, "Iran Strategy Stirs Debate at White House," *New York Times*, June 16, 2007; Norman Podhoretz, "The Case for Bombing Iran," commentarymagazine.com, June 1, 2007; and interviews with David Wurmser, March 2010.

50. Joseph Lieberman, Address to Christians United For Israel, Washington, D.C., July 16, 2007.

51. Interview with Elliott Abrams, November 2009; and interview with former senior U.S. official.

52. Interview with J. Scott Carpenter, November 2009; and interviews with David Wurmser, March 2010.

53. Interview with Stephen Hadley, January 2010; and Cooper and Sanger, "Iran Strategy Stirs Debate at White House"; Podhoretz, "The Case for Bombing Iran"; and interviews with David Wurmser, March 2010.

54. Interview with Stephen Hadley, January 2010.

55. Ibid.; Helene Cooper and David Cloud, "Saudi Arabia Says it May Meet Israel," *New York Times*, August 2, 2007; and Helen Cooper, "Saudi Asks Israel to Abandon Barrier as a Gesture to Arabs," *New York Times*, September 27, 2007.

56. Interview with Stephen Hadley, January 2010.

57. Interview with former senior U.S. official.

58. Interview with Stephen Hadley, January 2010.

59. Ibid.

60. Helen Cooper, "Bush to Bolster Abbas and to Seek Peace Talks," *New York Times*, July 17, 2007.

61. Helene Cooper, "Rice Backs Appointed Palestinian Premier and Mideast Democracy," *New York Times*, August 3, 2007.

62. Steven Erlanger, "Gains Unclear as Israeli and Palestinian Leaders Meet," *New York Times*, August 29, 2007.

63. Farah Stockman, "U.S. Unit Created to Pressure Iran, Syria Disbanded," *Boston Globe*, May 26, 2007.

64. Helene Cooper, "In Bush Speech, Signs of Split on Iran Policy," *New York Times*, September 16, 2007.

65. Robin Wright, "Iranian Unit to Be Labeled 'Terrorist'," *Washington Post*, August 15, 2007.

66. David Cloud and Helene Cooper, "Israel's Protests Are Said to Stall the Gulf Arms Sale," *New York Times*, April 5, 2007.

67. Steven Erlanger, "Israel to Get $30 Billion in Military Aid From U.S.," *New York Times*, August 17, 2007; and Cloud and Cooper, "Israel's Protests Are Said to Stall the Gulf Arms Sale."

68. Steven Lee Myers and Steven Erlanger, "Bush Declines to Lift Veil of Secrecy Over Israeli Airstrike on Syria," *New York Times*, September 21, 2007; and George W. Bush, *Decision Points* (New York: Crown, 2010), pp. 420–422.

69. Brian Knowlton, "Bush Discusses Report on Syria Strike," *New York Times*, April 30, 2008.

70. Mark Mazzetti and Helene Cooper, "An Israeli Strike On Syria Kindles Debate in the U.S.," *New York Times*, October 10, 2007; and David Sanger and Mark Mazzetti, "Israel Struck Syrian Nuclear Project, Analysts Say," *New York Times*, October 14, 2007.

71. Helene Cooper, "U.S. Will Invite Syria to Peace Conference," September 24, 2007.

72. Interview with Stephen Krasner, November 2009; and Steven Erlanger, "Bush Optimistic on Mideast Peace Despite Discord," *New York Times,* October 18, 2007.

73. "Report: Rice Compares Life In U.S. South to Palestinians' Plight," *Ha'aretz*, November 29, 2007.

74. Interview with Hussein Agha, September 2009.

75. Steven Erlanger, "U.S. Pushes for Turnout at Middle East Conference," *New York Times*, November 19, 2007.

76. Interview with Hussein Agha, September 2009.

77. George W. Bush, Remarks at the Annapolis Mideast Conference, Annapolis, Maryland, NYTimes.com, November 27, 2007; and Joint Understanding Read By George W. Bush at Annapolis Conference, Annapolis, Maryland, November 27, 2007, georgewbush-whitehouse.archives.gov.

78. Ibid.

79. Condoleezza Rice, Remarks at the Annapolis Conference, Annapolis, Maryland, November 27, 2007.

80. Mahmoud Abbas, Speech at the Annapolis Conference, Annapolis, Maryland, November 27, 2007, http://transparency.aljazeera.net/en/projects/thepalestinepapers/.

81. Ehud Olmert, Speech at the Annapolis Conference, Annapolis, Maryland, November 27, 2007.

82. Elaine Sciolino, "$7.5 Billion Pledged for Palestinians," *New York Times*, December 18, 2007.

83. Isabel Kershner, "Israel Rejects Hamas Overture, and Presses Housing Construction," *New York Times*, December 24, 2007.

84. Steven Erlanger, "Nudged By Bush, Israel Talks of Removing Illegal Outposts," *New York Times*, January 5, 2008; emphasis added.

85. Steven Lee Myers, "Bush Outlines Mideast Peace Plan," *New York Times*, January 11, 2008.

86. Steven Lee Myers, "In Heart of Islamic World, Bush Puts Forth His Faith," *New York Times*, January 15, 2008.

87. President Bush Discusses Israeli-Palestinian Peace Process, King David Hotel, Jerusalem, January 10, 2008, georgewbush-whitehouse.archives.gov.

88. Steven Erlanger and Steven Lee Myers, "Bush, Leaving Israel, Keeps Up Push for Peace Treaty," *New York Times*, January 12, 2008.

89. George W. Bush, Speech on the Importance of Freedom in the Middle East, Emirates Palace Hotel, United Arab Emirates, January 13, 2008, georgewbush-whitehouse.archives.gov.

90. Ibid.; emphasis added.

91. "Egypt Reseals Gaza Border Breach," BBCnews.com, February 3, 2008; and "Trapped in Gaza," *New York Times*, January 24, 2008; and Steven Erlanger, "Israel's Experimental Pressure Backfires," *New York Times*, January 27, 2008.

92. Isabel Kershner, "18 Palestinians Killed in Gaza Clashes," *New York Times*, January 16, 2008.

93. Tim Butcher, "Israeli Minister Vows Palestinian 'Holocaust'," *Telegraph*, February 29, 2008; Tim Butcher, "Peace Talks Halted as Israel Moves Into Gaza," *Telegraph*, March 3, 2008; and Helene Cooper, "Abbas Rebuffs Call by Rice to Return to Talks," *New York Times*, March 5, 2008.

94. Ibid.

95. Helene Cooper, "Gaza Pitfalls in Every Path," *New York Times*, March 3, 2008.

96. Helene Cooper, "U.S. May Relent on Hamas Role In Talks," *New York Times*, March 19, 2008.

97. Isabel Kershner, "Cheney Meets Israelis and Palestinians to Promote Peace," *New York Times*, March 24, 2008.

98. Ibid.

99. Helene Cooper, "In Mideast, Rice Urges Cooperation on Security," *New York Times*, March 20, 2008.

100. Isabel Kershner, "Middle East Peace Talks Resume," *New York Times*, April 8, 2008.

101. George W. Bush, Remarks to Members of the Knesset, Jerusalem, online.wsj.com, May 15, 2008; Isabel Kershner, "Israel and Syria Hint at Progress on Golan Heights Deal," *New York Times*, April 24, 2008; interview with Hrair Balian, February 2010; interviews with David Welch, November and December 2009; and Sheryl Gay Stolberg, "Bush and Jordan's King Meet on Mideast," *New York Times*, April 24, 2008.

102. George W. Bush, Remarks Before the World Economic Forum, Sharm El-Sheikh, Egypt, May 18, 2008.

103. Interview with Hrair Balian, February 2010; Isabel Kershner, "Israel Agrees to Truce With Hamas on Gaza," *New York Times*, June 18, 2008; Michael Shwirtz and William Bond, "Rice Warns that U.S. Will Defend Allies," *New York Times*, June 11, 2008; and Isabel Kershner, "U.S. Army Deploys Radar System in Israel," *New York Times*, September 29, 2008.

104. Elliott Abrams, *Tested By Zion: The Bush Administration and the Israeli-Palestinian Conflict* (New York: Cambridge University Press, 2013), p. 288. Abrams indicated that the offer was made on September 13, 2008, rather than in May as suggested by Rice.

105. Interview with Condoleezza Rice, December 2009.

106. Ibid.

107. Ibid.; interview with senior U.S. official; and Isabel Kershner, "Olmert to Quit After Elections in September," *New York Times*, July 31, 2008.

108. Interview with Stephen Hadley, January 2010.

109. Interview with Condoleezza Rice, December 2009.

110. Helene Cooper, "Israel's Political Situation Dims Hopes for Peace Deal," *New York*

Times, August 1, 2008.

111. Ethan Bronner, "Israeli Party Leader Seeks Early Elections," *New York Times*, October 26, 2008.

112. This phrase is borrowed from Christopher Patten.

113. Though a few random rockets were fired each month during the truce, the Hamas leadership was not responsible for them. As Hrair Balian noted in our February 2010 interview, what few rockets were launched were sent from disgruntled members of Hamas, criminal elements, or groups looking to discredit Hamas.

114. Interview with Hrair Balian, February 2010; Isabel Kershner, "Israel Agrees to Truce With Hamas on Gaza," *New York Times*, June 18, 2008; Rory McCarthy, "Gaza Truce Broken as Israeli Raid Kills Six Hamas Gunmen," *Guardian*, November 5, 2008; "Gaza Truce in Jeopardy after Hamas-Israeli Clashes," *New York Times*, October 5, 2008; and "Israelis and Palestinians Suffer Under Bombardments," Transcript, CNN Newsroom, December 31, 2008, http://transcripts.cnn.com/TRANSCRIPTS/0812/31/cnr.07.html.

115. "Israeli leaders 'to topple Hamas'," BBCnews.com, December 22, 2008.

116. James Hider, "Israel Vows to Sweep Hamas From Power," *London Times*, December 30, 2008.

117. Interview with former senior U.S. official.

118. "George Bush 'Shamed' Condoleezza Rice, Says Ehud Olmert," *Telegraph*, January 12, 2009; and Mark Landler, "Olmert Says He Made Rice Change Vote," January 12, 2009.

119. Richard Goldstone et al., "Report of the United Nations Fact-Finding Mission on the Gaza Conflict" ("Goldstone Report"), United Nations Human Rights Council, September 25, 2009, pp. 31–32, 202–203, http://www2.ohchr.org/english/bodies/hrcouncil/docs/12session/A-HRC-12-48.pdf; and "Gaza Looks Like an 'Earthquake Zone,'" BBCnews.com, January 20, 2009.

120. Margaret Coker, "Gaza's Isolation Slows Rebuilding Efforts," *Wall Street Journal*, February 5, 2009.

121. Goldstone Report, pp. 10–11.

122. Avi Shlaim, "Israel's War Against Hamas: Rhetoric and Reality," in Avi Shlaim, *Israel and Palestine: Reappraisals, Revisions, and Refutations* (London, Verso, 2010); and Fawaz Gerges, "Hamas Rising," *Dissent*, January 21, 2009, http://www.dissentmagazine.org/online_articles/hamas-rising.

123. Cornelius Tacitus, *Dialogus, Agricola, Germania* (London: Macmillan, 1914), p. 221.

CHAPTER 8

1. This prayer for realism is commonly used by Alcoholics Anonymous and is attributed to Reinhold Niebuhr.

2. Linda Bilmes and Joseph Stiglitz, *The Three Trillion Dollar War: The True Cost of the Iraq Conflict* (New York: Norton, 2008); and "Budget and Economic Outlook: Historical Budget Data," Congressional Budget Office, Washington, D.C., January 2010, http://www.cbo.gov/sites/default/files/cbofiles/ftpdocs/108xx/doc10871/historicaltables.pdf.

3. Victor Davis Hanson, "Losing the Enlightenment," Remarks at the Claremont Institute's Annual Churchill Dinner, Claremont, Calif., November 10, 2006, www.claremont.org/events/pageid.2047/default.asp.

4. Interview with Leon Panetta, February 2010.

5. Condoleezza Rice, "A Balance of Power that Favors Freedom," Wriston Lecture, Manhattan Institute, New York City, New York, October 1, 20

SELECTED BIBLIOGRAPHY

Abrams, Elliott et al., eds. *The Influence of Faith: Religious Groups and U.S. Foreign Policy* (Lanham, Md.: Rowman and Littlefield, 2001).

———. *Faith or Fear: How Jews Can Survive in a Christian America* (New York: Free Press, 1997).

Abrams, Elliott, and David G. Dalin, eds. *Secularism, Spirituality, and the Future of American Jewry* (Washington D.C.: Ethics and Public Policy Center, 1999).

Acton, John. *The History of Freedom and Other Essays* (London: MacMillan, 1907).

Adler, Emanuel. "Seizing the Middle Ground: Constructivism in World Politics," *European Journal of International Relations*, Vol. 3, No. 3 (September 1997).

Agha, Hussein, Shai Feldman, Ahmad Khalidi, and Zeev Schiff. *Track-II Diplomacy: Lessons from the Middle East* (Cambridge, Mass: The MIT Press, 2003).

Ammerman, Nancy T. "North American Protestant Fundamentalism," in *Fundamentalism Observed,* ed. Martin Marty and Scott Appleby (Chicago: University of Chicago Press, 1994).

Appleby, Scott. *The Ambivalence of the Sacred: Religion, Violence, and Reconciliation* (Lanham, Md.: Rowman and Littlefield, 2000).

Aruri, Naseer. *Dishonest Broker: The U.S. Role in Israel and Palestine* (Cambridge, Mass.: South End Press, 2003).

Asad, Talal. *On Suicide Bombing* (New York: Columbia University Press, 2007).

Augustine. *City of God Against the Pagans*, trans. Gillian Rosemary Evans and Henry Bettenson (London: Penguin, 1971).

Babik, Milan. "In Pursuit of Salvation: Woodrow Wilson and American Liberal Internationalism as Secularized Eschatology," DPhil Thesis, University of Oxford, 2009.

——. "Nazism as Secular Religion," *History and Theory*, Vol. 45 (October 2006).

Bacon, Francis. *The Advancement of Learning* (Oxford: Clarendon Press, 1876).

Bates, David. "Political Theology and the Nazi State: Carl Schmitt's Concept of the Institution," *Modern Intellectual History*, Vol. 3, No. 3 (November 2006).

Beilin, Yossi. *The Path to Geneva: The Quest for a Permanent Agreement, 1996–2004* (New York: RDV/Akashik Books, 2004).

Benvenisti, Meron. *Intimate Enemies: Jews and Arabs in a Shared Land* (Berkeley: University of California Press, 1995).

Ben-Ami, Shlomo. *Scars of War, Wounds of Peace: The Israeli-Arab Tragedy* (New York: Oxford University Press, 2006).

Bilmes, Linda, and Joseph Stiglitz. *The Three Trillion Dollar War: The True Cost of the Iraq Conflict* (New York: W.W. Norton, 2008).

Blumenberg, Hans. *The Legitimacy of the Modern Age* (Cambridge, Mass.: The MIT Press, 1985).

Blumenthal, Sidney. *How Bush Rules: Chronicles of a Radical Regime* (Princeton, N.J.: Princeton University Press, 2006).

Boyer, Paul. *When Time Shall Be No More: Prophecy Belief in Modern American Culture* (Cambridge, Mass.: Harvard University Press, 1992).

Bozeman, Adda. *Politics and Culture in International History: From the Ancient Near East to the Opening of the Modern Age,* 2nd ed. (New Brunswick: Transaction Publishers, 1994).

Budget and Economic Outlook: Historical Budget Data, Congressional Budget Office, Washington, D.C., January 2010.

Bull, Malcolm, ed. *Apocalypse Theory and the Ends of the World* (Oxford: Blackwell, 1995).

Bury, John Bagnell. *The Idea of Progress: An Inquiry Into its Origin and Growth* (New York: Macmillan, 1932).

Bury, R.G. "Plato and History," *Classical Quarterly*, Vol. 1, No. 1/2 (January–April 1951).

Bush, George W. *A Charge to Keep: My Journey to the White House* (New York: Harper, 2001).

——. *Decision Points* (New York: Crown, 2010).

Byrnes, Timothy A., and Peter J. Katzenstein, *Religion in an Expanding Europe* (Cambridge: Cambridge University Press, 2006).

Carr, E.H., and Michael Cox, eds. *The Twenty Years' Crisis: An Introduction to the Study of International Relations* (New York: Palgrave, 1939).

Clark, Victoria. *Allies for Armageddon: The Rise of Christian Zionism* (New Haven, Conn.: Yale University Press, 2007).

Clinton, Bill. *My Life: The Presidential Years* (New York: Random House, 2004).

Cohn, Norman. *The Pursuit of the Millennium: Revolutionary Millenarians and Mystical Anarchists of the Middle Ages* (London: Paladin, 1957).

Comte, Auguste. *The Positive Philosophy of Auguste Comte*, trans. Harriet Martineau (London: Kegan Paul, Trench, Trubner and Company, 1893).

Coveney, Peter, and Roger Highfield, *The Arrow of Time: The Quest to Solve Science's Great Mystery* (London: W.H. Allen, 1991).

Crunden, Robert. *Ministers of Reform: The Progressives' Achievement in American Civilization, 1889–1920* (New York: Basic Books, 1982).

Daley, Brian E. "Apocalypticism in the Early Church," in *The Encyclopedia of Apocalypticism: Apocalypticism in Western History and Culture*, Vol. II, ed. Bernard McGinn et al. (New York: Continuum, 2000).

Darby, John. *Studies on the Book of Daniel: A Course of Lectures,* 3rd ed. (Boston: John B. Bateman, 1864).

Darwin, Charles. *On the Origin of Species,* ed. Joseph Carroll (Toronto: Broadview Press, 2003).

Dessler, David. "Constructivism Within a Positive Social Science," *Review of International Studies*, Vol. 25, No. 1 (January 1999).

Dionysius, "The Extant Fragments of the Works and the Epistles of Dionysius, Bishop of Alexandria," in *The Writings of Gregory Thaumaturgus, Dionysius of Alexandria, and Archelaus*, ed. James Donaldson and Alexander Roberts (Edinburgh: T and T Clark, 1871).

Dorrien, Gary. *Imperial Design: Neoconservatism and the New Pax Americana* (New York: Taylor and Francis, 2004).

Drew, Elizabeth. "The Neocons in Power," *New York Review of Books*, June 12, 2003.

Edwards, Jonathan. *History of Redemption on a Plan Entirely Original: Exhibiting the Gradual Discovery of the Divine Purposes in the Salvation of Man; Including a Comprehensive View of Church History, and the Fulfillment of Scripture Prophecies* (New York: T. and J. Swords, 1793).

Ellis, John. *The Sharp End: The Fighting Man in World War II* (London: Book Club Associates, 1980).

Falwell, Jerry. "Future-word: An Agenda for the Eighties," in *Evangelicalism and Fundamentalism: A Documentary Reader*, ed. Barry Hankins (New York: New York University Press, 2008).

Farriss, Nancy. "Remembering the Future, Anticipating the Past: History, Time and Cosmology among the Maya of Yucatan," *Comparative Studies in Society and History*, Vol. 29, No. 3 (July 1987).

Fausto, Carlos. "Of Enemies and Pets: Warfare and Shamanism in Amazonia," *American Ethnologist*, Vol. 26, No. 4 (November 1999).

Finkelstein, Norman. *Image and Reality of the Israeli-Palestinian Conflict* (London: Verso, 2003).

Foucault, Michel. *Society must be defended: Lectures at the Collège de France, 1975–76*, ed. Mauro Bertani (New York: Macmillan, 2003).

Frankel, Benjamin. *Roots of Realism* (London: Frank Cass, 1996).

Freedman, Robert O. *The Middle East and the Peace Process: The Impact of the Oslo Accords* (Gainesville: University of Florida, 1998).

———. "The Bush Administration and the Arab-Israeli Conflict: The Record of its First Four Years," *Middle East Review of International Affairs*, Vol. 9, No. 1 (March 2005).

Fredriksen, Paula. "Apocalypse and Redemption in Early Christianity: From John of Patmos to Augustine of Hippo," *Vigiliae Christianae*, Vol. 45, No. 2 (1991).

Frum, David. *The Right Man: The Surprise Presidency of George W. Bush* (New York: Random House, 2003).

Frum, David, and Richard Perle. *An End To Evil: How to Win the War on Terror* (New York: Random House, 2003).

Fukuyama, Francis. "The End of History?" *National Interest* (Summer 1989).

———. *The End of History and the Last Man* (New York: Free Press, 1992).

———. "The Neoconservative Moment," *National Interest,* No. 76 (Summer 2004), p. 57.

George, Jim. "Leo Strauss, Neoconservatism and U.S. Foreign Policy: Esoteric Nihilism and the Bush Doctrine," *International Politics*, Vol. 42, No. 2 (June 2005).

Golding, William. *Lord of the Flies* (London: Faber and Faber, 1954).

Goldstein, Judith, and Robert Keohane. *Ideas and Foreign Policy: Beliefs, Institutions, and Political Change* (Ithaca, N.Y.: Cornell University Press, 1993).

Gray, John. *Black Mass: Apocalyptic Religion and the Death of Utopia* (London: Penguin Books, 2007).

Haass, Richard, and Martin Indyk. *Restoring the Balance: A New Strategy for the Next President* (Washington, D.C.: Brookings, 2008).

Halevy, Efraim. *Man in the Shadows: Inside the Middle East Crisis With the Man Who Led the Mossad* (New York: St. Martin's Press, 2006).

Halper, Stefan, and Jonathan Clarke. *America Alone: The Neo-conservatives and the Global Order* (Cambridge: Cambridge University Press, 2004).

Halsell, Grace. *Prophecy and Politics: Militant Evangelists on the Road to Nuclear War* (Westport, Conn.: Lawrence Hill, 1986).

Harrison, Simon. "The Symbolic Construction of Aggression and War in a Sepik River Community," *Man*, Vol. 24, No. 4 (December 1989).

Hayek, Friedrich August von. "Scientism and the Study of Society," *Economica*, Vol. 9, No. 35 (August 1942).

Hegel, George Wilhelm Friedrich. *The Philosophy of History,* trans. J. Sibree (New York: American Home Library Company, 1902).

Hill, David. *Greek Words and Hebrew Meanings* (London: Cambridge University Press, 1967).

Hobbes, Thomas. *Leviathan* (London: Routledge, 1889).

Hudson, Valerie. *Foreign Policy Analysis* (Lanham, Md.: Rowman and Littlefield, 2006).

Huntington, Samuel. *The Clash of Civilizations and the Remaking of World Order* (New York: Simon and Schuster, 1996).

Hurst, Steven. "Myths of Neoconservatism: George W. Bush's 'Neo-conservative' Foreign Policy Revisited," *International Politics*, Vol. 42, No. 76 (2005).

Indyk, Martin. *Innocent Abroad: An Intimate Account of American Peace Diplomacy in the Middle East* (New York: Simon and Schuster, 2009).

Kant, Immanuel. *Critique of Pure Reason,* trans. W. Pluhar (Indianapolis: Hackett Publishing, 1996).

———. *Perpetual Peace: A Philosophical Sketch* (London: Swan Sonnenschein, 1795).

———. "Religion Within the Boundaries of Mere Reason," in *Religion and Rational Theology,* trans. and ed. Allen W. Wood and George Di Giovanni (Cambridge: Cambridge University Press, 1996).

Kant, Immanuel, and Hans Siegbert Riess. "Idea for a Universal History with a Cosmopolitan Purpose," in *Kant: Political Writings* (Cambridge: Cambridge University Press, 1991).

Kepel, Gilles. *The Revenge of God: The Resurgence of Islam, Christianity and Judaism in the Modern World* (London: Polity Press, 1994).

Kessler, Glenn. *The Confidante: Condoleezza Rice and the Creation of the Bush Legacy* (New York: St. Martin's, 2007).

Keynes, John Maynard. *The Economic Consequences of the Peace* (New York: Harcourt, Brace and Howe, 1920).

Khaldun, Ibn. *The Muqaddimah,* ed. F. Rozenthal (Princeton, N.J.: Princeton University Press, 1958).

Khalidi, Rashid. *The Iron Cage: The Story of the Palestinian Struggle for Statehood* (Boston: Beacon Press, 2006).

———. *Resurrecting Empire: Western Footprints and America's Perilous Path in the Middle East* (London: I.B. Taurus, 2004).

Khong, Yuen Foong. "Neoconservatism and the Domestic Sources of American Foreign Policy: The Role of Ideas in Operation Iraqi Freedom," in *Foreign Policy: Theories, Actors, Cases,* ed. Steve Smith, Amelia Hadfield, Tim Dunne (Oxford: Oxford University Press, 2008).

Kimmerling, Baruch. *Politicide: Ariel Sharon's War Against the Palestinians* (London: Verso, 2003).

Klieman, Aaron S. *Compromising Palestine: A Guide to Final Status Negotiations* (New York: Columbia University Press, 2000).

Knutsen, Torbjørn L. *A History of International Relations Theory* (Manchester, UK: Manchester University Press, 1997).

Krauthammer, Charles. "Democractic Realism: An American Foreign Policy for a Unipolar World," Irving Kristol Lecture, American Enterprise Institute, Washington, D.C., February 2004.

Kristol, Irving. "The Neoconservative Persuasion," *Weekly Standard*, August 25, 2003.

LaHaye, Tim, and Jerry Jenkins. *Left Behind: A Novel of the Earth's Last Days* (Wheaton, Ill: Tyndale House, 1995).

Lapid, Yosef, and Friedrich Kratochwil. *The Return of Culture and Identity in International Relations Theory* (London: Lynne Rienner, 1996).

Leach, Edmund. *Custom, Law, and Terrorist Violence* (Edinburgh: Edinburgh University Press, 1977).

Lebow, Ned. *A Cultural Theory of International Relations* (New York: Cambridge University Press, 2008).

Lerner, Robert E. "Millenialism," in *The Encyclopedia of Apocalypticism: Apocalypticism in Western History and Culture,* Vol. II, ed. Bernard McGinn (New York: Continuum, 2000).

Lewis, Bernard. "The Roots of Muslim Rage," *Atlantic*, September 1990.

———. "What Went Wrong," *Atlantic*, January 2002.

———. *What Went Wrong: Western Impact and Middle Eastern Response* (Oxford: Oxford University Press, 2002).

Link, Arthur S. *The Higher Realism of Woodrow Wilson and Other Essays* (Nashville, Tenn.: Vanderbilt University Press, 1971).

Lovin, Robin. *Reinhold Niebuhr and Christian Realism* (Cambridge: Cambridge University Press).

Löwith, Karl. *Meaning in History: The Theological Implications for the Philosophy of History* (Chicago: University of Chicago Press, 1949).

Machiavelli, Niccolo. *The Prince,* trans. Angelo M. Codevilla (New Haven, Conn.: Yale University Press, 1997).

Mann, James. *Rise of the Vulcans: The History of Bush's War Cabinet* (New York: Viking Press, 2004).

Marsden, George. *Fundamentalism and American Culture*, 2nd ed. (Oxford: Oxford University Press, 2006).

Marx, Karl. *Capital: A Critique of Political Economy,* ed. Ernest Mandel (London: Penguin Classics, 1990).

————. "Towards the Critique of Hegel's Philosophy of Law: Introduction," in *Writings of the Young Marx on Philosophy and Society,* eds. Lloyd David Easton and Kurt H. Guddat (Indianapolis: Doubleday, 1967).

Marx, Karl, and Friedrich Engels. *The Communist Manifesto* (London: Penguin, 1848).

————. *The German Ideology,* ed. Christopher J. Arthur (New York International Publishers, 1964).

Mead, Walter Russell. "The New Israel and the Old: Why Gentile Americans Back the Jewish State," *Foreign Affairs* (July/August 2008).

Mendel, Arthur P. *Vision and Violence* (Michigan: University of Michigan Press, 1999).

Miller, Aaron David. *The Much Too Promised Land: America's Elusive Search for Arab-Israeli Peace* (New York: Bantam, 2008).

Mishal, Shaul, and Avraham Sela. *The Palestinian Hamas: Vision, Violence, and Coexistence* (New York: Columbia University Press, 2000).

Mitchell, George et al. Sharm El-Sheikh Fact-Finding Committee Report (The Mitchell Report), May 4, 2001.

Moltmann, Jürgen. *The Coming of God: Christian Eschatology,* trans. Margaret Kohl (London: SCM Press, 1995).

Morgenthau, Hans. "The Influence of Reinhold Niebuhr in American Political Life and Thought," in *Reinhold Niebuhr: A Prophetic Voice in Our Time*, ed. Paul Tillich (Greenwich, Conn.: Seabury Press, 1962).

———. *Politics Among Nations: The Struggle For Power and Peace* (Boston: McGraw Hill, 1948).

Mounce, Robert H. *The Book of Revelation: The New International Commentary on the New Testament,* rev. ed. (Cambridge: William B. Eerdmans Publishing, 1997).

Muasher, Marwan. *The Arab Center: The Promise of Moderation* (New Haven, Conn.: Yale University Press, 2008).

Netanyahu, Benjamin et al., *The Jerusalem Alternative: Moral Clarity for Ending the Arab-Israeli Conflict* (Green Forest, Ark.: Balfour Books, 2005).

Niebuhr, Reinhold. *The Children of Light and the Children of Darkness: A Vindication of Democracy and a Critique of Its Traditional Defense* (New York: Charles Scribner's Sons, 1960).

———. "Christian Faith and Political Controversy," in *Love and Justice: Selections from the Shorter Writings of Reinhold Niebuhr,* ed. D.B. Robertson (Louisville, Ky.: Westminster John Knox Press, 1957).

———. *Christian Realism and Political Problems* (New York: Charles Scribner's Sons, 1953).

———. *Faith and History: A Comparison of Christian and Modern Views of History* (New York: Charles Scribner's Sons, 1949).

———. Letter to June Bingham, October 26, 1961. Reinhold Niebuhr Papers, Box 26–27, U.S. Library of Congress, Washington, D.C.

———. "The Moral Issue in International Relations." Reinhold Niebuhr Papers, Box 16, U.S. Library of Congress, Washington, D.C.

———. *Moral Man and Immoral Society: A Study in Ethics and Politics* (London: SCM, 1932).

———. *The Nature and Destiny of Man: A Christian Interpretation* (London: Nisbet, 1943).

Nietzsche, Friedrich. *The Gay Science,* trans. J. Nauckhoff (Cambridge: Cambridge University Press, 1882).

———. *The Will to Power,* trans. Walter Kaufmann and R.J. Hollingdale (New York: Vintage Books, 1968).

Palmer, Earl. *1, 2, 3, John and Revelation* (Waco, Texas: W Publishing, 1991).

Parsi, Trita. *Treacherous Alliance: The Secret Dealings of Israel, Iran, and the United States* (New Haven, Conn.: Yale University Press, 2007).

Perle, Richard et al., "A Clean Break: A New Strategy for Securing the Realm," Institute for Advanced Strategic and Political Studies, Washington, D.C., July 1996.

Petito, Fabio, and P. Hatzopoulos, eds. *Religion in International Relations: The Return from Exile* (New York: Palgrave, 2003).

Plato. *The Republic*, Book VIII, trans. Allen David Bloom (New York: Basic Books, 1968).

———. *The Laws*, Book IV, trans. Thomas Pangle (Chicago: University of Chicago, 1980).

———. *Timaeus and Critias,* trans. Robin Waterfield and Andrew Gregory (Oxford: Oxford University Press, 2008).

Pocock, David. "The Anthropology of Time Reckoning," in *Myth and Cosmos,* ed. J. Middleton (New York: Natural History Press, 1964).

Popper, Karl. *The Open Society and Its Enemies, Volume I: The Spell of Plato* (Abingdon, UK: Routledge, 1945).

———. *The Poverty of Historicism* (London: Routledge and Kegan Paul, 1957).

Quandt, William B. *Peace Process: American Diplomacy and the Arab-Israeli Conflict Since 1967*, 3rd ed. (Washington D.C.: Brookings, 2005).

Rabinovich, Itamar. *Waging Peace: Israeli and the Arabs, 1948–2003* (Princeton, N.J.: Princeton University Press, 2004).

Rauch, Jonathan. "After Iraq, The Left Has a New Agenda: Contain America First," *Jewish World Review*, May 29, 2003.

Rauschenbusch, Walter. *A Theology for the Social Gospel* (New York: Macmillan Company, 1922).

Report of the Commission of Inquiry into the Events at the Refugee Camps in Beirut, *Jerusalem Post*, February 8, 1983.

Rice, Daniel F. *Reinhold Niebuhr and John Dewey: An American Odyssey* (New York: SUNY Press, 1993).

Ross, Dennis. *The Missing Peace: The Inside Story of the Fight for Middle East Peace* (New

York: Farrar, Straus and Giroux, 2004).

Rouleau, Eric. "Trouble in the Kingdom," *Foreign Affairs* (July/August 2002).

Rousseau, Jean-Jacques. *The Social Contract,* trans. Maurice Cranston (London: Penguin Books, 1968).

Rowland, Christopher. *Revelation* (London: Epworth Press, 1993).

Ruggie, John Gerard. "What Makes the World Hang Together: Neo-utilitarianism and the Social Constructivist Challenge," *International Organization*, Vol. 54, No. 4 (Autumn 1998).

Sahlins, Marshall. *The Use and Abuse of Biology: An Anthropological Critique of Socio-biology* (Ann Arbor: University of Michigan Press, 1976).

Said, Edward. "Michael Waltzer's 'Exodus and Revolution': A Canaanite Reading," *Grand Street*, Vol. 5, No. 2 (Winter 1986).

———. *Peace and its Discontents: Gaza-Jericho, 1993–1995* (London: Vintage, 1995).

Sandeen, Ernest. *The Roots of Fundamentalism: British and American Millenarianism, 1800–1930*, (Chicago: University of Chicago Press: 1970).

Sayigh, Yezid. "The Palestinian Paradox: Statehood, Security and Institutional Reform," *Conflict, Security & Development*, Vol. 1, No. 1 (April 2001).

Schopenhauer, Arthur. *On Human Nature,* trans. T.B. Saunders (London: George Allen, 1913).

Sha'ban, Fuad. *For Zion's Sake: The Judeo-Christian Tradition in American Culture* (London: Pluto Press, 2005).

Sharansky, Natan. "Democracy for Peace" speech, American Enterprise Institute World Forum, Beaver, Colo., June 20, 2002.

Sharansky, Natan. *Defending Identity: Its Indispensable Role in Protecting Democracy,* with Shira Wolosky Weiss (New York: PublicAffairs, 2009).

Sharansky, Natan, and Ron Dermer, *The Case for Democracy: The Power of Freedom to Overcome Tyranny and Terror* (New York: Public Affairs, 2004).

Shikaki, Khalil. "The Future of Palestine," *Foreign Affairs* (November/December 2004).

———. "With Hamas in Power: Impact of Palestinian Domestic Developments on Options for the Peace Process," Working Paper 1, Crown Center for Middle East Studies, Brandeis University, Waltham, Mass., February 2007.

Shlaim, Avi. *The Iron Wall: Israel and the Arab World* (New York: W.W. Norton, 2000).

———. *Israel and Palestine: Reflections, Revisions, Refutations* (London: Verso, 2009).

Smith, W. Robertson. *The Religion of the Ancient Semites* (London: Adam and Charles Black, 1907).

Solzhenitsyn, Alexander. *The Gulag Archipelago* (New York: Harper & Row, 1973).

Spector, Stephen. *Evangelicals and Israel: The Inside Story of American Christian Zionism* (Oxford: Oxford University Press, 2007).

Swisher, Clayton. *The Truth About Camp David: The Untold Story About the Collapse of the Middle East Peace Process* (New York: Nation Books, 2004).

Tacitus, Cornelius. *The Annals of Imperial Rome,* trans. Michael Grant (London: Penguin, 1956).

Tenet, George. *At the Center of the Storm: My Years at the CIA* (New York: HarperCollins, 2008).

Thucydides. *History of the Peloponnesian War,* trans. Rex Warner (New York: Penguin, 1954).

———. *The Peloponnesian War,* trans. Martin Hammond (Oxford: Oxford University Press, 2009).

Tolstoy, Leo. *War and Peace: A Novel* (London: W. Heinemann, 1925).

Tuveson, Ernest Lee. *Millennium and Utopia: A Study In the Background of the Idea of Progress* (Berkeley: University of California Press, 1949).

Usher, Graham. *Dispatches From Palestine: The Rise and Fall of the Oslo Peace Process* (London: Pluto Press, 1997).

Voegelin, Eric. *The New Science of Politics: An Introduction* (Chicago: University of Chicago, 1952).

Waltz, Kenneth. *Theory of International Politics* (Reading, Mass.: Addison-Wesley, 1979).

Waltzer, Michael. *Exodus and Revolution* (New York: Basic Books, 1986).

Weber, Max. *The Vocation Lectures* (Indianapolis: Hackett Publishing, 2004)

Weber, Timothy. *Living in the Shadow of the Second Coming: American Premillennialism 1875–1982*, (Chicago: University of Chicago Press, 1983).

———. *On the Road to Armageddon: How Evangelicals Became Israel's Best Friend* (Grand Rapids, Mich.: Baker Press, 2004).

Wendt, Alexander. *Social Theory of International Politics* (New York: Cambridge University Press, 1999).

Whitby, Daniel. *A treatise of the True Millennium: Showing that it is not a Reign of Persons Raised from the Dead, but of the Church flourishing Gloriously for a Thousand Years after the Conversion of the Jews, and the Flowing in of all Nations to them thus converted to the Christian Faith*, 1727.

Wilkinson, Paul. *For Zion's Sake: Christian Zionism and the Role of John Nelson Darby* (Colorado Springs, Colo.: Paternoster, 2007).

Williams, Michael C. "What is the National Interest? The Neoconservative Challenge in IR Theory," *European Journal of International Relations*, Vol. 11, No. 3 (September 2005).

Wilson, Woodrow. *A New Freedom: The Emancipation of the Generous Energies of a People* (Garden City, N.Y.: Doubleday, Page, and Co., 1921).

Winthrop, John. "*A Model of Christian Charity*," in *The Journal of John Winthrop, 1630–1649*, ed. Richard S. Dunn and Laetitia Yeandle (Cambridge, Mass.: Harvard University Press, 1996).

Wittes, Tamara Cofman. "The New U.S. Proposal for a Greater Middle East: An Evaluation," Middle East Memo No. 2, May 10, Saban Center, Brookings Institution, Washington, D.C., 2004.

Woodward, Bob. *Bush at War: Inside the Bush White House* (New York: Simon and Schuster, 2002).

———. *State of Denial*, (New York: Simon and Schuster, 2004).

———. *The War Within* (New York: Simon and Schuster, 2008),

Wurmser, David. *Tyranny's Ally: America's Failure to Defeat Saddam Hussein* (Washington D.C.: AEI Press, 1999).

INTERVIEWS

⌗

Interviewee	Principal Post	Location	Date
Elliott Abrams	Deputy National Security Advisor for Global Democracy Strategy	Telephone interview	November 6, 2009
Hussein Agha	Advisor to Yasser Arafat	London	September 14, 2009
Sir Mark Allen	British Foreign Office	London	September 8, 2009
Kofi Annan	UN Secretary General	Telephone interview	November 18, 2010
Jawad Annani	Jordanian Foreign Minister	Amman, Jordan	September 16, 2009
Richard Armitage	Deputy Secretary of State	Arlington, VA	February 2, 2010
Hrair Balian	Director, Carter Center Conflict Resolution Program	Telephone interview	February 4, 2010

Interviewee	Principal Post	Location	Date
John Bellinger III	Legal Advisor to the State Department and Legal Advisor to the National Security Council	Telephone interview	February 12, 2010
Shlomo Ben-Ami	Israeli Foreign Minister	Telephone interview	December 9, 2009, December 11, 2009
William J. Burns	Undersecretary of State for Political Affairs	Telephone interview	September 15, 2010
J. Scott Carpenter	Deputy Assistant Secretary of State for Near Eastern Affairs	Washington, D.C.	November 11, 2009
Mohammad Dahlan	Palestinian National Security Advisor	Written correspondence	January 12, 2010
Tom DeLay	House Majority Leader	Telephone interview	May 11, 2010
Michael Doran	Senior Director for Near East and North African Affairs, National Security Council	New York	November 4, 2009
Salam Fayyad	Palestinian Prime Minister	Ramallah, West Bank	December 23, 2009

Interviewee	*Principal Post*	*Location*	*Date*
Douglas Feith	Undersecretary of Defense for Policy	Washington, D.C. and written correspondence	November 12, 2009
Larry Garber	Director of USAID, West Bank/Gaza Mission	Jerusalem	July 16, 2007
Jean Geran	Director for Democracy and Human Rights, National Security Council	London	September 3, 2009
Michael Gerson	Assistant to the President for Speechwriting and Policy Advisor	Arlington, VA	December 10, 2009
Tim Goeglein	Special Assistant to the President and Deputy Director of the White House Office of Public Liaison	Washington, D.C.	November 13, 2009
Richard Haass	Director of Policy Planning, State Department	New York	November 2, 2009
Stephen Hadley	Assistant to the President for National Security Affairs	Washington, D.C.	January 28, 2010

Interviewee	Principal Post	Location	Date
Chuck Hagel	Senator and Secretary of Defense	Washington, D.C.	November 25, 2009
William Inboden	Senior Director for Strategic Planning, National Security Council	London	September 2, 2009
Stephen Krasner	Director of Policy Planning, State Department	Stanford, CA	November 2, 2009
Daniel Kurtzer	U.S. Ambassador to Israel	Telephone interview and written correspondence	December 7, 2009
Abdelsalam Majali	Jordanian Prime Minister	Amman, Jordan	September 16, 2009
Sir Christopher Meyer	British Ambassador to the United States	London	September 14, 2009
Amr Moussa	Jordanian Deputy Prime Minister	Washington, D.C.	November 11, 2009
Marwan Muasher	Jordanian Deputy Prime Minister	Washington, D.C.	February 26, 2010
Leon Panetta	Secretary of Defense and CIA Director	Telephone interview	July 5, 2013

Interviewee	Principal Post	Location	Date
Lord Patten	EU Commissioner for External Affairs	Telephone interview	September 1, 2009
Richard Perle	Chairman of the Defense Policy Board	Chevy Chase, MD	November 18, 2009
Colin Powell	Secretary of State	Telephone interview	January 7, 2010
Jonathan Powell	Chief of Staff to Prime Minister Tony Blair	London	September 7, 2009
Condoleezza Rice	Secretary of State	Stanford, CA	December 3, 2009
Ayman Safadi	Advisor to His Majesty King Abdullah II	Amman, Jordan	September 16, 2009
Ryan Streeter	Special Assistant to President Bush for Domestic Policy	London	September 3, 2009
Fayaz Tarawneh	Jordanian Prime Minister	Amman, Jordan	September 23, 2009
David Welch	Assistant Secretary of State for Near Eastern Affairs	London, written correspondence, and telephone interviews	November 20, 2009, November 30, 2009, December 15, 2009

Interviewee	Principal Post	Location	Date
Rowan Williams	Archbishop of Canterbury	London	September 7, 2009
James Wolfensohn	President of the World Bank and Quartet Middle East Envoy	New York	November 2, 2009
Paul Wolfowitz	President of the World Bank and Deputy Secretary of Defense	Washington, D.C.	February 19, 2010
David Wurmser	Principal Deputy National Security Advisor to Vice President Cheney	Telephone interviews	March 3, 2010, March 4, 2010
Elias Zananiri	Advisor to Mohammad Dahlan	Jerusalem and written correspondence	December 24, 2009
Phillip Zelikow	State Department Counselor	Telephone interview	January 5, 2010
Anthony Zinni	U.S. Special Envoy (Israel/PA)	Reston, VA	December 1, 2009

ABOUT THE AUTHOR

Daniel E. Zoughbie is Sultan Postdoctoral Fellow and Lecturer in International and Area Studies at the Center for Middle Eastern Studies, University of California at Berkeley. Previously, he was an International Security Program Postdoctoral Fellow at the Belfer Center for Science and International Affairs at the Harvard Kennedy School, a Visiting Scholar at Stanford University's Center on Democracy, Development, and the Rule of Law, and a Visiting Researcher at Georgetown University's Berkley Center for Religion, Peace, and World Affairs. He was named a TED Fellow, a PopTech Fellow, a Rainer Arnhold Fellow, a Haas Scholar, and a Strauss Scholar, recipient of the College of Environmental Design Professional Promise Award at the University of California at Berkeley and of a Do Something Award. Zoughbie graduated Phi Beta Kappa and with highest honors from the University of California at Berkeley. He studied social anthropology at Oxford on a Marshall Scholarship and completed his doctorate in international relations, also at Oxford, as a Weidenfeld Scholar. He is a member of the Board of Directors of the San Mateo County Community Colleges Foundation, which serves 40,000 students, and is also the founder and CEO of Microclinic International, a non-profit organization which promotes access to health care in underserved communities around the world.

INDEX

Belfer Center Studies in International Security

Published by The MIT Press

Sean M. Lynn-Jones and Steven E. Miller, series editors
Karen Motley, executive editor
Belfer Center for Science and International Affairs
Harvard Kennedy School

Acharya, Amitav, and Evelyn Goh, eds., *Reassessing Security Cooperation in the Asia-Pacific* (2007)

Agha, Hussein, Shai Feldman, Ahmad Khalidi, and Zeev Schiff, *Track-II Diplomacy: Lessons from the Middle East* (2003)

Allison, Graham, and Robert D. Blackwill, with Ali Wyne, *Lee Kuan Yew: The Grand Master's Insights on China, the United States, and the World* (2012)

Allison, Graham T., Owen R. Coté, Jr., Richard A. Falkenrath, and Steven E. Miller, *Avoiding Nuclear Anarchy: Containing the Threat of Loose Russian Nuclear Weapons and Fissile Material* (1996)

Allison, Graham T., and Kalypso Nicolaïdis, eds., *The Greek Paradox: Promise vs. Performance* (1996)

Arbatov, Alexei, Abram Chayes, Antonia Handler Chayes, and Lara Olson, eds., *Managing Conflict in the Former Soviet Union: Russian and American Perspectives* (1997)

Bennett, Andrew, *Condemned to Repetition? The Rise, Fall, and Reprise of Soviet-Russian Military Interventionism, 1973–1996* (1999)

Blackwill, Robert D., and Michael Stürmer, eds., *Allies Divided: Transatlantic Policies for the Greater Middle East* (1997)

Blackwill, Robert D., and Paul Dibb, eds., *America's Asian Alliances* (2000)

Blum, Gabriella, and Philip B. Heymann, *Laws, Outlaws, and Terrorists: Lessons from the War on Terrorism* (2010)

Brom, Shlomo, and Yiftah Shapir, eds., *The Middle East Military Balance 1999–2000* (1999)

Brom, Shlomo, and Yiftah Shapir, eds., *The Middle East Military Balance 2001–2002* (2002)

Brown, Michael E., ed., *The International Dimensions of Internal Conflict* (1996)

Brown, Michael E., and Šumit Ganguly, eds., *Fighting Words: Language Policy and Ethnic Relations in Asia* (2003)

Brown, Michael E., and Šumit Ganguly, eds., *Government Policies and Ethnic Relations in Asia and the Pacific* (1997)

Carter, Ashton B., and John P. White, eds., *Keeping the Edge: Managing Defense for the Future* (2001)

Chenoweth, Erica, and Adria Lawrence, eds., *Rethinking Violence: State and Non-state Actors in Conflict* (2010)

de Nevers, Renée, *Comrades No More: The Seeds of Political Change in Eastern Europe* (2003)

Elman, Colin, and Miriam Fendius Elman, eds., *Bridges and Boundaries: Historians, Political Scientists, and the Study of International Relations* (2001)

Elman, Colin, and Miriam Fendius Elman, eds., *Progress in International Relations Theory: Appraising the Field* (2003)

Elman, Miriam Fendius, ed., *Paths to Peace: Is Democracy the Answer?* (1997)

Falkenrath, Richard A., *Shaping Europe's Military Order: The Origins and Consequences of the CFE Treaty* (1994)

Falkenrath, Richard A., Robert D. Newman, and Bradley A. Thayer, *America's Achilles' Heel: Nuclear, Biological, and Chemical Terrorism and Covert Attack* (1998)

Feaver, Peter D., and Richard H. Kohn, eds., *Soldiers and Civilians: The Civil-Military Gap and American National Security* (2001)

Feldman, Shai, *Nuclear Weapons and Arms Control in the Middle East* (1996)

Feldman, Shai, and Yiftah Shapir, eds., *The Middle East Military Balance 2000–2001* (2001)

Forsberg, Randall, ed., *The Arms Production Dilemma: Contraction and Restraint in the World Combat Aircraft Industry* (1994)

George, Alexander L., and Andrew Bennett, *Case Studies and Theory Development in the Social Sciences* (2005)

Gilroy, Curtis, and Cindy Williams, eds., *Service to Country: Personnel Policy and the Transformation of Western Militaries* (2007)

Hagerty, Devin T., *The Consequences of Nuclear Proliferation: Lessons from South Asia* (1998)

Heymann, Philip B., *Terrorism and America: A Commonsense Strategy for a Democratic Society* (1998)

Heymann, Philip B., *Terrorism, Freedom, and Security: Winning without War* (2003)

Heymann, Philip B., and Juliette N. Kayyem, *Protecting Liberty in an Age of Terror* (2005)

Howitt, Arnold M., and Robyn L. Pangi, eds., *Countering Terrorism: Dimensions of Preparedness* (2003)

Hudson, Valerie M., and Andrea M. den Boer, *Bare Branches: The Security Implications of Asia's Surplus Male Population* (2004)

Kayyem, Juliette N., and Robyn L. Pangi, eds., *First to Arrive: State and Local Responses to Terrorism* (2003)

Kokoshin, Andrei A., *Soviet Strategic Thought, 1917–91* (1998)

Lederberg, Joshua, ed., *Biological Weapons: Limiting the Threat* (1999)

Mansfield, Edward D., and Jack Snyder, *Electing to Fight: Why Emerging Democracies Go to War* (2005)

Martin, Lenore G., and Dimitris Keridis, eds., *The Future of Turkish Foreign Policy* (2004)

May, Ernest R., and Philip D. Zelikow, eds., *Dealing with Dictators: Dilemmas of U.S. Diplomacy and Intelligence Analysis, 1945–1990* (2007)

Phillips, David L., *Liberating Kosovo: Coercive Diplomacy and U.S. Intervention* (2012)

Shaffer, Brenda, *Borders and Brethren: Iran and the Challenge of Azerbaijani Identity* (2002)

Shaffer, Brenda, ed., *The Limits of Culture: Islam and Foreign Policy* (2006)

Shields, John M., and William C. Potter, eds., *Dismantling the Cold War: U.S. and NIS Perspectives on the Nunn-Lugar Cooperative Threat Reduction Program* (1997)

Tucker, Jonathan B., ed., *Toxic Terror: Assessing Terrorist Use of Chemical and Biological Weapons* (2000)

Utgoff, Victor A., ed., *The Coming Crisis: Nuclear Proliferation, U.S. Interests, and World Order* (2000)

Weiner, Sharon K., *Our Own Worst Enemy? Institutional Interests and the Proliferation of Nuclear Weapons Expertise* (2011)

Williams, Cindy, ed., *Filling the Ranks: Transforming the U.S. Military Personnel System* (2004)

Williams, Cindy, ed., *Holding the Line: U.S. Defense Alternatives for the Early 21st Century* (2001)

Zoughbie, Daniel E., *Indecision Points: George W. Bush and the Israeli-Palestinian Conflict* (2014)

Belfer Center for Science and International Affairs

Graham Allison, Director
Harvard Kennedy School
Harvard University
79 JFK Street, Cambridge, MA 02138
Tel: (617) 495-1400; Fax: (617) 495-8963
http://belfercenter.ksg.harvard.edu   belfer_center@hks.harvard.edu

The Belfer Center is the hub of the Harvard Kennedy School's research, teaching, and training in international security affairs, environmental and resource issues, and science and technology policy.

The Center has a dual mission: (1) to provide leadership in advancing policy-relevant knowledge about the most important challenges of international security and other critical issues where science, technology, environmental policy, and international affairs intersect; and (2) to prepare future generations of leaders for these arenas. Center researchers not only conduct scholarly research, but also develop prescriptions for policy reform. Faculty and fellows analyze global challenges from nuclear proliferation and terrorism to climate change and energy policy.

The Belfer Center's leadership begins with the recognition of science and technology as driving forces constantly transforming both the challenges we face and the opportunities for problem solving. Building on the vision of founder Paul Doty, the Center addresses serious global concerns by integrating insights and research of social scientists, natural scientists, technologists, and practitioners in government, diplomacy, the military, and business.

The heart of the Belfer Center is its resident research community of more than 150 scholars, including Harvard faculty, researchers, practitioners, and each year a new, international, interdisciplinary group of research fellows. Through publications and policy discussions, workshops, seminars, and conferences, the Center promotes innovative solutions to significant national and international challenges.

The Center's International Security Program, directed by Steven E. Miller, publishes the Belfer Center Studies in International Security, and sponsors and edits the quarterly journal *International Security*.

The Center is supported by an endowment established with funds from Robert and Renée Belfer, the Ford Foundation, and Harvard University, by foundation grants, by individual gifts, and by occasional government contracts.